Quince Duncan

NICARAGUA
Caribbean Sea
COSTA RICA
LIMÓN PROVINCE
Limón
San José
Pacific Ocean
PANAMA
N

Quince Duncan

Writing Afro-Costa Rican and Caribbean Identity

Dorothy E. Mosby

THE UNIVERSITY OF ALABAMA PRESS
Tuscaloosa

Manufactured in the United States of America

Typeface: Garamond and Baskerville

Cover photograph: Detail from mural located in Vargas Park, Puerto Limón, Costa Rica, ca. 1996. Used with permission from Guadalupe Alvarez Rojas. Photo courtesy of Joseph Powell.
Cover design: James Elkin Buttram/Metanoia Design

∞

The paper on which this book is printed meets the minimum requirements of American National Standard for Information Sciences—Permanence of Paper for Printed Library Materials, ANSI Z39.48-1984.

Library of Congress Cataloging-in-Publication Data

Mosby, Dorothy E., 1970–
Quince Duncan : Writing Afro-Costa Rican and Caribbean Identity / Dorothy E. Mosby.
pages cm
Includes bibliographical references and index.
ISBN 978-0-8173-1349-4 (trade cloth : alk. paper) — ISBN 978-0-8173-8722-8 (e book)
1. Duncan, Quince, 1940—Criticism and interpretation. 2. Costa Rican literature—Black authors—History and criticism. I. Title.
PQ7489.2.D8Z77 2014
863'.64—dc23

2013020405

To my parents, James and Helen,
for launching me out into the world with support and love

Contents

Acknowledgments

This project has been many years in the making and there are many people to whom I am grateful for their encouragement and assistance: Marvin A. Lewis and M. J. Muratore, the progenitors of this project; Franklin Perry, Dlia. McDonald, and Guadalupe Álvarez Rojas for their unyielding support; Carol Knight for her devotion; Sheridan Wigginton for her constant motivation; and, of course, Quince Duncan, for his generosity and patience.

Abbreviations

CM	*Una canción en la madrugada*
FC	*Final de calle*
HA	*Los cuentos del Hermano Araña*
HC	*Hombres curtidos*
KM	*Kimbo*
LCE	*Los cuatro espejos*
LP	*La paz del pueblo*
MR	*A Message from Rosa / Un mensaje de Rosa*
PC	*El pozo y una carta*
RP	*La Rebelión Pocomía y otros relatos*
TBS	*The Best Short Stories of Quince Duncan / Las mejores historias de Quince Duncan*
TR	*El trepasolo*

Quince Duncan

Introduction

> What the son wishes to forget the grandson wishes to remember.
>
> —Marcus Lee Hansen, "The Problem of the Third Generation Immigrant" (1938)

Recognized as Costa Rica's first novelist of African descent, Quince Duncan is one of his nation's most esteemed contemporary writers.[1] The grandson of Jamaican and Barbadian immigrants, Duncan "remembers" the experience of the first generation of Afro–West Indian immigrants and that of their descendants in Costa Rica.[2] Through his art and storytelling, Duncan has become an important literary and cultural presence in a country that has forged a national identity around the mythologies of the *leyenda blanca*, the "white legend" of a rural democracy established by a homogeneous group of white, Catholic, Spanish peasants. This view is succinctly stated in Carlos Monge Alfaro's text *Historia de Costa Rica* (History of Costa Rica): "Costa Rica was a country of peasants, owners of small parcels of land. In Costa Rica there were no slaves or servants; all were persons whose worth was in their quality as human beings" (1966, 111).[3] This traditional view of Costa Rican history and national identity denies the existence of African slavery during the colonial period and minimizes or omits the significant contributions of West Indian immigrants to the nation's modern development. Richard L. Jackson observes in *The Black Image in Latin American Literature*, "Duncan deals with this problem of neglect as well as with the problem of identity, and his work is hailed by the Costa Rican national press as the product of a writer who is giving voice to a part of the country's ethnic mosaic that has not always been favorably treated" (1976, 128).

His novels, short stories, recompilations of oral literature, and essays collectively tell the history of people of Afro–West Indian descent in Costa Rica. Echoing immigration historian Marcus Lee Hansen's familiar aphorism, "What the son wishes to forget the grandson wishes to remember," Duncan "remembers" and intimately conveys the experiences of the first generation of Afro–West Indian contract laborers and the struggles of their descendants to be recognized as citizens of the nation they helped bring into modernity. Duncan's works are an effort to write the story of West Indian migration into the official literary discourse of Costa Rica by presenting legends and stories of Limón Province, as well as complicated issues of identity, citizenship, belonging, and cultural exile. His novels, *Hombres curtidos* (1971) and *Los cuatro espejos* (1973) in particular, portray the Afro–West Indian community in Limón and the cultural intolerance those blacks encountered who migrated from the Caribbean province to the national capital in the Central Highlands. His work follows the historical trajectory of the first West Indian laborers to contemporary concerns resulting from cultural change. The history of Afro–West Indian migration to Costa Rica—and to some extent Central America—comes from the author's intimate knowledge of this history and is a constant in the majority of Duncan's work.

West Indians in Costa Rica: An Overview

The descendants of Afro–West Indian contract laborers who first began to migrate at the end of the nineteenth century comprise the majority of the contemporary Afro–Costa Rican population. These early workers arrived in Costa Rica to construct a railroad from San José in the coffee rich Central Valley to the port city of Puerto Limón located in Limón Province on the Caribbean coast. During the first three decades of the twentieth century, many laborers remained and new workers arrived to work for the United Fruit Company, which became a leading exporter of bananas to the United States and other global consumer markets.

During the early years of migration through the years following World War II, the history of West Indian blacks in Costa Rica was characterized by its ethnic and linguistic separation from the national population. The West Indians and their American and British employers formed an enclave in Limón Province that stretched along the Caribbean coast. An air of provisionality infiltrated this enclave, since the laborers who arrived intended merely to fulfill the terms of their labor contracts, and then triumphantly return home with their earnings. The community they formed centered on the province's principal city, Puerto Limón, and, since the majority of workers were Anglophone West Indians and British subjects, the community identified strongly with the British Empire. The enclave became in many ways an extension of the British Empire rather than an integral part of Costa Rican society. The workers maintained their ethnolinguistic difference by supporting their own "English" schools and Protestant churches with teachers and ministers contracted from Jamaica and other parts of the British West Indies. Goods were imported from Jamaica and England, which ensured a sense of colonial continuity. The Afro–West Indians discouraged their children from learning Spanish and mixing with the local population, since such interactions would make the return home and reintegration more difficult. Consequently, the prejudices the centuries-old anti-Spanish attitudes of the British Empire fostered were preserved in Limón. Many of the West Indian workers were literate, and as British colonial subjects they considered themselves possessors of a culture far superior to that of the average Costa Rican.

Conversely, Costa Rica did not want to foster any notions of permanency for the West Indians. Historian Carlos Meléndez states, "the attitude of the blacks with respect to Costa Rica was for a long time one of lack of interest. The truth is that the same was also true of Costa Rica's attitude towards them." Citizens' groups decried what they saw as the "Africanization" of the province, which was seen as a threat to the nation's perceived whiteness (Meléndez and Duncan 1993, 89; Harpelle 2001, 71). A 1933 petition to the Costa Rican Congress by self-identified white workers portrayed the presence of blacks as an economic and cultural threat:

> We wish to refer especially to the black problem, which is of transcendental importance, because in the province of Limón it constitutes a situation of privilege for this race and of manifest inferiority for the white race which we belong to. It is not possible to get along [convivir] with them, because their evil ways do not permit it. For them the family does not exist, nor does the honor of the woman, and thus they live in an overcrowding [hacinamiento] and a promiscuity which is dangerous for our homes, founded in accordance with the precepts of religion and of the honorable customs [buenas costumbres] of the Costa Ricans.
>
> The blacks are now invading the cities of the central plateau, because in truth these towns are congested with blacks, and we do not exaggerate when we affirm that over 70% of the inhabitants are blacks, in comparison with the white race. (qtd. in Chomsky 1996, 237)

Groups of white Costa Rican workers and citizens sought to "contain" blackness and prevent the population from migrating into the Central Valley from coastal towns, which were supposedly "congested with blacks." It was not just concerned Costa Rican citizens who desired to maintain the nation's homogenous culture and racially "pure" body, but also the state. The need for exclusion was expressed in official legislation in Article 3 of Law 31 signed by President Ricardo Jiménez on December 10, 1934. This law prohibited black workers from moving with United Fruit to its Pacific coast operations when blight severely diminished banana production on the Caribbean coast.[4] This effort to protect national labor and eliminate black foreign labor had a devastating and lasting effect on the Afro–West Indian population. During the course of contract negotiations, the United Fruit Company "was quite willing to forego its West Indian labour force in order to maintain a profitable enterprise. United Fruit simply abandoned the community that it had helped to create" (Harpelle 2001, 88). With discrimination now written into law, many West Indian workers and their families chose to exploit more promising opportunities in Panama and Cuba or to return home to their islands of origin. Some, however, remained in the land they worked so hard to settle and began to harvest cacao and other products.

Although scholars have not located an actual written legal code, black West Indians were discouraged from settling en masse in the capital, San José, or in other areas of the Central Valley.[5] Even in the absence of a law prohibiting blacks from migrating to San José, blacks were not encouraged to remain in the capital for more than seventy-two hours when on business or seeking medical attention. The town of Turrialba, situated between San José and Puerto Limón on the railroad line, constituted the ethnolinguistic borderland where the train personnel would rotate from white and mestizo to West Indian on the journey to Limón.

Many of the West Indian residents who remained in Limón maintained the dream of returning to their islands of origin. However, with the birth of successive generations on Costa Rican soil, that dream became more and more distant. The second generation of Costa Rican–born blacks of West Indian heritage, described as the "lost generation," faced an even more complex situation: "They are not Costa Rican. They are not Jamaican. Great Britain does not recognize them as citizens because they were born in a foreign country. Costa Rica does not recognize them as citizens because they are black, children of Jamaicans. The blacks of the second generation are, for a long time, a people without a country, without a recognized identity" (Meléndez and Duncan 1993, 134, my translation).[6] Although some Costa Rican–born Afro–West Indians applied for and were granted citizenship, this situation would not improve until a watershed moment in the nation's history; the civil war brought changes for the third generation—Duncan's generation—and succeeding generations of blacks of West Indian descent in Costa Rica (Meléndez and Duncan 1993, 134).[7]

The year 1948 was pivotal for Costa Rica and the Afro–West Indian population. That year a civil war erupted between the government of President Teodoro Picado, heavily influenced by his predecessor President Rafael Calderón Guardia, and the government's opponents. The opposition denounced electoral fraud during Calderón Guardia's attempt at a second term in office and the president's compromised alliance with the Catholic Church and the Communist Party. The vast majority of blacks in Limón shunned the war, claiming it was not their war to fight. However, the triumph of José María Figueres Ferrer and the Army of

National Liberation embraced a strategy of political and social integration that would have an impact on the black population, especially the third generation of Afro–West Indian descent that includes Duncan. The new constitution of 1949 and successive legislative decrees ushered in several reforms, including the naturalization of blacks born in Costa Rica. New citizenship launched a wave of internal migration as *afrolimonenses* began seeking opportunities in the capital, but these Afro–West Indians, who once comprised a majority in the coastal province, became part of an ethnolinguistic minority in San José and other parts of the Central Valley. Although Limón Province remained the "cradle" of Afro–Costa Rican culture and history, the capital became the site of economic opportunity, cultural contact, and culture clash.

Quince Duncan's Biography

Like many Costa Ricans of Afro–West Indian descent, Duncan's story begins with a dream of progress and prosperity that seemed impossible, but one that each successive generation slowly began to realize. Dreams of prosperity and a secure future attracted thousands of Jamaicans to Central America, where they found work building canals and railroads and later in the agricultural sector. Dreams both deferred and fulfilled mark the author's family history. His maternal great-grandfather was born a slave, but he dreamed of bringing forth a generation of children who would be better educated than previous generations and who would become part of the professional class. The former slave's son, James Duncan, wanted to study engines, particularly steam engines, but the family did not have enough resources to support such an endeavor. James's father migrated to Panama to work on the construction of the canal in order to earn money to finance his son's education. When James traveled to Panama to see his father, he learned that his father had died and that there was no money left to fund his education. James Duncan decided to cross the border into Costa Rica where several other relatives lived, and he never returned to Jamaica. There, he married Elvira Moodie and a daughter, Eunice Duncan Moodie, was born.

Quince Duncan Moodie, the son of Eunice Duncan and Adolfo Robinson, was born in San José, Costa Rica, at San Juan de Dios Hospital on December 5, 1940. His father, a Panamanian, died when Quince was just two years old. Like many of his generation, Duncan was not considered Costa Rican even though he was born in the country. The author notes that his original birth certificate declared him as Jamaican because he was born at a time when children born to women of West Indian descent were recorded as "Jamaican" in the birth registry. After the war of 1948, the new governing junta initiated reforms that included an act to promote the naturalization and enfranchisement of blacks of West

Indian origin who were born in Costa Rica. Duncan's Limonese-born mother was then recognized as a citizen, and her son was automatically naturalized as a Costa Rican citizen as well. Although the original birth certificate is lost, Quince Duncan jokingly comments: "My first birth certificate says that I had been born in Jamaica—that I was Jamaican by birth. I find it humorous when I hear preachers saying, 'You have to be born again,' because I was born twice—once in Costa Rica and once in Jamaica on the same day at the same hour" (Duncan 1997, personal interview).

Shortly after her son's birth, Eunice Duncan traveled back to her family home in Estrada, Limón. This small provincial village would provide the grist for Quince's prose fiction and essays. For the first eight years of his life, his maternal grandparents, James Duncan and Elvira Moodie, raised him. When his grandmother died he spent eight months with his mother, but he soon returned to his grandfather's home. At the age of thirteen, Quince was introduced to his grandfather's library, which had been previously locked and considered off-limits. Duncan recalls his grandfather's fondness for reading: "My grandfather had a good collection of books. Jim Pa was an atypical small farmer, likely to not attend to the farm on the day he received a book, a magazine from England, or the *Gleaner* newspaper from Jamaica" (Duncan 1996, *Un señor* 44). His grandfather's library opened up new worlds for Duncan, who read voraciously. Books such as *Uncle Tom's Cabin*, Dante's *Inferno*, and tales of Ivanhoe and King Arthur supplemented his readings in school and the orally transmitted Anancy stories. Miss Rob, a neighbor, also encouraged his interest in literature: "Nevertheless, the definite impulse towards literature came from Miss Rob. She was the matron of the village, and ever since I was a child she told me that I would go far. It occurred to her to give me a push and she made me read books of short stories. The demands were very simple: 'Read a story and when you pass by here, tell it to me.'" According to Duncan, his neighbor's request: "awoke in me a mountain of fantasy with her Arabian tales" (Duncan 1996, *Un señor* 45–46). Around this time Duncan begins to write stories of his own.

He was fifteen when his grandfather passed away, and soon after the elder Duncan's death, Quince left Estrada and traveled to San José to live with his mother. Eunice Duncan, like her father and grandfather before her, was not a professional herself but maintained the dream of having professionals in the family. She worked hard to ensure an education for Duncan and his siblings. Growing up in Estrada, Duncan hoped to become a carpenter, a profession that carried a certain status in the eyes of the young Duncan. However, in San José he was unable to learn his preferred trade and studied cabinetmaking instead. Although he attended "Spanish school" at the age of ten, his previous schooling in Limón was not recognized in San José, and Duncan was obligated to repeat his primary education at the Escuela Nocturna Ricardo Jiménez and his secondary education at the Liceo de Costa Rica. Duncan then attended the Seminario Bíblico Latinoamericano and planned to become an ordained Anglican priest. He married his first wife, Flora Linch, in 1963, and the union produced threes sons, Andrés, Jaime, and Pablo. The marriage began to deteriorate, however, and Duncan withdrew from the ministry feeling that he could no longer continue to set an example for the church. In 1974 the couple divorced after ten years of marriage. Duncan remarried in 1975 and had two daughters, Shara Eunice and Denise, with his second wife Ileana Villalobos Ellis. Observing the progress his family has made over the generations, Duncan notes, "the old man's dream became a reality three generations later" (Duncan 2002, personal interview). As a result of their continual efforts to succeed, the author, his siblings, and their children had become professionals, thus finally realizing his great-grandfather's dream.

During the 1970s, Duncan attended the Escuela Normal Superior in order to become an English teacher. He attended the school at an important historical moment, because students and faculty participated in a movement to transform the institution into the Universidad Nacional (UNA). Duncan was on the board that organized the university, and when UNA officially opened in 1972, he became the first president of the student body. He would also become an adjunct professor of Latin American studies at the university, a post he held until his retirement in 1998 after twenty-five years of service. Although he has officially retired from his academic position at UNA, Duncan continues to be an active writer and scholar, publishing articles, presenting lectures, and participating in national and international congresses. Additionally, Duncan has a long-standing engagement with the education of Costa Rica's youth, holding positions as director at several prominent secondary institutions in the Central Valley, including Colegio St. Clare, Colegio West, Colegio Santa Fe, and the Centro Educativo Yurusti in Heredia.

His recognition as a writer, human rights activist, and educator within and outside Costa Rica is evidenced through the numerous invitations and honors he has received. Duncan has been a visiting professor at several universities in North America, including the University of Alabama at Birmingham, Indiana University of Pennsylvania, and Purdue University. In recognition of his achievements and his fight for human rights, St. Olaf's College in Northfield, Minnesota, granted him an honorary doctorate in 2001. He has traveled to Europe, Africa, and throughout the Americas, lecturing and attending conferences addressing issues of literature, history, culture, racism, and human rights.

Duncan currently lives in Heredia, Costa Rica, where he has lived with his family for many years. In addition to remaining an active scholar and writer since retiring from the university, Duncan has dedicated some of his time to the study and practice of alternative medicine, to human rights initiatives with UNESCO, and to local nongovernmental organizations, such as Proyecto Caribe, and progressive politics.[8]

Duncan's Place in Costa Rican Literature and *Afrorealismo*

It is precisely the social and cultural trajectory of West Indians and their descendants that Duncan center-stages in his work. His perspective on Afro–Costa Rican culture was unheard of in mainstream Costa Rican letters before his first major publication in 1969. Prior to Duncan, representations of black characters were found in works by notable figures such as Carmen Lyra ("Bananos y hombres," 1931); Carlos Luis Fallas (*Mamita Yunai*, 1941; *Gente y gentecillas*, 1947), Joaquín Gutiérrez (*Manglar*, 1947; *Cocorí*, 1947; *Puerto Limón*, 1950; *Murámonos, Federico*, 1973); and Fabián Dobles (*La Rescoldera*, 1947; *Historias de Tata Mundo*, 1955). However, these writers present an outsider's perspective that Ian Smart refers to as "a view from beneath the bed" (1984, 24). As one of the most respected writers of his nation, Duncan gives a fictionalized account to the long-ignored history of people of Afro–West Indian descent in Costa Rica.

Duncan's writing is most notable perhaps for its dismantling of the myth of Costa Rican exceptionalism (equality, democracy, homogeneity) and for its focus on Costa Rica's discriminatory treatment toward blacks. Like his literary contemporary, Afro–Costa Rican poet Eulalia Bernard (b. 1935), Duncan draws attention to the discrepancy between Costa Rica's rhetoric of inclusion for all its citizens and its treatment of black citizens. His writing also calls attention to the process of "cultural hybridization" that occurs when successive generations lose contact with the ancestral homeland. Duncan's novels *Hombres curtidos* (1971) and *Los cuatro espejos* (1973) examine the complex weave of ethnic, national, and cultural identity that was previously unexplored in Costa Rican literature. These two novels in particular depict a shifting sense of identity that calls to mind Stuart Hall's assertion that identity transforms and adapts over time. Identity, he argues is never fixed but changes with historical and cultural circumstances, as well as representational discourses (Hall 1997).

Duncan excels in the production of prose fiction, having written seven novels, six collections of short stories, and only one dramatic text to date. His contributions to Costa Rican letters also include anthologies and nonfiction studies such as *El negro en la literatura costarricense* (Blacks in Costa Rican Literature, 1975), *Contra el silencio: Afrodescendientes y racismo en el caribe continental hispánico* (Against Silence: Descendants of Africans and Racism in the Caribbean, 2001), and *El pueblo afrodescendiente: Diálogos con el abuelo Juan Bautista Yayah* (Afro-

Descendant Peoples: Dialogues with the Elder Juan Bautista Yayah, 2012), an introduction to the African Diaspora studies that uses the format of a fictional dialogue between Juan Bautista and his pupils. Duncan also has published children's literature. He introduced Afro–West Indian "Anancy stories" in the Spanish language to young audiences. In 1975 he initiated this project with the release of *Los cuentos del Hermano Araña* (Anancy Stories), which was followed in 1988 by *Los cuentos de Jack Mantorra* (The Stories of Jack Mantorra). He was also one of the compilers of the multilingual (Limonese Creole, English, and Spanish) collection of Afro–Costa Rican folktales, *Cuentos tradicionales afrolimonenses* in 1995. Many of these stories involve the trickster figure Anancy (also called Anansi or Nancy), a small but wily spider who, along with other animals, displays the positive and negative traits of humanity.[9] Additionally, his collaborative work includes the landmark social and historical examination, *El negro en Costa Rica* (Blacks in Costa Rica, 1972), cowritten with noted historian Carlos Meléndez, and *Teoría y práctica del racismo* (The Theory and Practice of Racism, 1988), coauthored with Lorein Powell. Duncan's other writings—essays, nonfiction, newspaper editorials, commentary, and academic articles—are also quite numerous. In this study, however, emphasis will be placed on his fictional work since he is best known for his novels.

Duncan has been a major figure in the Costa Rican national literary scene since 1968. Subsequently, he has been involved in shaping the country's literary direction, having served as president of the Asociación de Autores de Obras Literarias, Artísticas y Científicas de Costa Rica and as a member of the Círculo de Escritores. He was a member of the Board of Directors of the Editorial Costa Rica from 1991 to 1993 and later served as its president. Duncan belongs to the important generation of Costa Rican prose writers, a group that includes Fernando Durán Ayanegui (b. 1939), Tatiana Lobo (b. 1939), Alfonso Chase (b. 1945), and Gerardo César Hurtado (b. 1949). These writers have infused the national literature with a new aesthetic dimension and a new thematic direction. This generation comes of age after the 1948 civil war and the reform-minded leadership of the Second Republic, which is marked by modernization, social democratic values, anticommunist rhetoric, and the growth of consumerism, with a particular fondness for imported goods. Collectively, they observe revolutionary movements, particularly the Cuban revolution that set off waves of protests by young people throughout the Western Hemisphere. At home, they witness staid conservatism, government corruption, growing class disparities, economic stagnation, and the rapidly expanding bureaucracy of Costa Rica's pro–United States national government. In the midst of this tumultuous political environment, increasing militarism of the national police, and social rebellion, Duncan's literary principles were taking shape. Alfonso Chase describes the cultural politics in Costa Rica during the late 1960s and 1970s, the period of Duncan's greatest production:

> [It] is an experimental literature, subject to the vicissitudes of experimentation for the sake of experimentation and also is the beginning of a long-term change that is not immediately perceived. The foundation of the Ministry of Culture, Youth and Sports [MCJD] fulfilled an important role in the dissemination of these yearnings, but did not find sufficient interest among artists in order to become an authentic cultural revolution. The problem of bureaucracy in cultural institutions made the work of the institution [MCJD] difficult in the national political playing field, besides the renewed artistic enthusiasm initiated in the 1960s had notably decreased. . . . In national history, the 1970s mark a process of political fragmentation that becomes translated in the area of culture. The Costa Rican artist has emerged to take refuge in his own self as a way of manifesting inconformity with the social body within which he must create his work. (Chase 1975, 113)

Absent in Costa Rica was the revolutionary fervor and protest that engendered a growing body of Latin American fiction that was translated and marketed for global consumption. While Costa Rican novelists and short story writers were aware of the "boom" in Latin American fiction that heightened the international profile of writers like Gabriel García Márquez (Colombia), Carlos Fuentes (Mexico), Guillermo Cabrera Infante (Cuba), Mario Vargas Llosa (Peru), and Julio Cortázar (Argentina), they could not command the same global attention because of the lack of revolutionary rhetoric and political turmoil in Costa Rica during 1960s and 1970s that drew interest to Colombia, Peru, Mexico, Argentina, and Cuba.[10]

Costa Rican narrative fiction of the 1960s and 1970s uses popular, urban language to present themes of social criticism and to describe the pains of modernization. Chase describes Costa Rican literature of this period:

> Without counting the re-editions, beginning in 1970 many more books of prose fiction are published that show the contradictions of class, political disorientation, and the social crisis that is confronting the nation at all levels. The narrative fiction that appears beginning in 1970 is a socially committed literature, not with social-agrarian reform, but rather with the urban social reality. Although rural analysis still endures, it is not in the aspect of the romance of the land and family life, but rather confronting

> more expansive motivations such as pressures of national and foreign companies to take land away from peasants, problems of squatters, and in general that life Quince Duncan correctly calls *Hombres curtidos* (Weathered men). (Chase 1975, 114–15)

However, while looking inward at a changing and increasingly urban society, Costa Rican writers were also influenced by the French postwar *nouveau roman*, the new novel, and postmodernism. As Alfonso Chase comments, "perhaps since 1965, the new ideas of the novel of the French vanguard—Nathalie Sarraute, Michel Butor, Claude Simon, Alain Robbe-Grillet—were discussed and practiced by many writers, particularly the younger writers" (Chase 1975, 109). The new novel and postmodernist narrative strategies challenged the linear structure, single omniscient narrator, and time/space unity of the traditional realist novel. In order to present a perspective that was more compatible with the alienation, marginality, and disconnect that characterized their rapidly changing world, some writers adopted techniques that moved the novel away from what Roland Barthes's characterized as a "readerly" text (accessible, predetermined structure, information supplied to a passive reader) toward the "writerly" text (narrative ambiguity inviting the reader to construct meaning and interpretation). The new novel was generally characterized by multiple perspectives or ambiguous voices; subversion of linear structures and chronological order; use of dream states, stream of consciousness, and interior monologues; blurring of the fictional world and reality; and the tendency to be self-referential and self-reflective, that is to say, to draw attention to the text's fundamental artifice and process of writing. Several writers also demonstrated some postmodernist narrative strategies that decentered cultural "truths" and looked at them not as absolutes but rather as constructs that were formed historically and have "naturalized." These strategies betray a particular skepticism of universalisms through the use of popular culture, the mixing of genres, the blending of fictional worlds and reality, and bricolage (using the old to form the new). Through the techniques of the new novel and postmodernism, these writers dismantled the myths that had previously defined "Costa Ricanness." By questioning history, problematizing issues of class, reexamining identity, interrogating the progress of social reform, and engaging with urban landscapes, they revitalized the Costa Rican narrative as well.

In presenting black characters who examine the meaning of their citizenship and who participate in the construction of the Costa Rican nation, Duncan destabilizes the *leyenda blanca* (white legend), the myth of a white homogenous nation. *Hombres curtidos*, *Los cuatro espejos*, *La paz del pueblo*, and *Final de calle*, published in 1971, 1973, 1976, and 1979 respectively, reflect the narrative tendencies of the time. Duncan's experimentation with the new novel challenges the widely accepted and reiterated notions of who is Costa Rican. His writing interrogates the country's discourses of democracy and equality by exposing the marginalization of some of its citizens and its recreation of oligarchic structures that reforms were meant to dismantle. Like Carlos Fuentes's *Death of Artemio Cruz*, Duncan's *Hombres curtidos* and *Los cuatro espejos* present the lonely Orphic journey of the self on a quest to explore issues of national identity. In *Hombres curtidos*, for example, the protagonist, Clif Duke, makes a return home to Limón Province after living in the Central Valley for over a decade. Duke is actually writing the story we read, drawing attention both to his West Indian cultural heritage (through oral culture and memory) and his Costa Rican citizenship as he writes his family's history into the national narrative. Through flashbacks and multiple narrative shifts, it becomes apparent in the text that the narration is not only Duke's individual story about finding and claiming place, but also that of his collective ancestry—and that of all Afro–Costa Ricans of West Indian descent. Similarly, in another Afro–Costa Rican themed novel, *Los cuatro espejos*, "the drama of identity" begins when one morning, Charles McForbes, a black man in San José, realizes he cannot see his reflection in the mirror. What follows is a fragmented, nonlinear novel that breaks the unity of time and space, a disjointed structure that "mirrors, so to speak, the fragmentation of the protagonist himself" (Mosby 2003b, 135).

Duncan's style is noted for the alteration of linear time and the presence of multiple narrators and multiple voices. He often employs stream-of-consciousness writing to capture the interior or subconscious thoughts of his characters along with dreams, flashbacks, and flash-forwards in order to expose their multiple layers of personality. However, unlike other writers with similar aesthetic tendencies, Duncan's characters do not exist exclusively within the frame of their own fictional universe. There is a relationship between Duncan's technically inventive writing and the broader issues of ethnic and national identity (Mosby 2003b, 122). This connection is what Duncan identifies as *afrorealista* (Afro-realist), a link between the word and the world, offering a certain correspondence between the fictional text and the reality of people of African descent in the Americas and other parts of the Diaspora.

Afrorealismo (Afro-realism), described by Dellita Martin-Ogunsola as "the theory of lived experience," is the term Duncan uses to distinguish not only his own position as an Afro-Hispanic writer and his approach to writing about black cultures in the Americas, but also the contributions of other writers of African descent in the Spanish-speaking world (Martin-Ogunsola 2004, 14). He first introduced the term in his 1996 publication of personal anecdotes, *Un señor de chocolate* (A Chocolate Man), and later expounded on the concept in conferences and publications in the United States and Central America.[11] Afro-realism in Quince Duncan's fiction reflects a tendency, also present in works by other writers of African descent in the Spanish-speaking world, to correlate the fictional world of the narrative with the reality of communities of peoples of African descent. This perspective allows writers to create representations of blackness and "otherness" in the discourse of national literatures. The writings of authors of African descent in the Spanish-speaking world, such as Lucía Charún Illescas (Peru), Nelson Estupiñán Bass (Ecuador), Adalberto Ortiz (Ecuador), Marta Rojas (Cuba), Manuel Zapata Olivella (Colombia), though rooted in a long tradition of oral literature in Africa before the transatlantic slave trade, are also anchored in the social, cultural, and historical realities of their respective countries. In *Un señor de chocolate*, Duncan states: "Afro-realism is the lived word. This means that it is based on experience. It is a construction and reconstruction of reality, without ceasing to be fiction, without losing the sense of fantasy that makes us feel delight when reading it." He continues:

> On the other hand, Afro-realism carries within it the word of the ancestors, all of those events that happened a long time ago and continue to affect us. These things that are passed from mouth to mouth and form our tradition give us identity that legitimizes our survival. Through these handed-down stories we know that we form part of a fragmented cultural collective. Our culture was ruptured by 500 years of oppression. Afro-realism announces the small piece of reality that is left. . . . It is not limited to showing that the African conscience is ruptured, but rather is concerned with its reconstruction. For that reason Afro-realism is the dream of the reconstructed word. (Duncan 1996, *Un señor* 10)

Afro-realism offers an alternative vocabulary particularly when talking about belief systems and phenomena often associated with the supernatural. The term carries a greater cultural significance than "magic realism," which sometimes appears in Latin American fiction, often as the coexistence of the living and the dead, but also has a connotation of the fantastic, without any necessary correlation to actual occurrences in diasporic belief systems. Rather than rely on traditional referents of canonical Latin American literature, such as Western mythology or techniques like magic realism, Afro-realism draws upon the "Africanizing subversion of the language, recurring references to previously unknown traditions or at least until now marginal such as Muntu, Samamfo, Ebe yiye, the vindication of Yemayá, and the incorporation of Atlantic Coast English Creole" (Duncan 2005, "El afrorealismo" 7).[12]

Duncan identifies six general points that are characteristic of Afro-realism:

(1) The restoration the Afro-American voice through the subversion of colonial language through strategies such as neo-African linguistic play, use of Africanisms, appropriation of the Creole to demonstrate cultural resistance, and recovery of the oral tradition.
(2) The vindication of the African symbolic memory by turning away from European symbols and relying on ancestral memory and African and neo-African belief systems.
(3) The restructuring of an informed historical memory of the African Diaspora by challenging the omissions, denials, and myths of the dominant culture, especially as it relates to Afro-descendants.
(4) The reaffirmation of the concept of ancestral community, which includes a dual concept of transnational blackness and connection with ancestral spirits. In "El afrorealismo: Una dimensión nueva de la literatura latinoamericana," Duncan argues that "the community is not just the nation, tribe, or clan. It encompasses all of Africa, all territory inhabited by people of African descent, together with historical events, their myths and legends. In this context, Afro-realist writers go beyond the level of caricature in order to construct true literary personages."
(5) The use of an "intra-centric" (intrinsic) narrative perspective, that is to say, a narrative voice from within the community that does not resort to stereotypes. Duncan decries the use of stereotyped, negrista representations, and he observed in his keynote address to the College Language Association that "there is a critical but proud assumption and confrontation of the Black experience: slavery, cultural heritage, racism, whether in the form of systematic exclusion from power structures and decision making processes; in the form of invisibility, that is, the suppression form of textbooks, census, etc. or be it regional marginalization and personal stigmatization in the press, or whatever form it may take."
(6) The search for and affirmation of a black identity that rejects identification with the colonizers by identifying with the colonized, and coming to terms with this history and the resulting social dynamics and hierarchies. It is also an attempt to destroy the inferiority complex produced by the primacy of Eurocentric whiteness of Hispano-Mestizo identities and fully recognize the diversity of the cultures of the Americas. (Duncan 2005, "Afrorealismo"; and 2004, "Afrorealista Manifesto")

According to Duncan, the incorporation of any or all of these elements of *afrorealismo* reveals an effort to counter the long history of the descendants of

Africans portrayed as objects or "decorative elements" in mainstream/canonical Latin American literature, particularly *negrista* literature. He states, "these elements, *are not decorative* in the work of these [Afro-realist] writers, but rather are fundamental in the search for identity, reconciliation with their stolen cultural heritage, and the assumption of their Afro-Hispanic ethnicity. And, contrary to some of their compatriots, they do not consider ethnic diversity as a danger to national unity, above all, they embrace it as a source of wealth" (Duncan 2004, "Afrorealista Manifesto" n.p.).

The Afro-realist approach to Afro–Latin American fiction casts works by this group of authors as counternarratives of the official discourse of the national literatures that tend to promote a vision of a national identity that is linked to racial exclusion and promotes stereotyped or folkloric representations of blackness that are regarded as peripheral to the nation. Afro–Latin American writers center the perspective of the marginalized, subaltern voice of the black and mulatto population and reveal a consciousness of the prevailing racial ideologies that divide blacks and mulattoes as well as their mestizo and indigenous brothers. Quince Duncan in his exploration of *afrorealismo* states: "the search for identity that characterizes Afro-realist authors, challenges the false white-black dichotomy in order to recover a repudiated part of their identity as descendants of Africans. In the process, this affirmation includes all of the variability of *mestizaje* (race mixture), including the European contribution. And in open repudiation of all ethnophobic positions, the Afrorealists take on the African, Latin, and Indigenous position without omitting the contributions of other ethnicities" (Duncan 1996, *Un señor* 10).

Duncan and other Afro-Hispanic authors tend to use the cultural reality of peoples on the periphery as their narrative subject and their communities as the geographical milieu of their works instead of turning to speculative or imagined worlds. This is also an act of what Paulette Ramsay describes as "cultural and literary marronage," or the resistance to degradation of Afro-descendants "demonstrated by the affirmation of their blackness and links with Africa through the highlighting of different aspects of the African heritage" (Ramsay 1994, 32). Through Afro-realism, Duncan articulates the link between the African roots of the Diaspora and the geographical realities of its consequence, such as the cultures of peoples of West Indian descent in Central America. Because of his engagement with critical issues of West Indian migration to Central America, cultural and national identity, and history, the prose of Costa Rican writer Quince Duncan exemplifies Afro-realist tendencies in Afro-Hispanic literature.

Duncan's work has garnered critical attention in Costa Rica and North America and has earned him several literary prizes and academic honors, including the Editorial Costa Rica prize in 1978 and the distinguished Aquileo J. Echeverría

National Prize in 1979 for *Final de calle*. In spite of the fact that Quince Duncan is perhaps one of the most gifted writers of Central American letters, he remains unknown to literary circles in the majority of the hemisphere. He has attracted a devoted public of mostly North American academics, but his appeal has not extended beyond that narrow audience because of the limited availability of his texts, particularly his novels in either Spanish or in translation.[13] In other parts of the Americas, lack of recognition may be due largely to the politics of literary production and the tendency to overlook black writers of the Hispanic world. Even in his native Costa Rica, Duncan has faced criticism based not on the quality of his work but on his ethnic difference. Because his Afro–Costa Rican characters defy Costa Rica's national self-image, some critics have labeled his work as "non–Costa Rican" and therefore not part of the official discourse. Some have accused Duncan of not using standard Costa Rican Spanish, a frequently hurled attack against Afro–Costa Ricans. Duncan dispelled this misconception with the publication of *Final de calle* in 1979. Duncan anonymously submitted this novel to a literary contest sponsored by Editorial Costa Rica where it won the prestigious Editorial Costa Rica prize. The revelation that Duncan authored the novel about the 1948 civil war and its consequences also served to quiet critics who had accused him of dealing with only black issues. It is striking to note that in spite of the praise Duncan received for being the first Afro–Costa Rican novelist to present authentic characters of West Indian descent, it is *Final de calle* that is his most widely read work within Costa Rica. In "Afrorealista Manifesto," the keynote address to the 2004 College Language Association Convention held in Nashville, Tennessee, Duncan shares an anecdote about the selection of *Final de calle* as one of the twenty-five novels chosen to commemorate the twenty-fifth anniversary of Editorial Costa Rica:

> I remember some time ago with the late Victor Hugo Peralta, who, mind you, was a dear friend. In the occasion of the celebration of the 25th anniversary of Editorial Costa Rica, a collection of twenty-five novels was put together in a special edition. *Final de calle*, my award-winning novel which has almost nothing to do with the Black community, was selected. I was not happy about that, because even the local critiques unanimously insisted that my work represented "la incorporación del negro a la literatura costarricense" [the incorporation of the black into Costa Rican literature]. After some hesitation and discussion his answer was very clear: "*Final de calle* es más *nuestro*" [*Final de calle* is more *ours*]. So I imagine that an appropriate word for my Black fiction would be "exotic." (Duncan 2004, "Afrorealista Manifesto" n.p.)

It appears that in spite of the author's efforts to insert Afro–Costa Rican themes into his nation's literary canon, he is most renowned in his homeland for a novel that only deals marginally with blackness and therefore is more acceptable by the Costa Rican mainstream. Nevertheless, Duncan continues to influence Costa Rican literature by providing a model for contemporary Afro–Costa Rican writers like poets Shirley Campbell Barr and Delia McDonald Woolery.

Quince Duncan is a writer shaped by the memory of his West Indian forebears and his Costa Rican home. He remains the leading Afro–Costa Rican prose fiction writer, and his writing "remembers," repeating Hansen's dictum, the journey of the first generations of West Indian migrants and their children. This process of remembering through the written word memorializes their struggles and reminds all Costa Ricans of a time in their collective past when West Indians and their descendants were not embraced as *hermaniticos* (brothers). His novels, in particular, examine the process of not only becoming a legal, juridical citizen, but also a cultural citizen. The first is a "simple" matter of law, and the second is a process that is still incomplete, as Duncan also reminds his readers that the efforts to attain citizenship have not erased racial prejudice. Writing Afro–West Indians into the broader narrative of Costa Rican literature is not only an act of inserting that which was omitted and advocating for greater inclusion, but also an act that prompts questioning of the national literary canon and national discourse of identity.

Nevertheless, Duncan's writing also extends outward from Costa Rica and the Caribbean to connect events in the region to a greater diasporic consciousness by relating events to other geographic locations of the African Diaspora. In his novels and short fiction he explores the symbolism of Africa, fictionalizes the culture of the Ashanti before and after colonial contact, and analyzes the impact of the slave trade and the lives of African descendants in Europe and the Americas. Theorizing the Diaspora highlights the interconnectedness and the cultural tensions that characterize the dispersal of Africans in Old and New Worlds.

While the majority of his writing addresses black cultures in Costa Rica and the African Diaspora, some of his fiction presents a wider critique of Costa Rican society. *Final de calle*, "El Mayor" (Big Chief), "El candidate" (The Candidate), "La noche de Arenal" (The Night Arenal Exploded), "El engranaje" (Family Ties), and *El trepasolo*, Duncan's only dramatic text, do not specifically take up questions of ethnic identity and racism but deal with themes of political corruption, government bureaucracy poverty, and social class. The issues of social and economic inequality, political injustice, and human rights found in these texts, in conjunction with his examination of ethnic, cultural, and identity in texts such as *Hombres curtidos* and "Un regalo para la abuela," connect to form a larger counternarrative. This counternarrative challenges the tendency in contemporary Costa Rican fiction to elide matters of ethnic and cultural difference, as well as the official national discourse on democracy and equality, while giving voice to those marginalized by the country's literary canon. Duncan endeavors to incorporate those previously relegated to the margins into the narrative mainstream.

1
Short Fiction

Before the release of his earlier novels, *Hombres curtidos* and *Los cuatro espejos*, Duncan published short stories in newspapers, journals, and in stand-alone collections. Several of the author's short stories address the peculiarities of the Costa Rican social and political landscape while others address more universal themes such as sudden loss, betrayal, and youth. However, Duncan is most noted for his themes of Afro–West Indian history, language, and culture on the Atlantic coast. His short story collections include *El pozo y una carta* ("The Pit and a Letter," 1969), *Bronce* ("Bronze," 1970), *Una canción en la madrugada* ("Dawn Song," 1970), *Mangonía* ("Mangoland," ca. 1971), *La Rebelión Pocomía y otros relatos* ("The Pocomía Rebellion and Other Stories," 1979), and *Cuentos escogidos* ("Selected Stories," 2004). Some themes presented in the short stories appear later in more developed treatments in his novels. For example, the short story "El pozo," about tragedy during the Costa Rican civil war, prefigures the publication of the award-winning novel *Final de calle*. The title story of the collection, *La Rebelión Pocomía y otros relatos*, foreshadows the themes of Afro–West Indian religious expression and resistance in Limón presented in the novel *La paz del pueblo* (1978).

El pozo y una carta (The Pit and a Letter)

The appearance of the two-story collection, *El pozo y una carta*, marks the beginning of Duncan's publishing career. Prior to the publication of *El pozo y una carta*, a few of Duncan's short stories appeared in Costa Rican periodicals. However, this first collection prompted national interest in his work. The collection of two short stories foretells the two directions of Duncan's prose fiction: (1) the impact of Costa Rica's 1948 civil war on the national consciousness, and (2) the engagement with Afro–West Indian history and cultural heritage in the question of Afro–Costa Rican identity. "El pozo" is a story about two friends, Gabriel and Carlos, whose idealism about the future of their nation leads them to join the revolutionary forces in the civil war. Their brotherhood is shattered when Carlos loses his life in battle. Gabriel, who is captured by government forces, is left with memories of their childhood and the haunting voice of the dying Carlos repeating his name, "Gabriel . . . Gabriel . . ."

This short story, published before the devastating civil wars of the 1970s and 1980s that plagued several Central American countries, conveys the universal message about the deep and permanent scars that civil war leaves on a nation struggling with democracy and progressive reform. However, it is also specifically a Costa Rican story that recalls the destruction that accompanied the 1948 revolution that pitted an implausible alliance of Catholics, conservatives, and communists against a group of liberal-minded reformers. While there are no explicit references to Costa Rica's 1948 revolution, the suggestion of a political climate hostile to the opposition and the identifiable geographic markers such as the Mercado Borbón, located in the center of San José, connects the text to this historical event.

The second story, "Una carta" is a marvelously concise work that captures the impact of internal migration of Afro–Costa Ricans from small provincial towns to larger, urban centers in the nation's Central Valley and abroad. The story also appears, with a few minor alterations, in the collection *Una canción en la madrugada*. "Una carta" follows the unhappy life of Miss Spence, an Afro–Costa Rican grandmother in the town of Siquirres in the coastal province of Limón. Miss Spence has three children and all three have moved away—two to Limón and one to San José—in search of better opportunities. Miss Spence is left to care for her son's seven children after he migrates to San José. For two years, she travels daily to await the arrival of the train from San José in hopes that a letter from her son will arrive with a remittance to care for his family.

One of the notable elements of the text is Duncan's use of language to describe the landscape and Miss Spence's daily routine to receive news from her son. The story opens with "It's boiling" ("Hierve") and a description of the boiling heat of the humid earth and the scorching wind (*PC* 11). The arrival of the train provides no relief, but rather "stifle[s] the lament of the oppressed land, overtaken by great need, anguish, and intense heat" ("sofoca la queja de la tierra oprimida por la mucha necesidad, la angustia e intenso calor"; *PC* 11, my translation). Miss Spence's languid and daily routine of waiting and hoping for relief from her own difficult circumstances in the form of a letter from her son is captured through the painful repetition of, "No Miss Spence, there is no letter for you today."

The heat of the region and Miss Spence's unfulfilled hopes are temporarily broken by the receipt of the letter from her son:

> She broke the seal of the letter while the little ones dispersed, and stood there looking at a beautiful paper bill that peeked out from the envelope.
>
> A light breeze softened the heat from the environment and disappeared, carrying with it prayers that quickly sought God's ears.
>
> Rompió el sello mientras los pequeños se dispersaban, y se quedó mirando un hermoso billete que asomaba de entre el sobre.
>
> Un ligero soplo de aire amortiguó el calor del medio ambiente, y se alejó portando preces, buscando aprisa [sic] los oídos de Dios. (*PC* 13; my translation)

In spite of this momentary relief from the heat and the financial struggle to support her son's children, the rhythmical pattern of her difficult life continues. Miss Spence caresses the long-awaited letter as the heat of the Caribbean province continues to boil. She takes the few *colones* inside the envelope to buy fish to prepare a meal for her grandchildren and a few lottery tickets in hopes of extending her fortune.

Una canción en la madrugada (Dawn Song)

Written in 1967 and published in 1970, *Una canción en la madrugada*[1] is a collection of ten stories dedicated "to Limón Province, to the people of Estrada, and especially to the sacred memory of James, Elvira, and Eunice." This connection with the Caribbean coast and its people, as well as the familial ties to his grandparents and mother, recur prominently in the collection's themes of Afro–West Indian culture in Limón Province. The stories in *Una canción en la madrugada* portray different aspects of life in the coastal region at different periods, most notably, the nineteenth-century arrival of West Indian laborers, the 1948 civil war, and the 1960s and early 1970s. The title story "Una canción en la madrugada" (Dawn Song) and "Las oropéndulas" (Swan Song) depict the complex relationship between human beings and the natural environment. Regional legends and folktales are recast in "Duelo entre amigos" (Duel between Friends) and "La luz del vigía" (The Watchman's Light). The history and customs of the province, as well as contemporary social issues such as sexual harassment, changing cultural values, immigration, and underemployment, appear as themes in "La mujer de la capa blanca" (Sophisticated Lady), "Un regalo para la abuela" (A Gift for Grandma), "Nueve días" (Nine Days), "Una carta" (A Letter), "Dos caminos" (Two Roads), and "Demasiado Peso" (When I Lay My Burden Down).

The opening story of the collection, "Una canción en la madrugada," tenderly describes in beautifully poetic language a few days in the life of a Limonese couple, Juan and Mayra. The story opens with a description of the dawn: "The crystalline clarity of the dawn penetrates the room in all its splendor, scattering its spots of light everywhere. Nothing disturbs the joy of the two lovers" ("La cristalina claridad del alba penetra al cuarto con todo su esplendor, esparciendo por doquier sus manchas de luz. Nada turba la felicidad de los dos enamorados"; *TBS* 37; *CM* 11). The remainder of the text is a portrait of life in Siquirres along the railroad line in which the natural splendor of the region serves not only as a backdrop but also as a central "character" present throughout the story. The loving warmth and affection the couple share with each other is interrupted by the workday. Juan must take the train to the banana plantation, and he rushes through the morning calm in order to prepare for his long workday. The symbolism of the natural environment presents a series of oppositions as observed by Dellita Martin-Ogunsola: "In 'Dawn Song' Duncan contrasts the searing innervating daytime, symbolized by the tropical heat, to the cool refreshing night when John and Mayra relax in bed, represented by the translucent aura of the sky. The author extends this symbolic chart of opposites to the natural world, for the banana tree, cocoa plants, machete, and swamp are associated with pain, lack of fulfillment, futility, and danger, while distant objects like sky, stars, moonlight, and clouds suggests joys, hopes, and dreams" (Martin-Ogunsola 2004, 32). The bodies of Juan and Mayra in love, labor, and the struggle to survive are depicted as part of the natural environment of the region, which underscores the bond and dependency of humans on nature. Implicitly, there is a message that the West Indians belong to this place and by extension the nation through the careful integration of markers of Afro–West Indian culture such as food, language, music, and religion. According to Richard L. Jackson in *The Black Image in Latin American Literature*, in Duncan's work, "The Anglo-Caribbean background is reflected through the portrayal of Black customs as well as through the use of the English language in words and idioms used by characters most often in exclamatory expressions provoked by undesirable conditions, frustrations, and resentments" (1976, 129). Mayra and Juan use the expression "cho," a Jamaican exclamation of annoyance, when Juan rushes to catch the train. She says to Juan: "Like a runnin' ant . . . ¡cho! And what makes me boil is you haven't even washed your face" ("Tanta prisa . . . ¡cho! Y lo que me da cólera es que ni siquiera te has lavado la cara"), and he responds, "Cho, woman gimme the tea, man and stop talking, man" ("Cho, dame el té, hombre, y dejá de hablar, hombre"; *CM* 13; my translations). After the workweek is over, we get a glimpse into their Sunday ritual of church services at the Catholic and Anglican churches, fishing on the Pacuare River, and dancing to the blues and calypso.

"Duelo entre amigos" tells the tale of two unlikely friends who become enemies, and in an ironic twist of fate they become forever linked in local lore. A rum-drinking Jamaican and a guaro-swigging Costa Rican from Cartago form a friendship during a time when West Indians and the "natives" did not mix socially. However, the two men develop a bond, a brotherhood united initially by the love of imbibing spirits. Their relationship takes a dramatic turn when a cultural clash occurs during one night of drinking. The Costa Rican is a guest in the Jamaican's home and he spits on the floor of his host. This action, an accepted practice among Costa Rican peasants, is considered a personal affront in the eyes of the Jamaican.[2] The friendship ends violently and ironically. Both men are buried facing each other, "so that they may share the land, cold, and rain" ("para que compartiesen la tierra, el frío y la lluvia"; *TBS* 53; *CM* 20). The two men become legends in the region, prompting stories that begin with the familiar "Once upon a time there was a Jamaican and a man from Cartago who were friends" ("Había una vez un jamaicano y un cartago que eran amigos"; *TBS* 53; *CM* 20).

The 1948 Costa Rican civil war provides the historical setting for "Un regalo para la abuela" (A Gift for Grandma). The humor of the tale is juxtaposed with the seriousness of the armed conflict being waged. The disputed results of the presidential election of 1948 between former president Rafael Angel Calderón Guardia and Otilio Ulate created a national crisis, and "open rebellion erupted throughout the Central Valley" (Harpelle 2001, 169). An armed conflict ensued between the forces of Liberación Nacional led by former exile and opposition leader José María Figueres against the supporters of Calderón. The small town of Estrada, Limón, where "Un regalo para la abuela" is set, is a town very far removed, both culturally and politically, from the national political tensions that are sweeping the Central Valley. However, the tranquility of the Limonese village is broken by the whistle of the train and news that the armed forces of Liberación Nacional are heading toward Estrada. The town is thrust into the middle of the armed revolt when nearby Puerto Limón falls under the control of the *liberacionista* forces led by Figueres. Many of the Afro–West Indian men have already fled the area, and Cocobello, the story's protagonist, is faced with the difficult dilemma of how to protect his family and stay out of the conflict.

It is well documented that both sides of the revolt, progovernment supporters of Calderón and the rebels under the control of Figueres, sought recruits among the black population. President Teodoro Picado, a supporter of Calderón's candidacy, believed that Costa Rican–born West Indians had an obligation to protect the current government. According to historian Ronald Harpelle: "At the beginning of the civil war, President Picado's government told all Costa Rican–born West Indians that their obligation was to defend the established order against Figueres and his supporters. The reaction of the majority of the community was to avoid taking sides. For example, when a rumor reached the coastal town of Cahuita that the government was sending soldiers to look for recruits, the young men fled. Most of the people in the community knew little about the intricacies of the political crisis; furthermore, they did not care. All they knew was that that trains were not running, the port was closed, and shots were being fired in Limón" (Harpelle 2001, 169).

With the news of the encroaching forces on their way to Estrada, Cocobello is noticeably shaken. Word has traveled fast that the rebels are looking for recruits in the village, and as a healthy, able-bodied man he is a prime candidate for forced recruitment. Many men have already escaped into the mountains to avoid being conscripted by the government and the *liberacionistas*. Earlier, he successfully avoided the government troops, but now he must also avoid being taken into the ranks of the revolutionaries: "Suddenly he was in the middle of a revolution whose cause he did not understand and whose consequences were to be feared. No way! He decided to repeat the trick that had served him well with the official government." ("De repente estaba en medio de una revolución cuya causa no comprendía, y cuyas consecuencias eran de temerse. Ni modo: decidió repetir la treta que le había servido con el ejército oficial." *TBS* 59; *CM* 24). He and his wife, Ruby, become "tricksters" and employ the same Anancy-like survival tactic to avoid the rebels that saved Cocobello from conscription into the government troops: he dresses as a harmless, old woman and takes on the persona of "La Abuela" (the Grandmother)(Martin-Ogunsola 2004, 38–39).

Cocobello is the father of six sons who are under the protection of his in-laws. The narrator reiterates Cocobello's desire to save his children from harm and to stay out of the war: "He won't let them fight in a war that's not theirs." ("El no les dejará para luchar en una guerra que no es suya." *TBS* 6; *CM* 25). The soldiers arrive and proclaim that they are "revolutionaries." They question Cocobello's wife, Ruby, about the whereabouts of the male members of the household. She reveals little information and claims that she knows nothing about the conflict and has nothing to share with the men. The language Duncan uses to recount Ruby's interaction with the white and mestizo soldiers, in contrast with the easy flow of conversation with her husband, captures the sounds of an Anglophone speaker attempting to communicate in a language that is not hers. She says, "si senior," instead of the standard "sí señor" (yes sir); "mi solo tener hijos no esposo," instead of "Solo tengo hijos, no tengo esposo" (I only have children, I don't have a husband); and "mi no saber . . . mi no entiende esta cosa," instead of "yo no sé . . . no entiendo esta cosa" (I don't know . . . I don't understand this thing) (*TBS* 61; *CM* 26).[3] Furthermore, Duncan communicates through the transcription of English words in the Spanish text that the family is clearly West Indian. For example, Ruby exclaims, "Chisas Kraist" (Jesus Christ) when she witnesses the soldiers approaching their home.

The soldiers set up camp on their property and engage in a firefight with the government that ends quickly. The soldiers are enchanted with the "grandmother" and promise that after their anticipated triumph at the end of the conflict, blacks will no longer be exploited: "We'll expropriate the railroads and give them to the blacks." ("Expropiaremos el ferrocarril y se lo entregaremos al negro." *TBS* 65; *CM* 28). Hearing this, "Cocobello thought the matter sounded good to him, and he swore to support the new regime." ("Cocobello pensó que el negocio era bueno. Y juró apoyar al nuevo régimen." *TBS* 65; *CM* 28).

As the soldiers depart, they exchange comments about their experience with the blacks. Exhibiting stereotypical attitudes of white and mestizo Costa Ricans toward the blacks of Limón, they note with surprise how clean the blacks are. When one states that he finds Ruth attractive, his companion observes, "Hey, who wanna work to take care of a bunch of lil' pickaninneys?" ("Quién quiere trabajar para mantener negritos?" *TBS* 65; *CM* 28). The soldier replies, "What the . . . ? Who said anything about workin'?" ("Ydiay . . . ¿quién habló de eso?" *TBS* 65; *CM* 28), implying that although the rebels' reformist rhetoric conveys a desire to "end the exploitation" of the West Indians, they will never be fully accepted as part of the nation. The comments between the two men further perpetuate the stereotype of the sexually available black woman and the sexual exploitation of the black female body. Upon leaving, they give "grandma" a present as a token of their goodwill. After the rebels leave, Cocobello opens the package and exclaims, "Güel-ai-bi-dam" (Well I be damned, my translation). "Grandma" receives silk panties and stockings from the soldiers, provoking laughter in Cocobello. At the end of the story, in spite of the brief interruption the rebel soldiers provide, Cocobello states, "Life is just as fine as it was yesterday." ("Todo está bien como lo estuvo ayer." *TBS* 65; *CM* 28).

Life also returns to a relative state of normalcy in "La luz de vigía" (The Watchman's Light). This story details an attempt to provide a scientific explanation for an unusual phenomenon near a Limonese village that has disquieting results. For years people in the town have witnessed an unusual light in the woods on the edge of town. The explanation older residents offer is that the light appeared after the sudden death of a railroad worker. This is dismissed by a group of boys in the village who want to use the power of logic and reason to explain the presence of the light. They devise a plan to surround and confront the individual carrying the light. However, just when the boys believe they have "captured" the light, it disappears and reappears some distance behind them. The boys flee the woods and head back to town: "Nobody stopped until he got to his own house, and no one tried to tell about their strange odyssey. Hermetic muteness from everyone, terrified by desperate panic." ("Nadie se detuvo hasta llegar a su respectiva casa, y nadie quiso contar la extraña odisea. Mutismo hermético en todos ellos, aterrados por el desesperante pánico." *TBS* 81; *CM* 39).

When the group returns to school the following day, they are visibly affected and crestfallen by the events of the night before. Their teacher notices their "tristeza general" (general depression) and attempts unsuccessfully to get an explanation from the boys:

> Nobody wanted to tell the story, that sad story that everyone was denying yet knowing it was true. Because telling it would be equivalent to recognizing that it had actually happened, and by admitting it, their grandparents would soon turn out to be the real heroes, and the old people's tale would stop being a mere legend. Science painstakingly learned in the classroom was in danger. They could not let that happen.
>
> *Nadie quería contar la historia. Esa triste historia que todos negaban sabiéndola cierta. Porque contarla equivaldría a reconocer que efectivamente había sucedido, y de admitirla, los abuelos iban a resultar de pronto héroes, y su historia dejaría de ser una simple leyenda. La ciencia adquirida en el aula estaba en peligro. Y eso no era permisible.* (*TBS* 83; *CM* 39–40)

Nevertheless, one of the boys speaks up and tells the teacher about their failed venture to dispel the legend of the watchman's light. The teacher, "caught between diametrically opposed value systems," is eager to prove the power of science and reason over superstition and ignorance and decides to accompany the boys on their second attempt to discredit the legend (Martin-Ogunsola 2004, 46). She proclaims: "I have fought against superstition in all your lessons; I welcome the opportunity of doing it at the very scene of the events you guys have imagined." ("He luchado contra la superstición en las lecciones, valga la oportunidad de hacerlo en el propio escenario de los hechos imaginados por ustedes." *TBS* 83; *CM* 40).

When the students and their teacher arrive in the forest that night, the watchman's light appears. The teacher follows the light with confidence and cries out, "Sir, sir" (Señor, señor). However, she receives no reply and she gets no closer to the light or the mystery of the watchman's light. Panic sets in when the light appears between the group and their path back to town. Again as they approach the light, it reappears behind them: "Sad, downcast, terrified, and pensive, each one went home, tasting the bitterness of defeat. Almighty Science and all its legion of apostles had been trampled underfoot." ("Tristes, cabizbajos, sobrecogidos y meditabundos, cada quien se dirigió a su casa, bebiendo el acíbar de la derrota. Pisaban bajo sus plantas la omnipresencia científica y toda la legión de sus apóstoles." *TBS* 87; *CM* 42).

Two stories in the collection, "Dos caminos" (Two Roads) and "Demasiado peso" (When I Lay My Burden Down), probe cultural identity, belonging, and economic struggle and serve as preludes to the themes in Duncan's later novels *Hombres curtidos* and *Los cuatro espejos*. In "Dos caminos" a fifteen-year-old Afro–Costa Rican boy in Limón becomes a man when faced with difficult choices about his future. An ancestral voice emerges, which later becomes embodied in the form of an old black woman with "a time-worn face that reflected history in all its profundity. She knew the causes, I, the terrible consequences." ("una cara campesina, que reflejaba la historia en toda su profundidad. Ella conocía las causas, yo, las terribles consecuencias." *TBS* 89; *CM* 44). She is the voice of *samamfo*, the Ashanti term Duncan uses in his work to describe the spiritual connection between the living and the ancestors who have passed on. Here, the presence of the old woman expresses "the idea of the ancestors intervening in the lives of the living to influence them in the direction that their lives should take" (Ramsay 1994, 36). The ancestral spirit in "Dos caminos" shares the wisdom of one who has lived and sees the struggle ahead. She informs the young man that he has two paths to choose, "the low road where you rot and die, and the high road, which is a constant struggle. Choose." ("el camino de cieno en donde se vegeta y muere, y el de la Gloria que es constante lucha. Escoja." *TBS* 91; *CM* 45). He may remain in the province with few opportunities to obtain an education or migrate to the capital in order to learn Spanish and begin the difficult climb to become part of the middle class. He chooses the more arduous road of immigrating to the capital, affirming "the risks of an uncertain odyssey were preferable to the bitterness of the mudhole." ("eran preferibles los riesgos de tan insegura odisea, a la amargura del cieno profundo." *TBS* 91; *CM* 45).

We are not invited to witness the protagonist's life in San José at the end of "Dos caminos"; however, "Demasiado peso" features Brayan, a young man who remains in Puerto Limón and is weighed down by the inequality and exploitation he witnesses daily. The story begins with the narrator's lament, "Always the same mudhole as yesterday. Each day and each hour, hurtin' eyes and dry hands from so much fightin', and all for nothin'." ("Siempre con el mismo lodazal de ayer. Cada día y cada hora, los ojos llenos de agonía y las manos secas por tanta lucha, y total para nada." *TBS* 93; *CM* 46). The narrator examines the economic injustice of his situation and questions the value of working land that legally does not belong to his family but has sustained them for at least two generations. He declares, "And they say you a bum, you don't like to work the land, and I ask you, work the land for what? All told, the land don't belong to us alter fifty years of working it." ("Y dicen que uno es vago, que no le gusta trabajar la tierra, y yo pregunto, ¿trabajar la tierra para qué? Total, la tierra no nos pertenece después de cincuenta años de trabajarla." *TBS* 93; *CM* 46). The narrator-protagonist faces the threat of a long-absent owner returning to reclaim the bit of earth his family works for sustenance. This text anticipates the theme of landownership presented in Duncan's

1971 novel, *Hombres curtidos*, where the protagonist, Clif Duke, is reminded by his grandfather that they do not have legal title to the land they have settled and cultivated.

Brayan of "Demasiado peso" also questions the worth of working at the docks, observing that the owners of the company, rather than his people, are the direct beneficiaries of their labor. The protagonist-narrator comments: "Day after day with live callouses rubbin' hard against dead cysts like fire and ash, yo' palms tired of producin' wealth for none of yo' own people." ("Día tras día con los callos vivos restregándose contra los callosidades muertas, como lumbre y ceniza, la palma, cansada de producir riqueza para ninguno de los míos." *TBS* 93; *CM* 46). In *Lo jamaicano y lo universal en la obra del costarricense Quince Duncan*, Donald K. Gordon observes: "In 'Demasiado peso' (*Una canción en la madrugada*), an overwhelming element that contributes to Brayan's solitary desperation is his awareness of injustice: that work on the docks is for the benefit of others; that land that does not belong to you after fifty years of working it is for others. The economic inequalities constitute a factor that leads Brayan to a gnawing solitude and to suicide under so much weight" (Gordon 1989, 54). The narrator is trapped in an economic impasse without the education or finances to escape. The need to work for others for the rest of his life becomes a condemnation that produces uncertainty and difficulty in the life of the protagonist and becomes a weight, or a burden on his shoulders and on his mind.

He complains of the presence of salt—in his eyes, in the air, on his palms/hands, in the sand. He declares, "Your whole life is loaded with salt." ("La vida entera está cargada de sal." *TBS* 95; *CM* 47). Salt is connected not only with the briny air of the coastal town but also with preservative qualities and the bringing of bad luck when spilled. All of these associations join together and contribute to the stagnation, agony, and self-sacrifice of the protagonist who decides to remain in his hometown. Instead of struggling as a new arrival to the capital or abroad, he struggles at home, surrounded by corruption, the coarseness of life, economic inequality, and a hostile climate. He is tired of the routine of everyday life, the insincerity of his acquaintances, and he realizes that he is alone with his burden. The story ends with his mysterious death, possibly a suicide.

La Rebelión Pocomía y otros relatos (The Pocomía Rebellion and Other Stories)

Although many of the eleven stories in this collection, including the title story, "La Rebelión Pocomía" (The Pocomía Rebellion), are set in Limón, several of the collection's stories range in setting as well as theme and present a myriad view of Costa Rica and beyond. In many of the stories in *La Rebelión Pocomía y otros relatos*, a small or sudden change in fortune, political conditions, or the environment results in a major alteration in the lives of the characters. The consequences of the changes that take place range from full catastrophe to a disquieting resolution that leaves both the characters and the reader unsettled at the conclusion. Nature becomes the foe in "La llena" (The Flood) and "La noche de Arenal" (The Night Arenal Exploded) when unexpected events lead to disastrous results for the already downtrodden human characters. Similar destinies await those in sociopolitical settings, such as the presidential candidate who faces the betrayal of an ally in "El candidato" (The Candidate) or the dissolution of the lives of four orphans in "El engranaje" (Family Ties) when they are exposed to life beyond their barrio. A disheartening change of fortune is the topic of "Mitos ancestrales" (Ancestral Myths), a postcolonial parable that addresses cultural syncretism and hybridity as well as the conquest of a people.

A tragic event sets off a cry for revolution in the title story, "La Rebelión Pocomía" (The Pocomía Rebellion). Impelled to take action after the labor-related death of his brother, Jean Paul leads a rebellion of Francophone and non-Jamaican workers to protest poor working conditions and the company's broken promises to pay and repatriate the workers. The appeal for justice is connected with the members of an Afro-Christian religious sect called Pocomía (Pukumina, Pocomania), or Revivalism, which has its roots in Jamaica.[4] The practitioners of Pocomía sing hymns accompanied by drumming and dance in a counterclockwise direction with some congregants falling into a trance as they are possessed by the spirit. Jean Paul requests the aid of Mamá Bull, the "Mother" of the sect, in order to enlist the unswerving support of her followers and her visionary powers as a spiritual leader. She is the "Shepherdess," and her word carries much power over the actions of her flock. As Jean Paul approaches the obeahman's farm where the Pocomía ritual is being held, the full moon, the predatory owl, and the nocturnal "melancholy sounds and profane laments" ("sonidos melancólicos y lamentos profundos") are omens of the death and violence that is to come (*TBS* 123; *RP* 7).

Through flashbacks, Jean Paul's life appears in fragments. He is a Saint Lucian laborer who was lured to Costa Rica by the company's promises of money and benefits, but the fairy tale becomes one of disenchantment when he experiences the reality of exploitation and dangerous working conditions. He is surrounded by death in the construction of the railroad: "Death cuts off a thousand lives in the first twenty-five miles. Death lurks in every nook and cranny." ("La muerte cercena mil vidas en las primeras veinticinco millas. La muerte acecha en cada recodo." *TBS* 125; *RP* 8). His own brother is crushed to death by a rafter while building a bridge across the Matina River. Jean Paul believes it was an accident that could have been prevented had it not been for the indifference of the English foreman: "His death was a direct consequence of the foreman's indifference, one of those white-jacketed Englishmen with a cigar in his mouth." (Su muerte fue una consecuencia directa de la indiferencia del capataz, un ingles de esos, de puro en boca y chaqueta blanca. *RP* 8; my translation). Jean Paul also decries the Jamaican workers' apathy toward their working conditions. He complains that the Jamaicans are "irresponsible," "yes-men," and "slaves" because they do not denounce the lack of safety or the risk of death they confront everyday while working. They do not object to the debt they incur at the company store, nor do they protest against laboring for three months without wages. In spite of it all, they remain loyal to Minor Keith and the company.[5]

Jean Paul organizes a strike to address the workers' grievances against the company. He gains the support of workers from St. Lucia and St. Kitts, but the Jamaicans refuse to participate in the strike. When it is time to initiate the strike, Jean Paul goes to the well-hidden temple where Mamá Bull presides over the Pocomía ceremonies. She speaks, "a few words that no mortal can understand" ("unas palabras que no pueden entender los mortals") and orders wood to be thrown on the bonfire (*TBS* 129; *RP* 10). The members of the sect sing a hymn about the River Jordan, and the ceremony begins with shouts and the movement of bodies. The congregants move in a counterclockwise motion to the sounds of their hymns and the rhythms of drums. Mamá Bull encourages her followers to do what Jean Paul says and, in spite of protests, not to bring harm to the Jamaicans regardless of their apparent complicity with the company. One of the members of the sect implores other followers to look at the Jamaicans as their brethren in the same struggle: "They black like us. And 'sides, there's some of them who done become our brothers." ("Son negros como nosotros. Y además, hay algunos que se han hecho hermanos nuestros." *TBS* 131; *RP* 11). Mamá Bull agrees: "And even though they low-bellied, they is workers and they suffer the same as us." ("Y aunque aguanten pasivamente son trabajadores y sufren igual que nosotros." *TBS* 131; *RP* 11).

After one month, the Pocomía Rebellion is violently crushed by the Hispanic national government's Civil Guard with the assistance of the Jamaicans who are loyal to the company. During the rebellion, Jean Paul dies at the hands of another black man and Mamá Bull curses her Jamaican assailants: "They gon' always be like crabs in a barrel . . . nobody gon' never be successful because the other gon' block him." ("Como cangrejos en barril serán siempre . . . ninguno saldrá nunca porque el otro se lo impedirá." *TBS* 133; *RP* 12). This is a remarkable change from previous pronouncements encouraging brotherhood and unity among Afro-Caribbean workers. Ironically, although Pocomía is associated with Jamaican culture, Mamá Bull's national origin is not mentioned in the text and Jean Paul is identified as a French-speaking Saint Lucian.

Like many of Duncan's narratives, there are references to intrahistorical occurrences and vernacular culture.[6] According to the oral history of Limón, the 1910

Pocomía Rebellion involved a group of Francophone workers who demanded that the company fulfill its promise of repatriation, a request that was met with violence from authorities from the Central Valley (Duncan and Powell 1988, 73).[7] Also, "La Rebelión Pocomía," like other previously published short stories, anticipates the themes of cultural marronage (resistance) of the Afro–West Indian community against repression. *La paz del pueblo* (1976) details West Indian laborers' resistance to the exploitative relationship between the workers and the company as well as the intraethnic conflict between West Indians of different castes who divide along the lines of mainstream religion like the Anglican church and Afro-Christian sects like Pocomía. Blackness and West Indianness might basically be viewed as potential unifiers against a common oppressor; however, in "La Rebelión Pocomía," the colonial dynamic causes the Jamaican workers to be complicitous agents in their own exploitation as they identify with the agents of their oppression, Northern Railway Company and the United Fruit Company.

"La leyenda de José Gordon" (The Legend of Joe Gordon) presents another story of revolutionary resistance against the company and intraethnic betrayal. With this "literary rendition of Afro-realism," Duncan brings to the Spanish-speaking audience a legendary folk hero of earlier generations of Afro–West Indians in Limón Province (Martin-Ogunsola 2004, 73). The legend is also immortalized in a poem by Afro–Costa Rican poet Alderman Johnson Roden.[8] José (Joe) Gordon is a worker at one of the United Fruit Company's many banana plantations. Instead of receiving praise from his supervisor for saving the life of a fellow worker in the field, this act of courage costs Gordon his job. The appropriately named Mr. Brutt (which suggests brute/*bruto*), the white American plantation manager, places the financial loss of a cart full of harvested bananas above the life of one of his workers. Although Gordon is humiliated by Mr. Brutt's callousness, the workers and residents of Limón afford him heroic status.

Mr. Brutt's heartlessness is countered by José Gordon's Robin Hood–like generosity as he redistributes the company's wealth on his own terms in order to help those most in need at the company's expense. Gordon recognizes the inequality between the white administrators like Mr. Brutt who live well in the "Zone" and the blacks and mestizos who occupy shacks along the railroad tracks and in town. He simultaneously challenges this order and avenges his own mistreatment and the exploitation of other workers by sending provisions from the company commissary to the poorest residents and charging the expenses to Mr. Brutt. Gordon, who has the support of the people, challenges the supervisor's authority: "Joe's words had turned into commands and everyone was blindly obeying him without question." ("La voz de José se había convertido en palabras de mando y todos le obedecían ciegamente y sin protesta." *TBS* 227; *RP* 62).

Residents and workers feel José Gordon's presence. His body emits an intense heat (perhaps prompted by interior rage) and an aroma of rotting tomatoes. Like other notable folk heroes such as Nanny of the Maroons (Jamaica) and John Henry (United States), as José Gordon's legend grows among the residents of Limón, so do his heroic qualities and deeds. He assaults a plantation administrator at the farm by tying the man to a tree and putting his feet in an anthill. This act is singled out by the narrator because "[it] was his only act of cruelty, . . . years later the town would heatedly discuss whether or not this incident could be included in the anthology of deeds that constituted the Legend of Joe Gordon" ("[Fue] su único acto de crueldad, . . . años después, el pueblo discutió acaloradamente si se incluía o no en la antología de hechos que conformaban a la leyenda de José Gordon." *TBS* 225; *RP* 61). This footnote by the narrator is a device of metafiction, a common technique of postmodernist writers like Duncan. By engaging the reader in the diffusion of the legend of José Gordon, the narrator demonstrates that he is keenly aware of the impact his story will have on posterity.

Gordon's heroic actions do not deter the company from continuing their abuse and exploitation of the workers. The company triples the bounty they have put on his head and terminates any employee who mentions Gordon's name. In response, Gordon continues his resistance by demanding better conditions and committing acts of sabotage against the company's property to clarify his demands. It becomes apparent that the company needs to keep the workers from revolting en masse against their exploitation in order to protect its profits and Costa Rica's national government. As Donald K. Gordon observes: "The company as well as the government could not tolerate Gordon; they had to free themselves of him because they feared that his doctrines would infect the Jamaicans, Nicaraguans, Belizeans, and Hondurans and that they would command revolutionary movements in their home countries" (Gordon 1989, 42).

In a humorous passage, José Gordon taunts Mr. Brutt and one of his traveling companions in order to deliver his message in a more pointed manner. Gordon ambushes the two white men who are taking an excursion to Puerto Limón to escape the heat of the plantation. They are traveling comfortably by handcar, a manually operated railcar driven by two black workers. José Gordon's hot presence is felt, and Mr. Brutt hears the voice that has haunted him for several months. Mr. Brutt offers Gordon money to repatriate back to Jamaica in order to rid himself of this growing problem. Instead of accepting the offer to return home, Gordon forces Mr. Brutt and his traveling companion to switch clothing and duties with the black drivers. The surprising sight of two white men driving a handcar with four black men enjoying the ride perhaps proved to be too much for Mr. Brutt to handle because he swiftly disappeared after the incident without a trace.

Mr. Brutt's disappearance proves not to be a fortuitous event because his replacement is even more abusive and violent than his predecessor. The folk hero dies as a result of a betrayal, although the identity of the traitor is uncertain. The narrator mentions one possibility is "his wife's silent complicity" ("la callada complicidad de su mujer"), but the people say the criminal was a light-skinned black man who "promised only to injure him, collect, and leave while the hero suffered the metamorphosis of his resurrection." ("tenía el compromiso de herirle, cobrar, e irse, mientras José Gordon sufría la metamorfosis de su resurrección." *TBS* 245; *RP* 70).

No black worker wants to bury Joe Gordon's body, perhaps sensing that his physical body has more heroic acts to carry out, and the Hispanic Costa Ricans are given the task. En route to the cemetery the corpse sneezes and bits of flesh are dispersed, "fertilizing" the earth of the plantation and feeding the legend of Joe Gordon. His "apostles" are surrounded by "an inexplicable coldness" and disappear. The white superintendent who replaced Mr. Brutt celebrates Gordon's apparent demise, while Gordon's wife kills herself. Much like the legendary figure Mackandal of the Haitian revolution in Alejo Carpentier's *El reino de este mundo* (A Kingdom of This World), the people do not "see" what the white oppressors see. In Carpentier's novel, the folk hero is burned alive, but the people "see" him transformed into a mosquito that will continue to lead their resistance while the French colonizers only observe a rebellious slave being executed. In "La leyenda de José Gordon," the people of Limón await the resurrection of the workingman's savior who will continue to exact his revenge from the company.

Instead of the exploitative enterprise of the man-made company, in two stories of *La Rebelión Pocomía y otros relatos*, "La llena" (The Flood) and "La noche de Arenal" (The Night Arenal Exploded), the forces of nature and the environment are featured as antagonists. The mighty Reventazón River appears as a foe in the natural world of the Atlantic coast in "La llena" (The Flood), a tragic story of the powerful force of nature and the changes it brings to the life of a Limonese family. When the banks of the Reventazón overflow, the house occupied by Rogelio, his wife, Marion, and their infant son is swept away by the current of the overflowing river. The family finds refuge in a tree, but nature proves to be ruthless. Sadly, the child disappears from his father's grip as he attempts to save his wife from the elements. When they are discovered the next morning, Marion is found in the tree next to Rogelio. When they lower Rogelio down from the tree, he is lovingly clutching the empty blanket that once held their child.

The uncompromising power of nature to destroy life and human dreams appears in "La noche de Arenal" (The Night Arenal Exploded). Two men from San José, Mario and Carlos, are trekking across the landscape of the active volcano. The narrator informs the reader that the two men are making this journey to make money and return to the village of San Carlos where Carlos has fallen in love with a girl named María. The narrator does not state the exact nature of the venture, but it is clear that Carlos is motivated by the love of María to improve his station in life. Mario, his friend, accompanies him out of obligation: "Before leaving San José, he [Carlos] knew what the risks were and it was really hard for him to convince Mario to repay him the favor he owed this way." ("Antes de salir de San José [Carlos] sabía cuáles eran los riesgos y le costó trabajo convencer a Mario que pagarse de este modo el favor debido." *TBS* 161; *RP* 27).

While the Arenal volcano's eerie presence looms in the background, Carlos's thoughts turn to the more bucolic side of nature and to the object of his affection, María. Suddenly his fantasy is violently interrupted when a rabid dog attacks him. When dawn arrives, Carlos attempts to mask the severity of his wounds from his companion. His condition has deteriorated and he has been infected with rabies while "in the distance, the Arenal volcano spits its anger to the sky." ("A lo lejos hierve el volcán su ira al cielo." *TBS* 163; *RP* 28). Although it was his wish to make money and then return to life as it was before climbing the volcano, Carlos realizes he will never return home. His final thought is of María's natural beauty, which is juxtaposed with the violent furor of the volcano, which "explodes his vision into a myriad of pieces." ("revienta su visión en miríadas de fracciones." *TBS* 163; *RP* 28). His body is conquered and engulfed by the violent volcano, showing that Mother Nature prevails in this harsh landscape.

A classic battle between political forces ensues in "El mayor" (Big Chief) when professional duties and personal relationships collide with distressing consequences. Fernando Lugones has risen in rank in the Civil Guard. His position and his own arrogance push him to enforce the law against a family friend and smuggler, Don Ornaldo, who had just praised him hours before. Hypocrisy and corruption pollute the political landscape. As a child Lugones learned how to defraud customers by mixing wax, lard, and oil to sell as butter and by adding cheaper grades of rice to the more expensive grade in order to "soften" it. However, once Lugones assumes a position of authority, he has a sudden awareness of what is right and what is expected of his position. When he requests to speak with Don Ornaldo, the hypocrisy of his righteousness intertwines with his memories of childhood. Lugones contemplates the helpful role Don Ornaldo played in his life: "He was very indebted to Don Ornaldo. Very much so." ("Tenía mucho agradecerle a don Ornaldo. Mucho." *TBS* 137; *RP* 14). Nevertheless, Lugones gives the order to bring Don Ornaldo to justice and declares, "Let's go get that dirty smuggler." ("Vamos a agarrar a ese cochino contrabandista." *TBS* 137; *RP* 14). He forsakes the bonds of trust and loyalty with Don Ornaldo to display his newfound political power, achieved with the help of the one he now threatens to prosecute.

"El Mayor" is followed by another critical assessment of power and betrayal in "El candidato" (The Candidate). This story issues a sharp criticism of the post-1948 power of the major political parties in Costa Rica, bureaucracy, the oligarchy, and the concept of "the people." It is told from the perspective of Olman, a political candidate who appears to have lost the election. Olman confronts his political partner, Chaves Montada, and asserts that there was fraud in the presidential election. Olman wants to appeal the results but Chaves Montada refuses to support him. Olman also suggests the possibility of a coup so that he will emerge victorious, but Chaves, a veteran of the 1948 revolution, wants no part in such an act:

> He had not gone through the mountains, jungles, swamps, to return victorious in defense of suffrage so that I, especially I, his old fighting buddy, could now try to bring all his efforts to ruin. Chaves Montada was no pirate.
>
> *Él no había ido a las montañas, a las selvas, a los suampos, para volver victorioso en defensa del sufragio, para que yo, precisamente yo, su antiguo compañero de armas, pretendiera ahora romper en pedazos su obra. Chaves Montada no era un pirata.* (*TBS* 145; *RP* 19)

Olman argues with Chaves Montada over the efficacy of the revolution, stating that the same ruling class of coffee growers dominated politics and the economy before and after the revolution. He feels that Chaves Montada's withdrawal of support is an act of betrayal, and in an interior monologue he denounces his former ally:

> Pal, I fought for you like a mule. I was never slack or careless in anything. Yes, I ran errands. Thirty years ago I delivered messages. I desperately sought out the vote. You know it's true. I deserve victory. If I don't win the presidency now, I'll die frustrated. I'll die completely frustrated because of you. Because at the worst moment of my life, you have denied me your support. Traitor.
>
> *Luché por vos como una yegua. Nunca aflojé ni eché atrás en nada. Hice mandados, sí. Treinta años atrás hice los mandados. Busqué los votos desesperadamente. Vos lo sabés. Merezco el triunfo. Si no gano la presidencia ahora, moriré frustrado. Definitivamente moriré por culpa tuya. Porque en el momento más terrible de mi vida, me has negado tu apoyo. Traidor.* (*TBS* 147; *RP* 20)

Angered by the betrayal, Olman paces the streets, consumed with thoughts of the oligarchy that will ultimately rule the nation and the need for rebellion. In this frustrated state his thoughts turn to the tender caresses of Marilú (Mary Lou), a teacher from Talamanca. Olman equates her affection with "the people's kisses" ("besos del pueblo"), symbolizing the hope that the country will make a political change. While fantasizing about this ideal future, he condemns his former ally and others like him to hell (*TBS* 151; *RP* 22).

"El partido" (Go-o-o-o-al!) is a story about racism, the desire to conform, and Costa Rica's national pastime, soccer. It opens with a player named Guabo who complains that others have defined his being, "Afrolatindigenous, black among whites, white Indian among blacks, a white Negro among the indigenous, but in any case, underdeveloped, a bum." ("afrolatindígena, negro entre blancos, blanco entre negros, blanquinegro entre los indígenas, y en todo caso, subdesarrollado, muerto de hambre." *TBS* 165; *RP* 29). His team, Sonora, confronts an obstacle in the championship game against the famed Saprissa soccer club (their star goalie is not playing), and the protagonist faces a personal obstacle when his coach (and friend), Aleluya Rodríguez, makes impossible demands after he loans the protagonist a large sum of money.

During the game the team faces a hostile crowd of Saprissa fans. The protagonist is the object of their taunts, "Marvin . . . stomp that nigger." ("Marvin . . . liquide a ese negro." *TBS* 171; *RP* 32). The protagonist yearns to have the supportive presence of his brother in the crowd and is discomforted by his estranged sister's attendance at the match. His sister is a successful prostitute: "She was black and, precisely because of that, exotic in a society of whites. Her success rested on such. Men are usually very curious when it comes to sex." ("Era negra, y precisamente por eso, exótica en una sociedad de blancos. En tal factor residía su éxito: los hombres suelen ser muy curiosos en cuanto al sexo." *TBS* 171; *RP 32*). He dislikes Aracely, especially after she appeared as an uninvited guest to his recent wedding to a blonde, blue-eyed woman. As a well-known sports figure with a public image that depends on conforming to the dominant culture, having a prostitute as a sister, and such a dark-skinned one at that, would damage his reputation.

The confrontation between Aracely and their older sister, Rita, at the wedding celebration touches on issues of class, color, and the racial ideology of *mejorando la raza*, or "improving the race," by choosing mates of a lighter skin color. Rita insists that their brother is "colored" (moreno) because of the traces of white ancestry, but Aracely disagrees: "He's black. . . . And his wife's an Indian." ("Es negro. . . . Y su mujer es india." *TBS* 173; *RP* 33). Aracely threatens not only to show up at the soccer match between Sonora and Saprissa but also to cheer on the opposing team. She proclaims, "I'm a Saprissa fan . . . and I'm gonna come to the stadium on Sunday to laugh at you and [Melico], you rot'n brothuh." ("Soy saprisista . . . y yo voy a ir al estadio el domingo para reírme de vos, y del idiota de Guabo, ¡mal hermano!" *TBS* 171; *RP* 33).

To everyone's surprise, the protagonist's team triumphs over Saprissa, and in an ironic twist, Aracely was actually praying to the nation's patron saint for a Sonora victory. The sister he despised for her profession and her darker complexion was the only family member in attendance, and she was praying to the dark-skinned Virgin of Los Angeles, also called "La Negrita" (The Black One), to intervene so that her brother's team would triumph in their match. If the family is considered a metaphor for the nation, the tensions present in the brother-sister relationship of Guabo and Aracely illustrate the complexity of color in the Costa Rican "family." All members are not treated the same in spite of the familial bond. Guabo is the recipient of racial epithets during the soccer match ("stomp that nigger") because of his racially marked physical difference. To achieve success he must project an acceptable image to the public, and he "negatively defines himself by what he does not want to be (black) or by what he is not (white)" (Martin-Ogunsola 2004, 65). He tries to diminish his own blackness by marrying a woman of lighter skin color and European features in order to "improve the race," a strategy his sister, Rita, supports. This requires him to disassociate himself from his darker sister Aracely, who represents all the negative significations of blackness: the debased, immoral, sinful, sexualized, and exotic Other. Aracely is the specter that reminds Guabo of his blackness, but she is also the one who silently prays for his redemption, prayers that are unrequited. By extension, blackness in Costa Rica is that part of the nation that is made invisible because it does not conform to the Western construct of "progress" and acceptability.

Issues of class and economic disparity are addressed in "El engranaje" (Family Ties) when the lives of four poor orphaned children are forever changed when they visit a wealthy family's home. Pablo, Paco, Andrea, and Lucho form a ragtag family with their adoptive mother Doña Drusilda, a woman who took in these abandoned and unwanted children. Their impoverished but idyllic lives are interrupted when Leticia, a blonde, blue-eyed woman, arrives at their barrio in a chauffer-driven car looking for Doña Drusilda. The only mother figure they have known is called away to work for a wealthy family and they feel twice abandoned. The four travel to see Doña Drusilda and get a glimpse of the material possibilities of life, and they become ashamed of their own poverty. After their adventure, they discover that they no longer fit comfortably into their impoverished surroundings: "the barrio will never be the same again, neither the stone, nor the river, nor the mud, nor the tree's simple bareness at dusk. They became hostile, jealous and suspicious of one another." ("el barrio nunca volvió a ser el barrio, ni la piedra ni el río, ni la sencilla desnudez del árbol al atardecer. Se volvieron hostiles, celosos, sospechosos los unos de los otros." *TBS* 189; *RP* 41). Lucho and Paco leave the family, shattering the idyllic childhood the four once shared with their surrogate mother.

Regis, the protagonist in "Las manchas del ojo" (Eyespots), receives devastating news that he has cancer at the age of forty. He perceives his diagnosis as a death sentence, and this provokes a series of reflections that span the past and the present, the mundane and the philosophical. The narrative style of the text, a mixture of first person and third person, as well as the theme of a life-altering condition, prefigures Duncan's later novel, *Los cuatro espejos*. In "Las manchas del ojo," Regis seeks medical attention, as does Charles McForbes in the novel; however, whereas the former receives a diagnosis of cancer, the latter suffers a psychological breakdown related to his crisis of identity.

The life-changing experiences theme continues in "Las voluntades" (Little Boy Blue). The twenty-four-year-old main character has gotten a young village girl named Lupe pregnant. The news throws his parents into a tailspin as they fight to protect their son and the family's reputation. A battle of wills (las voluntades) occurs between the protagonist-narrator and his parents over the matter of responsibility and family honor. His parents question the girl's worthiness, morality, and purity, and they wonder if the pregnancy is just a ruse to trap their son in a marriage that will be socially beneficial for her. The young man, however, insists on marrying Lupe: "I made a promise in her womb; and she didn't try to trick me into marrying her." ("Forjé en su vientre una promesa. Y no es una mosquita muerta que ha tratado de casarme." *TBS* 207; *RP* 51). Nevertheless, the determination, resolve, and responsibility of the adult son dissolve into a childlike submission when his father, Santos, beats him. After the bloody assault, the protagonist-narrator reverts to a child of "Mommy and Daddy" (*hijo de mamí y papí*), an adult child spoiled and sheltered by overprotective parents:

> They've finally stopped the bleeding. Santos is at my side now. My mama's fondling my hair. They've begged me to forgive them. They've talked about allowance money for the baby. I remember Santos's voice in the clear dark of my childhood dreams. I remember my mama's breasts in my little mouth. And once I come to my senses here in my parents' house, I realize that I'm not gonna get married to Lupe next Thursday evening at 7:30 like I had planned to, because my daddy's calling her up on the telephone to tell her no.
>
> *Han logrado al fin detener la hemorragia. Santos está a mi lado ahora. Mi madre me acaricia los cabellos. Han hablado de perdones. Han hablado de pensiones alimenticias para el niño. Recuerdo la voz de Santos en el claroscuro de mis sueños infantiles. Recuerdo las glándulas mamarias de mi madre en mi boca pequeña. Y en casa descubro que no me casaré con Lupe el jueves a las*

> *siete y media como había previsto, porque mi padre la llama por teléfono y se lo dice.* (*TBS* 211; *RP* 53)

The young man is not only the heir to his parents' material wealth, but he will also carry on the family name, reputation, and legitimate bloodline; therefore, he must conform to their desires and social expectations. His parents adhere to the notion that "sons are not meant to nurse old people, but to prolong the species." ("los hijos no son para nutrir vejeces, sino para prolongar la especie." *TBS* 209; *RP* 52). In spite of his determination to go against bourgeois social convention and marry a girl of a lower class who has not received the approval of his parents, the son acquiesces to parental authority.

The subject of change is again present in the postcolonial parable "Los mitos ancestrales" (Ancestral Myths), a novella that closes the collection *La Rebelión Pocomía y otros relatos*. Donald K. Gordon in *Lo jamaicano y lo universal en la obra del costarricense Quince Duncan* observes that this story represents the struggle for identity through the "true-myth" tone presented in the text, similar to that Jorge Luis Borges and Carlos Fuentes practice. It opens with a quote by Sri Lankan/British human rights activist A. Sivanandan, which introduces the novella's premise about colonization and the postcolonial hybrid identities it produces: "On the margin of European culture . . . the 'coloured' intellectual is an artifact of colonial history. . . . He is a creature of two worlds, and of none" (*RP* 73). "Los mitos ancestrales" chronicles the impact and changes that result from the initial contact with a European explorer named Germanson in the African land of Kumasi and the eventual conquest and colonization of its people (Gordon 1989, 19).[9] The encounter has dire consequences and leads to the destruction of the narrator's native culture, but has the potential to create a syncretic one that incorporates elements of both the conquered and the conquerors. The griot-like narrator speaks from his prison of the past, preserving the memory of the traditional, precolonial culture. The use of Africanisms makes allusions to the gods and territory associated with the Ashanti, including a reference to Anansi/Anancy. He travels to Paris where he sees artifacts from his culture displayed alongside those of other conquered peoples. The narrator learns more about Germanson's manipulation of his culture's valorization of the written word and about the unwitting complicity of his own people that led to their subjugation. He speaks not only as one who has a connection to the past, but also as one who is aware that a new syncretic culture must be forged if the descendants of the conquered and the conquerors are both to survive.

The narrator sees the precolonial past as idyllic: "I, a young boy, used to dream while rapturously watching the adults dance, while intently listening to the virile story played out by the Tom-Tom, and while joyfully witnessing the performance of men who knew no greed, of men who never touched what was their neighbor's, of men who had never broken a promise." ("suspiraba contemplando la danza de los mayores, oyendo el cuento vigoroso del Tam-tam y mirando extasiado la demostración de los hombres que no codician, de los que nunca tocan lo ajeno, de los que jamás han roto el juramento." *TBS* 251, 253; *RP* 75). He values *samamfo*, an Ashanti term frequently used in this text and others by Duncan to describe the collective spirit and legacy of the ancestors, as well as the coexistence of the living with the spirits of their departed ancestors.

Samamfo becomes a force of resistance to the enslavement of the narrator's people. He criticizes the colonizers' attempts to put their culture on display in Western museums, which the narrator refers to as "a vain effort to gather from this land the remains of our Samamfo held captive in another country next to the captive Samamfo of others." ("Inútil esfuerzo por recoger de la tierra los restos de nuestro Samamfo cautivo en otra tierra, junto al Samamfo cautivo de otros pueblos." *TBS* 251; *RP* 74). He also describes the postcolonial dilemma of having to choose between the cultural legacy of his people, represented by the element gold, and the culture imposed upon them by their conquerors, represented by silver. He stands between the colonized and the colonizer: "Cursed be the fingers that now point and oblige me to choose between gold and silver, between light and shadow, between vigilance and sleep." ("Malditos dedos que apuntan ahora y me obligan a escoger entre el oro y la plata, entre la luz y el claroscuro, entre la vigilancia y el sueño." *TBS* 253; *RP* 75).

In his account of the history of the people of Kumasi, the arrival of Germanson, a European explorer, is a watershed moment. Germanson is described as the "herald of my country's agony and the beginning of this circle of solitude." ("un heraldo de la agonía de mi pueblo y el inicio de este círculo de soledad." *TBS* 253; *RP* 75). The griot-narrator discovers on a visit to London that Germanson wrote three letters describing his travels to Kumasi. Not unlike correspondence left by Columbus and other European explorers, each of the three letters presents a different perspective of the same occurrence for different audiences and purposes, an attempt to manipulate the perception of the Other through the West's highly valued written culture. Germanson's first draft, which is more "objective" and factual, is then altered in the second draft, written the following day, that dehumanizes his hosts by highlighting their primitivism, their "otherness." The Kumasi hospitality is distorted as Germanson places himself in the narrative as someone being mistaken for a pagan god—a clear allusion to the conquest of the Americas. The third letter Germanson produces is the final, "official" version that presents the natives as primitive and barbaric Others worthy of obliteration, and he asks specifically for compensation for tolerating the "indecency" he witnessed. The narrator also learns that Germanson plans to exploit the discord between the Kumasi king and his brother, Omowa, by appealing to Omowa's greed in order to divide and conquer the kingdom. With Germanson's encouragement, Omowa challenges his nephew, the prince, to a duel that leads to the latter's death. The European conquistador uses the disharmony among the people of Kumasi to impose his own order, and the people are unable to resist the Europeans' advanced weaponry. Omowa realizes Germanson's intentions too late and dies in the struggle against the invading army. Germanson removes the gold from Kumasi and gives the natives silver crosses, thus beginning "El mito de cautiverio," or the colonization of Kumasi.

The narrator speaks of the arrival of colonists from Europe, the process of learning the language of the colonizer, and the adoption of their customs. The colonial arrivals install an exploitative economic order and a diet that relies on European products, creating considerable wealth for the metropolitan center. He also addresses the tribulations of the underground anticolonial movement, as well as evidence that the people of Kumasi are abandoning their traditional ways.

The narrator and his son are then executed for their resistance to the colonizer, but he returns many years later after what he describes as a "deep dreamless sleep" ("un sueño profundo sin sueño"). He finds himself "reborn" in the "master's house" as the child of a servant in the governor's house (*TBS* 267; *RP* 82). In this ancestral return, he finds that everything is different—as if his culture had been obliterated. He is raised in another Germanson's house bearing the name "Governor" instead of "Conqueror," and learns from within the "big house" "all of the tricks of science and good manners" ("todos los trucos de la ciencia y los buenos modales"; *TBS* 267; *RP* 82). Although the narrator has latent memories of the precolonial era and the conquest, he finds that most have no such recollection of the past, particularly of the resistance and struggle to keep alive the Kumasi traditions. Only the peasants in rural villages retain some cultural memories. The conquered peoples are prohibited from owning weapons without special permission from the governor. Sunday, rather than Monday, is declared the first day of the week, a change that represents the invaders' revision and erasure of the culture of his people:

> No one remembered the dormant history of the Tom-Tom [drum]. The people's songs still possessed the cadence of Samamfo, for no one called them by name, but instead "our heritage." The Tom-Tom had lost its centuries-old clarity and now talked of monotony. Of an almost incoherent monotony. Of arrested words.

> *Nadie se acordaba de mi torpe historia sobre el Tam-tam. Los cantos del pueblo, tenían aún la cadencia de Semanfo [*sic*], pero nadie los llamaba por su nombre, sino "nuestra herencia." El Tam-tam había perdido su claridad de siglos, y solo hablaban de monotonía. De monotonía casi incoherente. De verbos presos.* (*TBS* 267, 269; *RP* 82)

The history of the people of Kumasi is no longer told from their perspective, but rather begins with the arrival of the conquerors. No one has memories of the past, and the conquerors have become the possessors and police of the written word, which is given precedence over the oral tradition. Without the traditional oral narratives of Kumasi's griots, the conquerors create a distorted history that places them at the center of Kumasi culture. It is a history that justifies their conquest:

> I would read another history in the textbooks. Germanson and his people were, by definition, superior to the people of Kumasi. We, the descendants of primitive peoples, were the sons of lost monkeys, humanoids, eternally in the process of humanization.
>
> *Leía en los textos otra historia. Germanson y su pueblo eran, por definición, superiores al pueblo de Kumasi. Nosotros, descendientes de primitivos, éramos los hijos de perdidos monos, humanoides, eternamente en proceso de humanización.* (*TBS* 269; *RP* 83)

In this "next life" the narrator becomes a portrait artist for the ruling elite, but his painting of the governor's daughter, Lucy, creates a controversy.[10] The symbols of the conquest appear in his painting: gold, which represents the traditional Kumasi culture through images of the sun and rebirth, while silver represents the imposition of the culture of the conquerors, which to him "is simply the present decadent civilization in crisis" (era simplemente la decadente civilización actual en crisis) (*TBS* 269; *RP* 83). The authorities immediately attempt to reeducate him on his use of artistic symbols and their "correct" interpretation according to the dominant culture. However, another servant in the governor's household overhears the complaints, and he takes the narrator to the countryside at night so he can see and hear the strong-willed peasants participating in traditional rites. He states, "For the first time I managed to coherently retrieve my pre-infantile memories. And I drank out of golden calabash cups with the peasants." ("Pude, por primera vez, recuperar con coherencia mis recuerdos pre-infantiles. Y bebí con los campesinos en jícaras de oro." *TBS* 271; *RP* 83). He shares his collective, or "preinfantile," memories of his culture with Lucy, who becomes a friend and confidante. He is ultimately exiled because of the controversial nature of his art, which depicts gold and silver together on the same canvas. The narrator eventually arrives in London where he learns more about science and technology and discovers historical information about Germanson and his family. Educated in the ways of the colonizer, he returns to Kumasi after his exile and people begin to call him "The Doctor" (El Doctor).

At this point, the narration switches from first person to third person, an indication of the protagonist's newly acquired status and the distance that separates him from his culture. The Doctor, who now speaks perfect English, gains the favor of Germanson and marries a Kumasi woman educated in France. He becomes a dignitary in the metropolis, representing the colonized nation on the Council of Protectorates, a group of other conquered peoples. During his time abroad, The Doctor renews his passion for art and begins to paint even larger golden suns and even more decay of the silver civilization that tried to destroy the Kumasi people. Although his wife demonstrated her opposition to his art by calling it "a dangerous pastime" ("una actividad peligrosa"), he continues to represent in his art the resistance of his people and "the ancient, occult rites of preservation became the modern, covert rites of liberation." ("los antiguos ritos ocultos de la conservación pasaron a ser nuevos ritos ocultos de la liberación." *TBS* 275; *RP* 85). The Doctor's art becomes an example of cultural marronage in a painting where a "small silver sun was losing itself in the immense golden horizon" (un pequeño sol de plata se perdía en el inmenso horizonte dorado), portraying the strength of the cultural resistance in Kumasi (*TBS* 275; *RP* 85).

Unable to manage the conflict between his political appointment and his art, The Doctor resigns his position and returns to his home without his wife, who refuses to leave Europe. He reconnects with the clandestine traditions the peasants practice and with the *samamfo* of his people. Inspired by the memory of the past's glory, he launches a political party, Partido de la Liberación Aurea (PALA), but the group is banned because of the threat it poses to the established order, and natives educated in Europe, like his wife, condemn it. A cultural revolt takes place wherein the people of Kumasi rediscover their traditions, their collective history, and their legacy of gold: "The Samamfo freed itself from the stagnant, old silver dust, and timeless gold surged forth again, purified by the rains of that year." ("El Samamfo se liberó de viejos polvos de plata y el oro intemporal surgió de nuevo, purificado por las lluvias de ese año." *TBS* 279; *RP* 87).

The people of Kumasi "reconquer" their land and their culture. The new regime erases the term "silver" from the national vocabulary and abolishes Western names. However, the narrator, who supports the recovery of Kumasi's culture, now questions the motivations behind the erasure of the colonizers' culture and the recovery of an authentic preconquest past. He returns to his art and paints a portrait with seven suns: four gold and three silver, which "produced infinite tones between gold and silver" ("producían infinitas tonalidades entre oro y plata"), demonstrating the mutual influences the two cultures have on each other (*TBS* 281; *RP* 88). His art elicits numerous interpretations. However, his own interpretation of the painting is the most controversial: "It was not enough to say that we were no longer the children of one Samamfo, but rather a hybrid of two." ("No bastó demostrar que ya no éramos hijos de un solo Samamfo, sino un híbrido de dos." *TBS* 281; *RP* 88). The representation of hybridity challenges PALA's attempt to recuperate a pure and authentic precolonial past. In the eyes of the narrator, the past cannot be fully recovered or restored to its former glory because of the syncretic culture that developed after the contact between Kumasi and Europe.

Having returned from Paris after independence, the narrator's wife, now a converted supporter of the PALA regime, turns him in to the government authorities for not conforming to the spirit of *samamfo*. He loses his status and position, and as punishment must paint seven hundred gold suns under his wife's supervision. He is exiled from Kumasi to the land of silver but returns again to his native land. Once back in Kumasi, he is exiled again for including silver in a government-commissioned piece, and he travels again to the land of silver where he is honored as a "genius" and a "great master." When he paints a golden moon with a background of silver, however, he angers the prince in the land of silver and is exiled to the basement of the palace. He muses:

> I have fallen into disgrace. I think. They have condemned me to solitude. I think. Seated like I am in this circle in the basement of the palace. I think. A circle of silver, I think. They have destroyed my painting, I think. It was my best painting, I think.
>
> *He caído en desgracia. Pienso. Me han condenado a la soledad. Pienso. Sentado como estoy en este círculo, en el sótano del palacio. Pienso. Un círculo de plata, pienso. Habrán destruido mi cuadro, pienso. Era mi mejor cuadro, pienso.* (*TBS* 281; *RP* 90)

During his imprisonment, he finds Lucy, who is also condemned for having rescued his painting. His wife appears in a vision and seeks to collect his "vanquished remains" (vencidos despojos) and return them to Kumasi. She retreats empty-handed, but retains her own version of history. The narrator states, "History will say that I abandoned her for a silver woman. And it will say at the end of my days, I violently cast away my golden dreams. It will say that I betrayed the most sacred part of Samamfo." ("La historia dirá que la abandoné por una mujer de plata. Y dirá que al final de mis días, renegué de mis sueños dorados. Dirá que he traicionado lo más sagrado del Samamfo." *TBS* 285; *RP* 90). However, he knows that he has struggled to keep the traditions of his people alive, and in the process he has been inculcated with the story of *samamfo*—he is a part of *samamfo* and *samamfo* is a part of him. He issues a curse to those who have spoken out against him: "If I die, someone will be responsible for my death, someone one day will be confronted with rejection by his own people as punishment." ("Si muero, alguien cargará con mi muerte, alguien enfrentará algún día su propia rebelión como un castigo." *TBS* 285; *RP* 91).

At the end of the story, he and Lucy join hands. The gold and silver cultures brought together initially by force and imposition are now forever linked. The narrator comments, "We have ceased weeping and Lucy is smiling. Suns of gold and silver radiate from our face. I know we will cry again as we continue on." ("Hemos dejado de llorar y Lucy sonríe. Soles de oro y plata devienen en nuestra sonrisa. Yo sé que en la lucha volveremos a llorar." *TBS* 287; *RP* 91). Although their tears have stopped, their struggle continues, and there will be more tears shed because there is no safe home for them until the "gold" and the "silver" recognize their syncretic culture. In the meantime, gold and silver reject each other and there is no place for the narrator and Lucy to dwell unless they are willing to make their own "third" space.

Much of the content of "Los mitos ancestrales" refers to the historic struggle of the Ashanti against the British during the nineteenth and twentieth centuries. There are many allusions to Ashanti history, including references to a warrior-queen (the historical Yaa Asantewa who led Ashanti fighters against the British until she was forced into exile in Seychelles by English forces), the famous gold of Kumasi, Ashanti deities (Nyame) and monarchs (Okomfo), and the most revered symbol of the Ashanti, the Golden Stool. Duncan, as a descendant of Ashanti/Akan peoples, uses this history in order to link the regions of the Diaspora in his narrative—Central America, the Caribbean, Europe, and Africa—and create a parable to discuss resistance. But the text may also be read as an allegory about cultural syncretism. The protagonist-narrator carries both the culture of the Kumasi and the culture of Germanson, a union that reflects not only the encounters between Africans and Europeans in the old world, but also the patterns of interaction and exchange between the conquered and the conquerors who together have forged the new cultures of the Americas.

Anancy Stories

Quince Duncan, like his Afro–Costa Rican literary predecessors, Dolores Joseph Montout and Alderman Johnson Roden, incorporates the oral tradition into his work. This oral tradition includes the famed Anancy stories, animal trickster tales, which passed from enslaved West Africans to the Caribbean, where they were adapted to mirror the conditions of plantation slavery and were then passed on to Central America with free laborers. In Central America, the Afro–West Indian workers and their families shared stories of Bredda Anancy, also called Hermano Araña (Brother Spider), which served not only to amuse but also as a means to teach survival in conditions of systematized oppression and exploitation. Entertaining and didactic, the stories demonstrate how the small spider outwits creatures larger and more powerful than himself. Joice Anglin, in her study "Anancy in Limón," notes, "The opponents of the trickster are generally chosen from those who supposedly are supreme in the forests: Tiger, Lion, Elephant. Their role in the story is that of animals that can be easily fooled. Trickster takes advantage of this weakness as often as he can" (Anglin Edwards 1993, 41).[11] The larger animals became representations of the whites who controlled production and maintained order on the plantation or on the railroad, while Anancy himself came to represent those who were subjugated. Because of his small size and physical weakness in comparison to other animals, Anancy has to use his intelligence and cunning in order to survive, an important lesson about how best to resist dominant forces. As Duncan states in *El negro en Costa Rica*: "Through their fables, the blacks taught their children—perhaps unconsciously—that astuteness is a virtue if one is black and if one lives in a racist, white, and oppressive society" (Meléndez and Duncan 1993, 126).

While the oral retelling of these animal tales and trickster stories is disappearing, Duncan introduces Anancy stories and other folktales to a new, Spanish-speaking generation of readers. The publication of *Cuentos de Hermano Araña* (The Stories of Brother Spider) and *Cuentos de Jack Mantorra* (The Stories of Jack Mantorra), in addition to the compilation *Cuentos tradicionales afrolimonenses*, demonstrates that "The bilingual versions of the stories that appear in written and oral forms reflect the wily spider's changing role in the transformation of a cultural identity through the retention of what is useful and adjustment to the new environment" (Mosby 2003b, 38). The adaptation to the contemporary culture of Costa Rica reflects the continual process of change the Anancy stories have undergone as peoples move and have contact with other cultures.

In his "new home," Anancy becomes "Hermano Araña" (Brother Spider), and the traditional ending to the Jamaican Anancy stories is altered to fit the new setting. The phrase "Jack Mandora, me no chose none," traditionally serves as an apology for the display of poor behavior by the trickster. The Jamaican folklorist Louise Bennett comments on the phrase: "At the end of each story, we had to say, 'Jack Mandora, me no chose none,' because Annancy sometimes did very wicked things . . . and we had to let Jack Mandora, the doorman at heaven's door, know that we were not in favor of Annancy's wicked ways. 'Me no chose none' means 'I don't choose to behave in any of these ways" (Bennett 1966, ix). In Duncan's recompilation of the trickster stories, he identifies his narrator as Jack Mantorra, a name that also has a greater assonance with the character's alias "La Cotorra," meaning parrot or chatterbox. Duncan adds his own version of Bennett's disclaimer: "Jack Mantorra says that if this story seems like something you have seen or heard, don't complain because after all, he is just the narrator" ("Jack Mantorra dice que si este cuento se parece a algo que ustedes hayan visto u oído, no lo reclamen, porque después de todo, él es solo una cotorra"), and "Jack Mantorra says being just the narrator he does not know if what he has said is certain or not." ("Dice Jack Mantorra, que siendo él simple cotorra no sabe si lo dicho es o no cierto." *HA* 6, 14).

In Duncan's version of the tradition, Jack Mantorra is further transformed from heaven's doorman to an old Jamaican storyteller and grandfather figure: "Jack Mantorra is a legendary character from the Caribbean and in a certain way represents the wizard or chief of the tribe who at nightfall was given the task of telling Anancy stories to the children. He represents the grandparent, in the Caribbean context of Limón, seated in his hammock rocking in the stifling afternoon air with children at his feet, hanging on his every word" (*HA* 2). He is also a traveling figure who goes from town to town sharing the stories he heard in Jamaica, along with ones he created to appeal to the children of Costa Rica. Duncan is keeping the tradition of these stories alive by adapting them to new circumstances.

There is often an element of comedy in the Anancy stories. In "El caballo de trote" (The Riding Horse), which appears in *Los cuentos del Hermano Araña*, the proud and beautiful Hermano Tigre (Brother Tiger) is tricked by the Spider with humorous results. Hermano Tigre, known for his white mane, attracts the attention of many of the women in the jungle for his good looks. Hermano Araña (Brother Spider), who is not as attractive as his romantic rival, is overcome with jealousy. He wants to cut Hermano Tigre's mane but realizes that he is too small and weak to contend with the tiger. Instead, Hermano Araña decides to heed the adage, "brains over brawn" ("más vale maña que fuerza") and chooses to attack Hermano Tigre's pride by claiming that the tiger is nothing more than his riding horse. The gossip spreads across the jungle and reaches Hermano Tigre. The tiger wants to clear up this matter and goes to Hermano Araña so that the two can publicly disclaim the rumor. Hermano Araña feigns illness but agrees to go with Hermano Tigre to town. He asks the tiger to carry him on his back because of his illness and insists that he needs a saddle, reins, and spurs to keep him stable on the ride into town. Unwittingly, Hermano Tigre makes the rumor a reality by becoming the spider's riding horse and demonstrating in the process that "intelligence is worth more than beauty" ("la inteligencia vale más que la guapura"; *HA* 23).

Anancy shows that in spite of his small size and physical weakness, he can satisfy his needs (and sometimes his greed) by his wit and astuteness. His goal is usually food (that belongs to other animals) or in more adult versions of the stories, the sexual conquest of other animals' wives or daughters. Anancy's humanlike traits help us readily identify with the characters and their reactions to adverse circumstances, which at times appear heroic and other times quite villainous. The Anancy stories can serve as lessons for empowering the weak, but Anancy's sometimes selfish behavior can also serve as an "antimodel," showing how not to behave. In "Anansi y la Olla Mágica" (Anancy and the Magic Pot), which appears in *Los cuentos de Jack Mantorra*, the spider's greed has troubling consequences. During a famine, Anancy finds a magic pot in the forest that prepares whatever he wants on demand. While other animals are walking skeletons, Anancy is getting big and fat, which of course raises suspicions. The other animals find Anancy's pot and have a feast, but to cover up their discovery, they wash the pot. Unknown to them, the magic power of the pot disappears if it is washed. Anancy returns to the pot, finding the scraps from the feast and the pot without food. Perhaps if Anancy had shared his good fortune, everyone would have continued to benefit from the magic pot.

Although Hermano Araña (Brother Spider) is most often the perpetrator of the trickery, sometimes he falls victim to the tricks of Toucuma, Tiger, other animals, or members of his own family. In one of the stories Duncan shares in *Los cuentos del hermano araña*, "A veces el guardia roba más que el ladrón" (Sometimes the guard steals more than the thief). Hermano Araña becomes the victim of his own greed. Hermano Tucumá (Brother Toucuma) realizes that the harvest from his crops is rapidly disappearing and decides to consult Hermano Araña, who in spite of his laziness is known throughout the region for his intelligence. Unaware that the thief is none other than Hermano Araña, Tucumá hires him to watch his crops at night. This becomes an ideal opportunity for Hermano Araña to steal Tucumá's food and collect payment for the night watchman's job. When Tucumá realizes his crops are still being pilfered, he becomes suspicious. Reminiscent of stories of the Ibo- and Yoruba-derived stories of Br'er Rabbit in the southern United States, Hermano Tucumá makes a large doll out of tar and places it in the field to catch the thief.

At nightfall, Hermano Araña begins his duty by filling his basket with the food Tucumá hired him to protect. While in the field, he sees the "person" and "thinks of capturing it and laying the blame on him for all of the robberies" (*HA* 5). When the person does not respond, Hermano Araña hits the "tar baby" until all eight of his legs are stuck. Hermano Tucumá discovers that Hermano Araña is the real thief and comments, "in this country, the guard steal more than the thief," a warning to always be vigilant (*HA* 5).

The presence of this tradition in Costa Rica serves as a foundation for Duncan's work by connecting the West Indian oral tradition to contemporary Afro–Costa Rican culture. Through Duncan's efforts to write these stories in Spanish, the Anancy stories are incorporated into the cultural patrimony of Costa Rica and exist in written form to be shared and passed on to forthcoming generations. Additionally, the stories continue to survive in Duncan's narrative fiction since several Anancy stories and references to Anancy tales appear in Duncan's novels, *Hombres curtidos*, *La paz del pueblo*, and *Kimbo*.

2
The Novels of Identity
Hombres curtidos and *Los cuatro espejos*

> Negroes are told in a language they cannot possibly misunderstand that their native land is not their own.
>
> —Richard Wright, *Black Boy (American Hunger)*

Duncan's first two novels, *Hombres curtidos* (1971) and *Los cuatro espejos* (1973) may be described as "novels of Afro–Costa Rican identity." These early works center on the reconciliation of national and cultural identities—the fact of being black of West Indian descent and Costa Rican, in defiance of the *leyenda blanca.* The author's depiction of West Indian characters, community, culture, and history from an intrinsic perspective mark an important moment in Costa Rican literature. The Afro–Costa Rican identity of the protagonists is shaped by the West Indian–influenced culture of Limón and the dominant Hispanic culture of the Central Valley. Set in the 1960s and 1970s, the novels feature characters who travel between these two locations in order to make peace between matters of national and ethnic identity through the motif of the journey between the two locations.

Hombres curtidos

Published in 1971, *Hombres curtidos* is widely acclaimed as the first published novel in Spanish by an Afro–Costa Rican of West Indian descent. *Hombres curtidos* is also the first novel to explore identity from the point of view of an Afro–West Indian subject in Costa Rica who evolves from foreigner to citizen, but yet remains an Other. The novel addresses the reconstruction of West Indian culture by Jamaican immigrants whose memories of the history of struggle and suffering of past generations constitute the primary building blocks. As Donald K. Gordon affirms in his *Lo jamaicano universal en la obra de Quince Duncan*, "[*Hombres cur-*

tidos] is the novel that concentrates most closely on the Jamaican–Costa Rican question" (Gordon 1989, 19) and represents a departure from works by Costa Rican writers of non–West Indian origin such as Carlos Luis Fallas and Joaquín Guitérrez that treat the black presence in the literature with superficial folkloric curiosity.

This contemporary novel explores the problem of national and cultural identity for the third generation of Costa Rican–born blacks of West Indian descent. The central character in the novel, Clif Duke, is the Afro–Costa Rican grandson of Jamaican immigrants and carries the burden of resolving the conflict between his Costa Rican citizenship and his "West Indianness." As an Afro–Costa Rican, Clif Duke's assertion of citizenship and belonging conflicts with his country's claim of whiteness and homogeneity. Clif must decide where to locate his "home" and how to define his identity in a space where he is considered an outsider because of his Afro–West Indian heritage, but he also finds himself estranged from the place of origin of his progenitors. It is up to Clif, armed with a cultural inheritance from his grandfather, Jakel Duke, an inheritance that includes sacrifice, hope, and an understanding of collective struggle symbolized literally by blood, sweat, and tears, to claim his place in the nation.[1] Through Clif Duke, who is a representative figure of the pivotal third generation, the novel develops its principal themes: the process of finding home, claiming an identity, and conserving cultural memory. *Hombres curtidos* also delves into the third generation's questioning of tradition and progress and presents issues of ancestral exile and displacement.

Structure and Themes

The novel is composed of twelve numbered and titled chapters divided into three parts. The narration, in the style of the "new novel" in Spanish American literature, frequently changes narrative perspective and alters linear chronology. A chapter may begin in first person, then shift to a flashback of a conversation or a childhood incident, and then shift again to a third-person-omniscient narrator. The first part of *Hombres curtidos* (chapters 1–6) establishes the return of the prodigal grandson to Estrada after a long absence and reconstructs the history of the Duke family. The action takes place in multiple spaces and with multiple identities shaped by family memories of different shores—Africa, Jamaica, Panama, and Costa Rica.

The second part of the novel (chapters 7–10) takes place entirely in Costa Rica and shifts between the grandfather on his deathbed and the grandson's struggles with his national and cultural identity. In this section, Clif contemplates his connection with the land, the collective history of West Indians in Costa Rica, his blood heritage, and his country. This section of the novel highlights the legacy of colonialism in the British West Indies, the immigration of West Indians to Central America, and the extension of Costa Rican citizenship to blacks born in Costa Rica after years of exclusion by the national government.

The third part of the novel (chapters 11–12) also unfolds in Costa Rica and focuses on Clif's arrival in Estrada. His vivid memories of his own struggles and painful recollections of racism experienced in San José unfurl at the end of the novel, ironically deepening his bond with his native land. Clif is able to claim Costa Rica as his home and assert his sense of belonging as he begins to write the exculpatory narrative of his grandfather's life and legacy as a foundation for his own. Clif Duke provides an Afro-Hispanic example of Hansen's aphorism regarding the third-generation immigrant, "What the son wishes to forget the grandson wishes to remember" (Hansen 1990, 195). Clif begins his narrative with: "The act of lifting the suitcase, hoisting up the child, and exiting the train is just one motion." ("El acto de levantar la valija, alzar el niño y bajarme del tren es uno solo." *HC* 3). At the end of the novel, this same phrase not only closes the text but also brings Clif full circle toward understanding his identity and raising the possibility for a new beginning as an Afro–Costa Rican.

In spite of the multiple narrative voices and perspectives in the text, Clif emerges as the novel's protagonist since he is the catalyst that sets the novel in motion. His return enables the story of his grandfather to be written. However, one can similarly argue that the novel has no single protagonist as such, but rather Clif is the figure who unites the narration of a collective consciousness. The narrative style of *Hombres curtidos* communicates a journey via collective cultural memory and the protagonist's discovery of his national and cultural identity. Through the voyage from the capital to his childhood home in Limón Province, Clif is able to complete his own story by revisiting his grandfather's history. Clif can only perform this search for his identity by returning to the place where this history begins—the house his Jamaican grandfather built with his own hands—in order to "reconcile with the mud" ("reconciliarme con el barro").

Plot. The return of Clif Duke to his home in Estrada, Limón, marks the beginning of "El Regreso," the first chapter of *Hombres curtidos*. After fourteen years of absence, the thirty-year-old man, accompanied by his wife and young son, leaves his comfortable, bourgeois life as a writer in the capital to return to the rural home his Jamaican grandfather built in the Atlantic province. Clif had constructed a life of artistic and social prestige in the urban center of San José. Initially, Clif's motives for the return are uncertain: "My wife contemplates the surrounding dwellings in silence. One could see in her eyes that she still doubts the cause for my return. No one knows, perhaps not even I know." ("Mi esposa contempla el caserío en silencio. Se le ve en los ojos que aún duda sobre la causa de mi retorno. Nadie lo sabe, tal vez ni yo mismo lo sé." *HC* 3). He returns to a town that has changed little, "Not even a sign of paint or repairs—nothing has changed. Here everything is static. Things just are—decaying, delving toward self-destruction, or simply resigned to the effect of erosion." ("Ni pintura, ni reparaciones; ningún cambio. Acá todo es estático. Las cosas son, decrecen, buceando la autodestrucción, o simplemente aceptando el efecto de la erosión." *HC* 3).

His friends in the capital are dismayed at his decision to return to his origins, equating the West Indian foreignness and blackness of Costa Rica's "last frontier" with barbarism and backwardness in comparison to the civilized cosmopolitan setting of Hispanic culture and whiteness the capital represents. In Estrada, Clif is greeted by neighbors carefully navigating wooden planks that cover the muddy soil underneath, a significant contrast to the anonymity offered by the city with its concrete sidewalks. Clif, who abandoned an unimportant village in a marginalized province to seek his fortune in the capital city, now returns from the prestigious capital to confront and reconstruct the past. He uproots himself and his family from their urban comforts to search for his roots and reconnect with his history and identity. Approaching the house where he grew up, Clif notes:

> The house emerges from between the fresh leaves of the cacao grove, and the sensation of returning overwhelms me, startles me. I am home. The nostalgia accumulated through the years, flows and frees itself. The memories are violent, and strike relentlessly. A tenuous largesse that explodes into a crossroads before my uncertain future. But I am home, that is important.
>
> *La casa surge de entre las hojas frescas del cacaotal, y la sensación del regreso me abruma, me sobrecoge. Estoy en casa. La nostalgia acumulada a través de los años, fluye, se libera. Los recuerdos son violentos, y golpean sin tregua. Largueza tenue que revienta cruz sobre mi futuro incierto. Pero estoy en casa, eso es importante.* (*HC* 5)

In representing Clif Duke's quest to discover his roots in Estrada, Duncan employs parallel imagery that links Clif's attempt to understand his position as a Costa Rican of Jamaican descent with memories of the past. For example, as Clif walks to the house with his slumbering young son clasping his neck, a similar image is evoked of himself as a child grasping his grandfather's neck. Memories of the past and the need to comprehend his future compel him to return to the place where he was raised to write his grandfather's story as the deceased man's only male heir and to clear his name. Jakel was accused of misappropriating money from the fraternal lodge's burial society.[2]

What begins to develop in the pages of the novel is the personal and collective history of the African Diaspora, the trauma of displacement, and the need to locate some place one can call home and forge a sense of belonging. While most of the novel's action takes place in Costa Rica, the narration recalls the collective memory of the African past with references to the Ashanti struggles against British colonization, the preabolition period of Jamaica, and culminates in the departure of many Afro–West Indians for opportunities for work in Central America. In Costa Rica, the first generation of West Indians and their children grapple with the problem of returning home to Jamaica or other points in the Anglophone Caribbean. Many are unable to return because they cannot afford the passage home; many decide not to return because of an evolving connection to the new land. Moreover, for those born in Costa Rica, the West Indies is a "foreign" place. It is not until the reforms of Costa Rica's Second Republic in the aftermath of the 1948 civil war that Costa Rican–born blacks are enfranchised. Nevertheless, citizenship fails to erase ethnic and cultural exclusion.

While Clif embarks on his journey to find himself through the exercise of writing, he also works to vindicate his grandfather and clear Jakel Duke's name (and consequently his own). The narration recounts the multiple migrations of his family in Jamaica and Central America all the while referring to Clif as the *heredero*, or heir to this Duke family legacy. The fatherless Clif Duke was raised by his mother, Grace, and her parents, Jakel and Gretl Duke. However, the grandfather treats the boy as if he were his son. Before Clif was born, "he felt pride since the child would carry the Duke name and he began to pray for it to be male-child." ("él sentía orgullo, por cuanto el bebé llevaría el apellido Duke, y empezó a rogar para que naciese varón." *HC* 7). When Clif was a child, Jakel Duke "Deposited in the mind of the young Clif the heritage and the increasing family glory so that one day he would pass it on with even greater glory to his children and continue on for decades until that moment among his lineage a pristine Ethiopian male will rise up to be the pride of his race and to cover the Duke name with radiance." ("Depositó pues, en la cabeza del joven Clif, la herencia y la gloria recibida y aumentada, para que éste la legue a su vez con mayor gloria a sus hijos, y sí por decenios, hasta que a caso de entre su estirpe se levante prístino varón etíope, para orgullo de su raza, y para cubrir de aureolas el apellido Duke." *HC* 7). He sees the boy as the bearer of the family name, as well as its blood, culture, and history. Clif is seen as the one who will eventually be responsible for the maintenance of the family's small farm, appropriately named Buena Esperanza, "Good Hope." Notions of inheritance and heritage are preoccupations that carry over into Clif's adulthood. Clif Duke's return to Estrada prompts feelings of nostalgia as he remembers his childhood while holding his own sleeping son.

The first part of the novel shifts between Clif's return to Estrada and his grandfather's past. The narration portrays Jakel Duke's point of view in order to tell the story of his voyage to foreign shores. Chapters 2, 3, and 4, respectively titled

"Danzas" (Dances), "Ayer" (Yesterday), and "Conociendo" (Knowing), explore Jakel's memories of life in Jamaica and immigration to Central America. Jakel Duke boards a ship in Montego Bay destined for Panama to collect his inheritance from his recently deceased father, Jonás, who immigrated to work on the canal. Jakel carries in his pocket the last communication from his father, a letter informing him of Jonás's impending death and a request to come as quickly as possible to Panama to claim his inheritance. Prompted by his dying father's last letter to him, Jakel contemplates his family's history. This unearthing of the past links the generations through a quest to understand the meaning of heritage, culture, and identity.

During Jakel's voyage to Panama, he recalls his father speaking to a white man named Mister Edwin, who he is ordered to address as, "tío abuelo" (great-uncle). Subsequently, the narration alternates between the lines of Jonás's letter and Jakel's childhood memories of his father. The interweaving of the dying man's letter and his son's memories uncovers another chapter of the family history: the disinheritance of Jonás's mother and the mystery of the white great-uncle. His mother was the natural daughter of a white Jamaican slave owner and his slave, Nicky. The slave owner had to sell his enslaved lover in order to repay his debts, and he is left with his legitimate white offspring, Mister Edwin, and two illegitimate black daughters, Jonás's mother and aunt. After their father's death, the black daughters were cheated out of their share of the estate by their half brother, Mister Edwin, the master's legitimate heir. Mister Edwin derisively gives Jonás's family a token amount of money, which he sees as a gesture of goodwill, but which is actually an act of penance, "as if that could erase the sin he committed from his conscience." ("como si eso pudiese borrar de la conciencia el pecado cometido." *HC* 13). He then deducts maintenance expenses of food, clothing, other miscellaneous costs and the "goodness" of finding his half sister employment with a Scotsman who would eventually become her lover: "He added with incredible cynicism—'one needs to be a Christian to do so much for a pair of Negresses.'" ("Añadió con increíble cinismo—se necesita ser cristiano para hacer tanto por un par de negras." *HC* 13). Jakel is astonished at his father's feigned smile in the face of such humiliation.

Aboard the ship from Jamaica, Jakel also reflects on the history of colonization and slavery and questions whether blacks have truly found freedom after emancipation. He observes that the emancipation decree Queen Victoria signed in 1838 simply served to replace one type of slavery with another (*HC* 15). Jakel rejects a fellow passenger's offer of *ganghá* (ganja/marijuana) on the ship, preferring not to alter his melancholy state. Also, during the sea voyage, several of the passengers engage in the rituals of *pocomía* (Pukumina/Pocomania), an Afro-Christian religious practice from Jamaica that blends Christian beliefs with dance, drumming, and spirit possession. A sailor-griot begins to sing a story so that those on the ship "could hear the glory of their tribe, the history known by all but silenced by shame and twisted by pens of the Caucasus." ("pudiesen oír la gloria de su tribu, la historia conocida por todos, y la otra parte callada por vergüenza, tergiversada por las plumas del Cáucaso." *HC* 18). The griot sings of the betrayal and conquest of the Ashanti by the British, of the Middle Passage that brought enslaved Africans to the plantations in the Americas, of the development of European domination, and of the racialization of the structures of power and economic opportunity. The griot reminds his listeners that history is written by the conquerors, and his retelling of the story reveals the formation of "a race weathered by the centuries. A mixture of legend and history, a confusion of purported truths, bound and amalgamated without remedy." ("una raza curtida en los siglos. Mezcla de leyenda e historia, confusión de verdades sobrepuestas, atadas, amalgamadas ya sin remedio." *HC* 21). As the griot tells his story, a Pukumina ceremony begins with the music and the trance of the priestess aided by the sounds of drums. Together the griot and the priestess represent the resistance of African descendants in the Americas to the erasure of their history and the ability to form syncretic cultural practices in the New World that are rooted in the African past.

When Jakel arrives in Panama, he is dismayed at the tiny sum of money the executrix has given him, "calculated by the neighbors as not even one-third of the original sum which was impossible to prove because it did not occur to Jonás to specify the amount in his last letter." ("calculada por los vecinos como apenas una tercera parte de la suma original, lo cual resultó imposible comprobar porque a Jonás no se le ocurrió especificar la suma en su postrera carta." *HC* 24). Jakel's dreams of studying mechanics disappear and he leaves Panama for Costa Rica to join his "brother," Walter. Jakel's grandmother adopted Walter, and Jakel and Walter grew up together in the house their grandmother shared with her Scottish lover. The death of the Scotsman at sea provided yet another blow to the prosperity and survival of the family. Although the Scotsman and Jakel's grandmother were together for thirty years, he never married her, for fear of losing clientele. Black women were accepted only as concubines or servants for white men, but not as legitimate wives. The sale of her own black mother, the death of her white father, the deaths of Jonás and the Scotsman, followed by the departures of Walter and Jakel himself leave Jakel's grandmother alone, abandoned, and disinherited in Jamaica.

The revelation of the troubling family history of disinheritance and entangled relationships poses a question that appears at least three other times in the novel: "why do the men of our race love so little?" ("¿por qué los hombres de nuestra raza aman tan poco?" *HC* 26). Jakel suggests during a conversation with Walter that for blacks love is just too complicated: "To love many with the fear of losing them in any moment—to distribute love in infinite pieces, for if one is lost, it goes never to return. Then to save your loved ones from the pain of loving us by pretending to be cold and hard. What a mess." ("Amar a muchos con el miedo de perderlos en cualquier momento. Repartir el amor en infinitos pedazos, por si en alguno se pierde, se va sin regreso. Luego ahorrarles a los seres queridos el dolor de querernos, fingiendo frialdad o dureza. Qué enredo." *HC* 28). The impact of slavery and forced separation is a powerful and tragic legacy. Even with the abolition of the practice of slavery, black Jamaicans remain shackled to this history: "Queen Victoria freed us and we remain captives." ("la Reina Victoria nos liberó y seguimos cautivos." *HC* 28). They remain captives of a legacy of slavery, colonialism, and a racial ideology that affirms the servitude of blacks through the promulgation of the myth of inferiority. This same ideology denied Jakel's grandmother her inheritance and barred the Scotsman from marrying the mulatto woman even after thirty years of concubinage.

In Costa Rica, Walter takes his "brother" around Limón and the English-speaking enclave formed by workers and the United Fruit Company. The West Indian culture is evident in the presence of the British consul, bridal agencies for single Jamaican men, the importation of goods from England and Jamaica, foods like ackee and oxtail, as well as calypso singing and calypso orchestras. Also present in the enclave is a historical prejudice against Hispanic culture and a color-based caste system, both legacies of British colonialism. In Costa Rica there are three principle antagonists in operation: the hostile land, the hostile nationals, and the hostile work conditions. During a hunting party to find and kill a *tepescuintle* (paca), they encounter the savagery of both the natural and the human environment. Jakel, Walter, Gregory, La Bala (Bullet), and Sidney, their guide, venture into the lowland jungle of the province and encounter Costa Ricans who react with fear and hostility to their presence. When the hunters encounter a mestizo woman washing clothes in a stream, trouble erupts. All of the negative stereotypes of the oversexed, predatory black male surface when the mestizo woman screams and flees upon seeing the group of black men.[3] The episode also signals ethnolinguistic and deep cultural differences between the Anglophone British West Indian and the isolated and provincial Spanish-speaking peasants. The West Indians deem the *paña*, or "Spanish," as backward and incapable of performing the work needed to build their nation's infrastructure.[4] The Costa Rican nationals view the black foreigners as a social, sexual, cultural, and economic threat. These opposing viewpoints collide when six Hispanic campesinos emerge from the forest with weapons, and the encounter between two ethnolinguistic groups becomes a full-blown attack. Gregory is mortally wounded by a machete, and one of the campesinos is killed, while another lies gravely wounded. Both groups flee the scene after the brutal encounter.

In chapter 5, "La herencia" (Heritage), the narrative then shifts to Clif's memories of his grandfather's last days. In a conversation with their neighbor, Miss Ann, Jakel announces that his time has come, a euphemism for his impending death. He states: "I have spent my life asking God to let me know the number of my days." ("Pasé mi vida pidiéndole a Dios que me hiciera conocer el número de mis días." *HC* 50). He indicates a desire to abandon his work and give up on life to the surprise of both Clif and Miss Ann. The grandfather also abandons the land because he has grown weary of life and the calumny unleashed against him. The memory of his grandfather's death is evoked:

> With determination Clif observed his noble figure laid out on the bed, his lips getting ready to speak as if ready to dictate in a single and sublime sentence the long history of poverty and angst: he murmured inaccessible phrases, distant from it all. He could not even recognize the voice of his only and dearly cherished daughter, Grace. His temples, silvered by the passage of time, seemed to announce the end of a life.
>
> *[Clif] observó determinadamente su hidalga figura tendida sobre la cama, sus labios en ademán de discurso, como si quisiera dictar en una sola y sublime oración la larga historia de penurias y de angustia: murmuraba sentencias inaccesibles. Ajeno de todo. Ni siquiera pudo reconocer la voz de Grace su única y tan estimada hija. Sus sienes, plateadas por el paso de la vida, parecían anunciar el fin de una biografía.* (*HC* 52)

Although Jakel's condition is deteriorating to the point that he has difficulty recognizing his loved ones, he manages to communicate to Clif the gift of his inheritance. He entrusts to his grandson the material fact of an inheritance, but with an understanding of the importance and implications of a work ethic that has aided the family's survival:

> You well know Clif that the land belongs to a family that never worked it. But also keep in mind if I had not received a title that guarantees it to me, I would not be able to pass on the right to you to cultivate it, so that's what a title is worth. The land, son, does not belong to any one person, but rather belongs to everyone. . . . We have brought nothing into this world Clif and we can take nothing with us except, do you know what? The little experience that we accumulate.
>
> *Bien sabes Clif que la tierra pertenece a una familia que nunca la trabajó. Pero también presente que, si yo no hubiese tenido un título que me la acreditase, no podría legarte el derecho de explotación, pues eso es lo que vale un*

> *título. La tierra hijo, no es posesión de nadie en particular, sino de todos . . . Nada podemos llevar con nosotros, salvo, ¿sabes qué? la poca experiencia que acumularemos.* (*HC* 55)

After withdrawing from the intimate scene with his grandfather, Clif notes the passing of his grandfather's generation, the first generation:

> Now, I remembered everything, the entirety of the past that died that afternoon, the remains of a culture descending into the tomb together with its kin, generously giving six feet of earth to each one.
>
> *Ahora, recordaba todo, todo el pasado que se moría esa tarde, los restos de una cultura descendiendo a la tumba junto a sus deudos, donando generosamente seis pies de tierra para cada uno.* (*HC* 57)

The narrative then shifts to Clif's perspective. He recalls his own departure and his return. He thinks to himself, "Nothing in my grandfather's history justifies my return." ("Nada en la historia del abuelo, justifica mi regreso." *HC* 52). The narration enters Clif's intimate thoughts, shifting the narration from third person to first. Clif remembers the last days of his grandfather on his deathbed and his weakening physical body.

"La vid" (The Vine), the pivotal sixth chapter of *Hombres curtidos*, ends the first part of the novel. This chapter, dense with significant details, describes the relationship of the children of the first generation of immigrants to Costa Rica and to the land of their parents, Jamaica. It reveals the uncertain future of the second generation and their struggle between cultures and countries. This portion of the narrative is told from the perspective of Clif's mother, Grace, who, while lamenting her father's grave condition, remembers a discussion with her boyfriend, Clovis. Their discussion takes place while they are facing the Caribbean Sea, the body of water that separates the second generation of Afro–West Indians in Costa Rica from the island homes of their parents. After Clovis asks for her hand in marriage, offering to be a paternal figure to the fatherless Clif, Grace rejects the proposal. Her thoughts drift back to the proposal of marriage presented to her by Clif's father, Clifton, who died suddenly before their union could be formalized.

Clovis and Grace enter into a heated debate about the identity of blacks in Limón and their relationship to the West Indies (the homeland of their parents) and to Costa Rica (the nation-state in which they were born, but that does not fully embrace them as citizens). Their intense conversation touches upon issues of exile, the Diaspora, language, and questions of ethnic, cultural, and national identity. In the novel, the unified struggle with the land of the first generation gives way to the identity crisis of the second generation—which home to claim, which identity to embrace? Clovis, who was born in Jamaica and brought to Costa Rica as a small child, identifies himself as Jamaican and desires to maintain cultural continuity with the island even though they are on "foreign" soil. Like the first generation, Clovis dreams of an eventual return to Jamaica. He speaks of conserving the English language and Jamaican customs while rejecting those of the *paña*, the white and mestizo Costa Rican nationals. When issues of the "local culture" emerge, he clings to the essentiality of blackness: "What is really important is the race, the blood-right that ties us to Jamaica as her heirs. It's like the situation of the Jews—dispersed all over the globe; they find unity in their race, religion and customs." ("Lo realmente importante es la raza, el derecho de sangre que nos liga a Jamaica como herederos. Es el caso de los judíos: dispersados por todo el orbe encuentran su unidad en la raza, en la religión y en las costumbres." *HC* 65). For him "race," language, and culture are irrefutable and unchangeable. He blames the deteriorating morality of the Limonese youth on "the terrible ideas of those who dedicate themselves to preaching that we Negroes must assimilate to the local culture." ("las nefastas ideas de quienes se dedican a predicar que los negros debemos de asimilar la cultura local." *HC* 64). Clovis declares, "We have to preserve our language at all costs." ("Tenemos que conservar nuestro idioma cueste lo que cueste." *HC* 65), and that above all he considers himself Jamaican.

Grace, who was born in Costa Rica, does not have the same attachment to her Jamaican identity as her companion. Jamaica is not her home; it is the place of origin of her parents. Unlike Clovis, she acknowledges that identity is not permanent and unchangeable, but rather undergoes a series of transformations through the successive generations. She feels it is unrealistic for their generation to continue the illusion that they are Jamaican, and she advocates that Afro–West Indians integrate with the dominant Hispanic culture by learning Spanish and accepting some of their practices. She urges Clovis to consider the distance that separates them from Jamaica and to keep elements of West Indian culture that are beneficial, but to remain open to the Hispanic culture: "we could have two cultures, fused together, united in such a way we could see the world in perspective" (*HC* 74). While both regard English as the language of the conqueror, Grace does not consider English as an indispensable cultural tool. She sees the separation from the land and culture of the original "home" as the primary factor contributing to the "loss" of West Indian culture: "The vine Clovis. . . . We cannot bear fruit because we are not connected to the vine—it has been cut off and we are separated at the very least and we are losing our West Indian culture little by little." ("La vid, Clovis. . . . No podemos dar fruto, porque no estamos unidos a la vid: ha sido cortada y por lo tanto nosotros estamos ¡separados! Y vamos perdiendo poco a poco la cultura antillana." *HC* 67).

Grace recounts a parable of two market women on their way to town to sell their wares as a metaphor for the condition of the second generation of West Indians in Costa Rica. In the story, one woman discovers a hole in her basket and she stops to mend it, while the other market woman, who also has a hole in her basket, instead of stopping to repair it, runs to the market as quickly as she can to sell whatever is left in her basket. She equates these women with the preservation of culture versus the need for progress, which implies not being preoccupied with what may be lost in the process of anticipated gains. Grace repeats the words of her parents, that it is not "inheritance based on blood, but rather work and the blood spilled in the process." ("no por herencia basada en la sangre, sino por el trabajo y la sangre derramada en el proceso." *HC* 68) that will establish their identity in the "new" land. She places the blame for poor conditions in Limón not on external forces, but on blacks themselves. In contrast, Clovis places the blame on the customs of the *paña,* which benefit those from "up over yonder" ("allí arriba"), or the agricultural producers in the Central Valley, as well as on the black West Indians themselves for assimilating: "The majority have lost the culture they have inherited through their own fault because they have assimilated too much of the local culture." ("La mayoría han perdido ya la cultura heredada, por propia culpa, porque han estado asimilando demasiado de la cultura local." *HC* 71). Clovis insists that following the ways of the white and mestizo Costa Ricans is not the path blacks should now follow: "We aren't descendants from Spain, but rather Jamaica." ("Nosotros no descendemos de España sino de Jamaica." *HC* 72). Grace, on the other hand, rejects the idea of Jamaica as her "home" because it was never her home—it was her parents' place of origin: "You go on with your Jamaica. Jamaica should be put in a museum. The nationality that you refer to has died." ("Usted sigue con su Jamaica. Jamaica debe ser puesta en nuestro museo. En cuanto a nuestra nacionalidad se refiere ha muerto." *HC* 72). As a solution, Grace posits that the blacks of West Indian descent make an effort to integrate themselves into the nation by adopting some of the practices of the national culture, and "conserve that which is good, absorb that which is better. That is the order for all of us: men and women, weathered by pain, suffering, the love for our neighbor and the soil, . . . Our baskets have broken and we must start running." ("conservar lo bueno, absorber lo mejor. Esa es la consigna para todos nosotros: hombres y mujeres, curtidos en el dolor, en el sufrimiento, en el amor al prójimo y al suelo. . . . Se han roto nuestras canastas y echémonos a correr." *HC* 73–74). Grace, unlike Clovis, accepts the reality that she cannot return to her parents' homeland but must forge her own cultural space and accept the fact that cultures in contact change and transform—absorbing and adapting. She entrusts the decision to further shape and define this new identity to her son Clif.

The second part of the novel begins with the seventh chapter "La incoherencia" (Incoherence), which focuses on Jakel's thoughts on his deathbed. He drifts in and out of consciousness, mixing references to the present with moments from long ago. He hears the voice of his deceased wife, Gretl, and his thoughts turn to her in order to have her by his side in his last hours. Jakel recalls the damaging flood that caused the residents of Estrada to lose everything they had worked so hard to produce. Nevertheless, he and Miss Ann, their neighbor, managed to laugh in the midst of their tragedy as livestock, crops, lives, and homes were lost. An indifferent nurse who is more occupied with her crossword puzzle than with an elderly black patient ignores his death moans. When help is requested for Jakel, she barks, "I'm coming. Can't you see I'm busy?" ("Ya voy, ¿no me ve que estoy ocupada?" *HC* 88). Jakel seems to separate from his body and is looking for his wife. He remembers her refusal to return to Jamaica. Gretl did not want to leave the province or the lives they had struggled to construct. "And your sweat Jakel? The blood spilled so many times, the innumerable wounds that I cured with so much devotion." ("¿Y tu sudor Jakel? La sangre derramada muchas veces. Las heridas innumerables que ha curado con tanta devoción." *HC* 89–90). She insisted they stay on the land the Costa Rican nationals found impossible to "civilize," but that they, the West Indians, had succeeded in cultivating through their labor and suffering. She reminds him of the sacrifice they made to provide a future for their daughter and declares that Costa Rica will be their home and that of their daughter Grace as well: "Perhaps with all of the sacrifice and the effort that has cost us, we have earned the right to the land for our children." ("Tal vez con todo el sacrificio y el esfuerzo que nos ha costado, hayamos ganado le [*sic*] derecho a la tierra para nuestros hijos." *HC* 90). The decision to remain in Costa Rica becomes a cultural affirmation and a legacy for Grace, who now studies Spanish and "already has the foundation so that she is not left behind" ("ya tiene las bases para no dejarse arrastrar"; *HC* 90). Jakel thinks of his original home, St. James Parish, the place that holds the memories of his father, his grandmother and her Scottish lover, and Walter. He remembers the many departures and homecomings he has witnessed over the course of his life.

The narrative moves back to Jakel's hospital bed. The old man is put on a respirator, and when the doctors speak to him, he answers, but his response is only audible in his own mind. He is trapped in his disintegrating body and experiences frustration at his inability to communicate with anyone but himself. He gives up on life. One of his last thoughts is of Clif, the grandchild he brought into the world and encouraged to embrace his native land, a country that "never decided if it wanted blacks or not." ("nunca decidió si quería o no a los negros." *HC* 94). Jakel's thoughts take him back to the humiliating racism he encountered in San José while looking for a bathroom: "I can't let you use it nigger, you'll scare the children." ("No puedo prestárselo negro: se asustan los niños." *HC* 94). He remembers accusations that "Blacks are pigs" ("los negros son unos cochinos"; *HC* 95) and of being degraded by a police officer who fined him for urinating in public. He thinks how difficult it is to change "a narcissistic society." ("una sociedad narcista." *HC* 96). He thinks of Clif for the last time and closes his eyes. At Jakel's funeral, Clif's mind reverberates with the question his grandfather posed to him: "Are you Costa Rican? Are you really? That is your problem right now." (¿Eres costarricense? ¿Lo eres realmente? Ese es tu problema de ahora. *HC* 99). It is the question of the hour for Clif and his generation. How does one establish identity and citizenship in their own land?

In "Brutus," the narrative presents the perspective of Clif as a thirty-year-old man who returns to Estrada and reflects on his grandfather's death and confronts the surging memories of the past. His wife inquires about the cause of Jakel's death. After some contemplation, he responds, "he did not die, they killed him" ("no murió, lo mataron") and that "perhaps that was the motive, the true cause for my return." ("tal vez allí estaba el motivo, la verdadera causa de mi regreso." *HC* 102). Before his death, Jakel Duke was involved in the lay governance of his church. The elders were asked to be the executors of an heirless woman's estate that was to be distributed to the school after her burial expenses, with a small sum destined for the committee as compensation for their efforts. Out of malice, Howard Bowman, one of the members of the committee, falsely accuses Jakel of appropriating some of the money. The fabricated story irrevocably tarnishes Jakel's reputation in the community, and the accusation becomes "a fatal blow—he could endure the inclemency of the land, the changing market, and his own failures, and through it all he always maintained his unblemished, good name. He never took anything that didn't belong to him" ("Un golpe fatal. Había podido aguantar la inclemencia de la tierra, los mercados variantes, los propios fracasos. Pero siempre mantuvo su nombre sin mácula. Jamás se apropió de lo ajeno"; *HC* 104). Howard Bowman, the false friend and fellow elder of the church, is likened to Judas Iscariot: "The role of Judas corresponded to Bowman. He executed it with frightening coldness, striking his friend where it hurt the most. Brutus, and you Brutus." ("El papel de Judás le correspondió a Bowman. Y lo ejecutó con espantos a frialdad, golpeando al amigo en el sitio donde más doliera 'Brutus, Brutus, aún tú." *HC* 106).

As a boy, Clif recalls eavesdropping on the discussions the church elders held about his grandfather and the distribution of the bequest. He feels that the controversy Bowman's rivalry and jealousy created precipitated his grandfather's death. He discovers now his purpose for returning to Estrada. Armed with his pistol, pen, and paper ("Tengo mi pistola. Tengo pluma y papel"; *HC* 106), he returns home as his grandfather's heir to avenge the elder Duke and clear his grandfather's (and consequently his own) name. As his motives to restore his family's honor become clearer, so does his evolving understanding of his identity in the context of his grandfather's life and his own place in the African Diaspora. He recalls the conversation he had with his grandfather about his blackness, cultural legacy, and making a place for himself in his own country. Jakel tells Clif that his blackness does not make him superior or inferior, but "it makes [him] the inheritor of a thousand years of persecution." ("[le] hace heredero de miles de años de persecución"). He goes on to affirm: "we blacks were not a unified people, nor are the Europeans, but there is a point of contact between us that is creating from many, one people. A point of contact Clif. It is something deeper than skin." ("los negros no éramos un pueblo—los europeos tampoco lo son—hay un punto de encuentro entre nosotros que está creando de muchos pueblos, uno. Un punto de encuentro Clif. Es algo más profundo que la piel." *HC* 107).

Although Jakel emphasizes the physical and social weakness of the Costa Rican nationals who could not construct their own infrastructure and underscores the difference between the literate, Afro-Saxon West Indians and the uncultured Costa Rican *cholos*, Jakel foresees an imminent integration of Costa Rica's ethnic populations.[5] Nevertheless, he also reminds his grandson that "we are weathered men, that's the fact of the matter. Weathered by pain and suffering. Weathered peoples are . . . they are more profound. But Clif, before you are black, you are a man. Take care not to hate." ("somos hombres curtidos Clif, eso es el asunto. Curtidos en el dolor y en el sufrimiento. Los pueblos curtidos son . . . son más hondos. Pero Clif, antes que negro, eres hombre. Cuídate del odio." *HC* 107).

The adolescent Clif contemplates Costa Rica as the land he "inherits" and his identity within it. He recalls the generations before him who tilled the soil and made great efforts to carve out a small piece of land to claim as their own in a hostile environment. The reflections cover the period of West Indian migration for the construction of the transcontinental railroad and include the numerous deaths from the harsh conditions. Overwhelmed by thoughts of the past, Clif meditates: "And in spite of everything . . . you stayed fighting, grandfather, as if you were going to receive great compensation. Ignorant from the start, coarsened by the hostility of the region, without contact with West Indian culture, like my mother said very well, you conquered the land, but lost your culture in the process and now you have none." ("Y a pesar de todo eso . . . permanecieron luchando, abuelo, como si fuesen a recibir una gran recompensa; ignorantes desde el principio. Embrutecidos por la hostilidad de la zona, sin contacto con la cultura antillana, como lo dice muy bien mi madre; conquistaron la tierra, pero perdieron su cultura, y hoy no tienen ninguna." *HC* 114). Fatal rail accidents, unremunerated work, exploitative conditions, accidents in the course of clearing the jungle, and dissipating dreams are just some of the arduous circumstances the Afro–West Indians encountered.

Clif remembers explaining to his grandfather as a young boy his understanding of displacement of the black West Indians: "And you all arrived in order to fulfill a contract. Then you cultivated the land, and, in spite of all the bad things that you had to put up with, you stayed here, and we without a country." ("Y ustedes llegaron para cumplir con un contrato. Luego cultivaron la tierra, y, a pesar de todo los males que hubieron de soportar, se quedaron aquí, y nosotros: apátridos." *HC* 115). Unlike his grandfather, a Jamaican, Clif feels like he is without a country and agrees with his mother that perhaps he too is without a culture. Clif is aware that he has no sense of place: "the intention of returning home as a middle-class people created a very particular mentality. But you cannot deny the value of the blood that was spilled, and the bones, and the sweat and even the tears that have served to fortify the earth." ("la intención de volver convertidos en burgueses creó una mentalidad muy particular. Pero no puedes negar el valor de la sangre derramada, y los huesos, y el sudor, y aún las lágrimas que han servido para abonar la tierra." *HC* 115). In spite of the desire of the first generation to return, collectively they sensed the need to stay in the new land because of their Herculean effort and the sacrifices required to make the land habitable. After all of this struggle, it would have been difficult to walk away and return to Jamaica.

Jakel declares to Clif as the young man departs for San José to start a new life in the capital: "This land is also yours. It is not mine, just like it didn't belong to the Spanish, and nevertheless, it does belong to your descendants with all rights. . . . Conquered by us, given to our grandchildren to be perpetually shared from generation to generation." ("Esta tierra es también tuya. No es la mía, como nunca lo fue de los españoles, y sin embargo, es de los descendientes suyos con toda propiedad. . . . Conquistada por nosotros, legada a nuestros nietos; para ser compartida perpetuamente de generación en generación." *HC* 116). He continues to encourage Clif: "You take possession of it, knowing that it is the product of effort and work, and that if any blood was shed, that blood was ours." ("Entras en la posesión de ella sabiendo que es el producto del esfuerzo y del trabajo, y que si alguna sangre fue derramada esa sangre fue la nuestra." *HC* 117). The need to pass on a legacy and history to benefit the succeeding generations leads Jakel to say, "we cultivated it for our children and grandchildren." ("cultivábamos para nuestros hijos y nietos." *HC* 118).

This explains in part the complex issues of migration and the immigrants' disinterest in learning about the local culture to the extent that people even hid their children from government officials. The officials sought to place Afro–West Indian children into "Spanish" schools run by national authorities. The need to conserve West Indian culture made the reluctance to learn Spanish understandable since, "Language was a key that would open the door to eventual integration: the culture that we came to know in the country, embodied largely in the *cholo* was not very attractive. . . . What would have happened with our children in Jamaica with a Latin culture? They would not have been able to adapt." ("El idioma era una llave que abriría la puerta a una eventual integración: y la cultura que nosotros conocíamos como del país, encarnada en el cholo principalmente, no era muy atractiva. . . . ¿Qué hubiera sido de nuestros hijos, en Jamaica, con cultura latina? No se hubieran podido adaptar." *HC* 118). Clif recalls being struck by the words of his Costa Rican teacher working to acculturate the children and grandchildren of Afro–West Indians: "Well Clif, you are Costa Rican. Jamaica is the land of your parents and you should love it as such." ("De modo pues Clif, eres costarricense. Jamaica es la tierra de tus padres. Amala como tal." *HC* 118–19). Clif is now more aware of his "Costa Ricanness" and ponders, "So, am I Costa Rican?" ("Entonces soy costarricense?" *HC* 119). He will repeat this several times in order to affirm his Costa Rican identity, but he will not forget his grandfather's roots and his labor in the country.

The third part of the novel begins with the chapter titled "La conquista" (The Conquest), when Clif Duke approaches a greater understanding of his attempts to belong to Costa Rican society and accept his ethnolinguistic difference. The narrator's perspective focuses on Clif's return to Estrada and the train ride to the provincial town. The beginning presents an interaction between Clif and his wife on the journey from San José to Limón. The wife asks Clif about his experience during his first few years in San José.[6] He does not want to invoke the painful memories of the discrimination and racism he experienced—racial epithets, racist taunts, damaging stereotypes—or the overt discrimination in his search for housing and employment. He responds by saying, "There's not much to tell" ("No hay mucho que contar"), but the memories overpower him and he tells her some of the difficulties he faced in San José where he learned how racist attitudes become socialized: "The mother teaches her child the knowledge that was passed on to her: blacks don't comb their hair, blacks don't bathe." ("La madre enseña al hijo la sabiduría que a su vez aprendió de los suyos: los negros no se peinan, no se bañan." *HC* 125). He recalls how other blacks "would cross the street in order to avoid one another in their desperate struggle to pass unnoticed" ("se cambiaban de acera para no toparse unos con otros, en su desesperada lucha por pasar inadvertidos"; *HC* 125), an ironic gesture considering that the descendants of Afro–West Indians bear the very evident marker of racial difference through their skin color.

When inquiring for employment at a hotel in the capital, he recalls the explicit preference for Chinese and white workers and the discrimination against black citizens. Looking for work was a struggle during his first months in San José, and Clif eventually had to abandon his studies. He hoped for the triumph of a specific political party in elections, which is implicitly understood as being the Partido de

Liberación Nacional (PLN), the political party of José María Figueres who supported the postwar integration of the nation's black population. He continued to struggle for survival in San José, which was also a struggle that pitted his desire to belong against the reality of being a minority:

> Thus valiantly, he conquered the city. He reduced her to his whims, sometimes painful, but always fighting. He wanted to change her, humanize her, make her compatible with the hallucinatory and idealistic dreams of old Jakel, but the city unfolded in the opposite way—she dehumanized him, repudiated him for the grave sin of being black.
>
> *Así valientemente, conquistó la ciudad. La redujo a su antojo, con dolor a veces; siempre en lucha. Quiso modificarla, humanizarla, hacerla compatible con los sueños alucinantes e idealistas del viejo Jakel, pero la ciudad realizó el proceso contrario, deshumanizándole, repudiándole por el grave pecado de ser negro.* (*HC* 133)

Because he feels his difference, Clif continues to question his identity: "But was I Costa Rican? Not the mechanical and involuntary question of having been born in a determined country, but rather, the fact that to be or not to be incorporated into national society—the real fact of his marginal situation." ("Pero: ¿era costarricense? No la cuestión mecánica e involuntaria de haber nacido en determinado país, sino el hecho de estar o no incorporado a la sociedad nacional. El hecho real de su situación marginal." *HC* 133). He continues to question the meaning of national identity: "What were the elements that in effect made one or not Costa Rican and what were the obstacles? *And what power gave him the right to claim his place*?" ("¿Cuáles eran los elementos que en efecto lo hacían o no costarricense? ¿y cuáles los obstáculos? *¿Y qué poder le daba derecho a reclamar su lugar*?" *HC* 133, my emphasis).

Clif also contemplates the pan-Africanist vision of Marcus Garvey. In a conversation with his grandfather, Jakel opposes the idea of a "return to Africa" Garvey's followers proposed, but he also recognizes the psychological and physical effects of colonialism: "they conquered us, raped our women, exploited the enormous wealth of our motherland, they enslaved us physically and they tyrannized us ideologically to the point that made many believe that we were an inferior race." ("nos conquistaron, violaron nuestras mujeres, explotaron las enormes riquezas de nuestra patria, nos esclavizaron físicamente y nos tiranizaron ideológicamente, hasta el punto de hacer creer a muchos que éramos una raza inferior." *HC* 134).

But a return to Africa seems even more problematic: "Where Clif? We don't even know from which part of the continent we come from and we would be foreigners in any part of Africa." ("¿Cuál tierra Clif? Ni siquiera sabemos de qué lugar del continente provenimos, y seríamos extraños en cualquier parte del África." *HC* 134). Jakel also recognizes the influence of native culture on the black Diaspora: "There is something in common among us. But also a black Cuban is more Cuban than African, and more like a Latino in his way of thinking than an Ethiopian." ("Hay algo común entre todos nosotros. Pero también un negro cubano es más cubano que africano, y más semejante a un latino en su manera de pensar que a un etíope." *HC* 134). He claims that there would be no place for blacks from the Diaspora in Africa because of the effects of Western ideologies and their geography of displacement: "They can't even say from which tribe or nation their ancestors came from." ("Ni pueden dar cuenta de qué tribu o nación provienen sus antecesores." *HC* 134).

In spite of the hardships Jakel, Gretl, and Grace faced, they chose to remain. Jakel poses a question to his young grandson and encourages him to form a link between his native land, his Jamaican cultural heritage, and his national identity: "Do you think after so many sacrifices we could simply pick up and leave for home? It was impossible for us to leave this land because we came to love it." ("¿Tú crees que después de tantos sacrificios podíamos simplemente levantarnos e irnos para la casa? Nos fue imposible dejar esta tierra, porque llegamos a amarla." *HC* 135).

The narrative perspective in "Algo importante" (Something important), the final chapter of *Hombres curtidos*, presents Clif's first person point of view as he again revisits his grandfather's history. The protagonist proclaims: "Everything in my grandfather's history justifies my return. Everything." ("Todo en la historia del abuelo justifica mi retorno. Todo." *HC* 138). This contrasts with his declaration in the first chapter where he declares that "Nothing in my grandfather's history justifies my return." ("Nada in la historia del abuelo justifica mi retorno." *HC* 52). As he sits in the house in which he grew up, built by Jakel's own hands, he catches a glimpse of his grandfather's traitorous friend, Howard Bowman, approaching the family's house. Now the reason for his return becomes increasingly more focused and clear: "I need to return to reconcile with the mud." ("Necesito regresar, reconciliarme con el barro." *HC* 138). His wife asks why he has returned to Estrada, and Clif responds, "I came to write about my grandfather's life." ("Vine a escribir la biografía del abuelo." *HC* 139). She is shocked by the response and threatens to leave while Bowman, his grandfather's nemesis, the man Clif holds responsible for his death, knocks on the door. Clif is the heir of his grandfather's history and struggle and "the true receiver of glory and hope." ("el verdadero depositario de la gloria y la esperanza." *HC* 138). He summons the courage of Jakel, the one who came before him, the one who came to Costa Rica, worked the land, and started a family. Clif must avenge the man whose strength was ended by Bowman's betrayal. But he puts aside the thoughts of using the pistol and turns to the power of pen and paper.

His wife fails to comprehend the task Clif feels he must accomplish. Meanwhile, Bowman grows tired of knocking at the door without a response and departs. After this Clif sits at the typewriter and begins to write "as if I had lived the history that I plan to tell." ("como si hubiera vivido la historia que me propongo a relatar." *HC* 140). He writes, "The act of lifting the suitcase, hoisting up the child, and exiting the train is just one motion" ("El acto de levantar la valija, alzar el niño y bajarme del tren es uno solo"; *HC* 140). These are the same lines that begin the novel, bringing the story of Clif and his quest to understand his identity has come full circle.

Analysis

Hombres curtidos examines the complex construction and negotiation of Afro–Costa Rican identity through three generations of the Duke family. The novel details the first generation's reconstruction of Jamaican culture in Costa Rica and the second and third generations' memories of this history of struggle and suffering to make the land they settled their new home. Clif Duke, a member of the third generation, remembers the struggles of his grandfather, a man who emigrated from Jamaica in search of a nonexistent inheritance and who unintentionally settled in Costa Rica to build a future for his descendants. Clif also witnesses the uncertainty experienced by his mother's generation, the second generation caught between a homeland they never knew and a country that rejects them. Clif draws upon the collective memories of the first and second generations, as well as his own individual memories of growing up in Estrada, in order to write not only his grandfather's life story and preserve the esteemed family name but also to construct his own identity through the experiences of earlier generations.

Hombres curtidos presents a contemporary dimension to the theory presented by sociologist Marcus Lee Hansen in his 1938 essay, "The Problem of the Third Generation Immigrant," wherein he notes the frequently quoted aphorism, "What the son wishes to forget the grandson wishes to remember" (Hansen 1990, 195).[7] The generations in Hansen's thesis are defined by a significant event and by their response or relationship to that event. Stanford M. Lyman observes, "from these moments he [Hansen] has counted generations and observed the generational period in which the original 'historical' moment of experience is erased from the collective mind and, later, in another generational period remembered" (Lyman 1990, 127). In terms of immigration and settlement into a new land, Hansen finds that the second generation, the "sons/daughters" of immigrants, hastens the process of assimilation by turning away from the language and cultural practices of their parents in order to lessen the differences between themselves and the dominant culture. However, the third generation, the grandchild of immigrants, is engaged in an act of cultural and historical recovery in order to restore value to the first generation's heritage and experience. Additionally, the revalidation of this experience "mak[es] it the central part of the heritage group as well as a source of its collective identity" (Hansen 1990, 195). Although simple and limited in its original approach, this postulate still has value in describing the experience of generations following a significant, defining event such as migration. While Hansen's theory focuses on the specific experience of European immigrants to the United States, some partial parallels may be made to express the contemporary phenomenon of West Indian migration to other parts of the Americas and to Great Britain.

In the context of *Hombres curtidos*, it is the arrival of thousands of workers from Jamaica, Barbados, Trinidad, and other parts of the Caribbean basin to work on the construction of the transcontinental railroad or for fruit exporters that forms the significant event that defines the first generation. The second generation, which Duncan eloquently depicts through the debate between Grace Duke and her partner, Clovis, as "nowhereans," are stateless individuals who are neither British subjects nor embraced as Costa Rican citizens (Perry and Sawyers Royal 1995, 218).[8] Carlos Meléndez and Quince Duncan in *El negro en Costa Rica* call this generation the "wounded generation" and observe: "The second generation, born in Costa Rica or brought at a young age does not know Jamaica, and little by little leaves the dream of 'the return.' But the process of socialization to which they have been subjected by their elders impedes their incorporation into national life. They continue to identify themselves as Jamaicans because that is the label to which they have become accustomed and Costa Rica also labels them as Jamaicans" (Meléndez and Duncan 1993, 130). The second generation loses the protection of British citizenship and is largely ignored by the Costa Rican national government until post-1948 reforms extend citizenship to Costa Rican–born blacks. Many members of this generation migrate to San José in search of better employment options and educational opportunities. During this process, some try to assimilate to the dominant culture by speaking Spanish and adopting Hispanic cultural practices. It is clear from the debate between Clovis and Grace that the idea of a fixed and unifying cultural identity with unchanging shared values and a common history begins to unravel with their integration into the nation's Hispanic culture.

It is this third generation, the generation of Clif Duke, that participates in the affirmation of their national and cultural identity. Like the previous generation, they make great efforts during the 1950s and 1960s to exploit the opportunities of their recently granted citizenship by migrating to the Central Valley, particularly San José. Clif Duke participates in this wave of internal migration, leaving his home in Limón province to return to Estrada fourteen years later as a thirty-year-old man who writes his grandfather's story.

Memory, both collective and individual, is a powerful force for the third generation of blacks of West Indian descent. They attempt to understand their identity within Costa Rican society by recovering and recalling the first generation. Drawing on the work of Maurice Halbwach's *The Collective Memory* (1950), Singh, Skerrett, and Hogan observe in *Memory, Narrative, and Identity*: "Memory is one of the ways our consciousness connects items and experiences in the net of language . . . we 'remember' not only things that have actually happened to us personally, but also, and perhaps even more importantly, we 'remember' events, language, actions, attitudes, and values that are aspects of our membership in groups" (1994, 17).

There is a (re)construction of identity through the examination of the self and the collective historical experience of the group and its memory. The collective experience of the past, expressed in Jakel Duke's sacrifice and the demands of the dominant culture to conform, are encountered by his daughter and grandson. The formation of a national and cultural identity requires memory, specifically a concept of collective memory, a necessary tool in the creation of the "new" self. This involves an understanding of the collective cultural past as well as issues of inclusion/exclusion as the developing national identity is negotiated. Clif recreates the past to remember the collective struggle as exemplified by his grandfather's personal history, which also enables him to understand the importance of cultural memory in the formation of his identity.

Duncan's use of metafiction, multiple voices, and narrative shifts in *Hombres curtidos* also supports the textual quest for an Afro–Costa Rican identity. According to Singh, Skerrett, and Hogan, "Memory interrupts linear, conventional narratives in order to make room for multiple voices and perspectives." The presence of multiple voices "is a means of creating community as part of the dialectic between past and the present in moving toward the future" (1994, 18). Duncan's constant alteration of chronological order through flashbacks, and the multiple narrative shifts in voice and perspective, reveal that the story of finding and claiming place is not just Clif Duke's individual story but also a collective one made up of individual and communal experiences and memories of Costa Ricans of Afro–West Indian descent.

The representation of the three generations of Afro–West Indian immigrants and their descendants in *Hombres curtidos* is a counterdiscursive endeavor intended to dismantle the myth of Costa Rica as a white, Spanish-speaking, Catholic nation while presenting an intrahistory of Afro–Costa Ricans.[9] Singh, Skerrett, and Hogan observe that "ethnic writers valorize the subjectivity of narratives and undermine the very nature of hegemonic constructions of history and culture. Memory in this context shapes narrative forms and strategies towards reclaiming a suppressed past and helps the process of re-visioning that is essential to gaining control over one's life and future" (1994, 19). The novel calls into question the *leyenda blanca* and the marginalization of Afro–Costa Rican cultural contributions in light of this ethnic group's economic contributions to the nation's development. *Hombres curtidos* is the first major narrative in Costa Rica's national literature by a person of Afro–West Indian descent to critically expose the stereotypes and assumptions that label Afro–Costa Rican as a the racially marked, foreign Other—the very antithesis of a *tico de pura cepa* (an authentic Costa Rican).

An essential component of Clif's writing and remembering is the notion of disinheritance and inheritance. The novel presents a continual pattern of disinheritance that deterritorialization, separation, and displacement creates that requires urgent resolution. Clif Duke's quest—his desire to find a home and finally claim a space of his own from which he cannot be dispossessed—is an attempt to reclaim this lost inheritance. Jakel hears myths of the Ashanti on his way to Panama that tell of the disinheritance of Africans who were forced into ancestral exile in the diaspora of the Americas, the disinherited black daughters of a white slave owner who are cheated by their half brother, the journey that leads Jakel Duke to Panama where he finds only a small fraction of the inheritance he expected, and of the inability of Jakel to be considered a citizen of Costa Rica in spite of his labor to make the land hospitable. These voices eventually lead Clif to answer his grandfather's question, "Are you Costa Rican?" (¿Eres costarricense?), and claim his heritage and the land of his birth as the legitimate legatee of both. This transfer of a legacy from one generation to another is spiritual and cultural rather than material. Jakel Duke stresses to Clif the importance of his heritage and birthright:

> At sixteen, he [Jakel] formally emancipated him so that he could take on the responsibility of his blood, his culture, and even more importantly the responsibility of maintaining the Duke name to the height that is befitting of it. . . . Now, fourteen years after that solemn morning, he was once again in his hometown.
>
> *A los dieciséis años, le otorgarse la emancipación formal, para que el hecho tomase sobre sí la herencia: la sangre, la cultura, y más importante aún la responsabilidad de mantener el apellido Duke a la altura que le correspondía. . . . Ahora, catorce años después de aquella solemne mañana, estaba de nuevo en su pueblo natal.* (*HC* 6)

Clif frequently hears "you are the heir" (vos sos el heredero). He is the only Duke grandson and the last generation to inherit his grandfather's teachings, his property, and the family name.

The need to remember the past and value the collective memory explain the novel's preoccupation with inheritance and land as part of the broad theme of identity, which, like material possessions, are passed on from one generation to the next. Jakel's and Clif's individual memories contribute to the construction and perpetuation of the collective memory. They are chapters that form part of the whole narrative experience of a people. In the constantly shifting narrative perspectives between first and third person—and between Clif and Jakel—these fragments of memory—about journeys, arrivals, struggles—form the greater story of the Afro–West Indians. This story describes those who came to Central America, the settlement of some in Costa Rica, the conditions in Jamaica, the reason why some chose to leave and why some could not or would not return home, and the difficult negotiation of identity of black West Indians.

Clif Duke returns to Estrada to find his own roots, but he must first reconstruct his grandfather's past, and in so doing, memorializes the collective struggle and collective memory of Jakel and the other first-generation immigrants who sacrificed to cultivate the land for the next generation. In the process of re-visioning history, Clif is better able to understand his place in it and his place in the Afro–West Indian collective memory. When Jakel speaks of passing on to Clif an inheritance, he is referring not just to the modest house and the land but also to the memory of struggle and the determination to survive, which is the true spirit of what it means to be an "hombre curtido" or a witness to the trials of life. To be an "hombre curtido" is to be a survivor and also to acknowledge the collective history and struggle that made survival possible.

While *Hombres curtidos* is not a flawless first novel—there are many questions, gaps, and undeveloped points—it is an important text in Costa Rican and Central American literature.[10] With *Hombres curtidos*, Duncan is not rewriting history, but he is writing the black West Indian presence into history. It is an act of remembering intended to chart a future path. As critic Terry DeHay claims, "Remembering is the process of reclaiming and protecting a past often suppressed by the dominant culture, and in this sense, as re-visioning, it is essential in the process of gaining control over one's life" (1994, 43–44). Clif's return is a union of individual and collective memory, of past and present, of his ethnically marked body that tags him as a "foreigner" in his native land and the dominant culture. If the national culture will not include him, he will claim it on his own, as his grandfather and his mother had done before him. Clif must venture to his origins and mediate between his individual and collective past and the present. History is presented as a mitigating factor in the mutability of cultural identity. Clif must understand his beginnings in order to determine his future. He resists the notion of assimilation but argues for tolerance, understanding, and adaptation without allowing complete obliteration of difference by the dominant culture—or fully embracing all its cultural practices.

Los cuatro espejos

Duncan's first novel of Afro–Costa Rican identity, *Hombres curtidos*, is about the efforts of a third-generation grandson to acknowledge the cultural history and identity of the first generation of Jamaican immigrants. The author's second novel, *Los cuatro espejos*, which relies heavily on the techniques of the new novel, portrays the psychological struggle of Afro–West Indians to integrate into the dominant culture. *Los cuatro espejos* was published in 1973 and is the most studied of the author's novels to date, garnering the attention of critics inside and outside of Costa Rica for its innovative technical style and themes. Although Duncan has claimed that he believes *Kimbo* to be his best novel, the quantity of articles and book chapters about *Los cuatro espejos* indicates that it is preferred by a number of critics (Duncan, personal interview 2002).[11] Dellita Martin-Ogunsola notes thematic echoes of *Invisible Man* by African American author Ralph Ellison in the protagonist's search for place and meaning in a culture that does not fully embrace his existence: "The exploits of Charles McForbes, like those of Ellison's *Invisible Man*, constitute the epic of the black man's search for a healthy, viable essence in the African diaspora of the New World. For this reason Duncan's character incorporates the double-consciousness and sense of duality classically articulated by DuBois in *The Souls of Black Folk* (1903), for McForbes' quest for an identity with which he can be comfortable illustrates the ongoing battle of the 'two warring forces in one dark body'" (Martin-Ogunsola 1987, 9).

The identity crisis for the light-complexioned protagonist, Charles McForbes, begins one morning after attending a lecture on the "desperate" condition of racial minorities in Costa Rica, including Afro–West Indian descendants like McForbes. After a series of disturbing dreams, McForbes awakens next to the sleeping white body of his second wife, Ester Centeno. When he approaches the bathroom mirror, he sees only blackness where his face should appear. The lecture from the previous night on ethnic minorities, his feelings of displacement, and his racially marked body alongside his wife's whiteness catalyze McForbes's identity crisis. This crisis launches McForbes on a journey through the streets of San José and to his hometown in Limón Province, a trip that forces the protagonist to examine the trajectory of his life and to confront his denial of his black roots. The journey from San José to his origins in Limón echoes the voyage Clif Duke took in *Hombres curtidos*. McForbes leaves the life he created with his second wife in the center of the nation's dominant Latin culture to the Afro–West Indian heritage of the province in which he lived with his first wife, Lorena Sam. The move highlights McForbes's conflicted self-consciousness, as Dellita Martin-Ogunsola observed. The tensions between the dual aspects of his identity and his attempt to negotiate between the city and the province reveal fissures in the protagonist's attempt to "pass" for Latin. Traveling between San José and Limón serves as a cultural bridge that allows McForbes to explore decisions he has made during his life and mute the dissonance created by his multiple identities—a light-skinned black man of Afro–West Indian ancestry who has adopted the language and behavior of the dominant Latin culture.

Structure and Themes

The two-part novel, set during the 1960s and 1970s, is divided into eleven chapters: the first six comprise part 1 and the remaining five chapters constitute part 2. Dellita Martin-Ogunsola notes, "chapters 1, 4, 6, 7 and 11 constitute the external structure of the work, which portrays Charles and Ester in upper-class society of San José, while the inner story, composed of chapters 2, 3, 5, 8, 9, and 10 depicts Charles and Lorena in rural Estrada" (Martin-Ogunsola 2004, 83). The first part of the novel details McForbes's psychological crisis, his life in the capital, and his marriage to Ester, and it offers clues about his past in Limón with his first wife, Lorena, and her tragic death. In this first part of the novel, only two chapters—chapters 1 and 4—are told from McForbes's point of view. The remaining chapters are narrated in third person with a shifting perspective, focusing at times on Charles, at times on other characters. The second part of the novel is narrated in first person by McForbes, and as Alan Persico observes, "this part constitutes about one-third of the work, but it is not surprisingly, the section where the protagonist seeks and finds his own psychological and cultural liberation" (Persico 1991, 16). In the second part of the novel McForbes confronts his blackness and travels to his old home in Limón to revisit his past where he discovers that he has not only abandoned his roots, but also his identity.

The first chapter, narrated by the protagonist, expresses his deteriorating mental condition as he faces the mirror. Since the initial focus is on McForbes's mental state, there are few signs that point toward the protagonist's ethnicity or skin color. As the narrative develops and McForbes sinks deeper into his crisis, the absence of physical description creates disquietude for the reader who is uncertain if the character is a white man who is becoming black or if the character is a black man who is in denial of his color. The protagonist's interior monologue and reaction to blacks suggest that he is not of Afro–Costa Rican descent, particularly when he uses of the pronoun *ellos* (they) and the possessives *su/sus* (their). However, when McForbes retraces memories of his life in Limón in the latter chapters of the first part of the novel, we learn unambiguously of his ethnic identity and cultural background with the marked shift in the use of the first-person plural pronoun *nosotros* (we) and the possessives *mi/mis* (my) and *nuestro* (our). This change signifies the protagonist's reconnection with his authentic identity and a narrowing of the distance he placed between himself and other blacks.

When McForbes's voice is at the center of the narrative, he speaks in a colloquial, informal tone, often repeating the words *cursi* (trite, corny), *rutina* (routine), *aburrimiento* (boredom), and *estoy aburrido* (I'm bored). He swears without hesitation, letting out *pucha* (damn) and *carajo* (crap) when expressing his frustrated thoughts. These words are also indicative of his mental state—the fatigue, the fragmentation, and the frustration that has resulted from his inability to reconcile the duality of his existence. Using popular language, McForbes appears at times to carry on a conversation with his inner self in the form of an interior monologue that at times appears to be directed to the reader: "My life has had its ups and downs, failures, endeavors, come-backs, so, I will tell you about them." ("Mi vida ha tendio sus altibajos, fracasos, esfuerzos, regresos, en fin, ya los iré contando." *LCE* 10). Frequent stream-of-consciousness passages that appear disjointed and fragmented also serve to illustrate his broken and disjointed condition during his crisis of identity.

Like Duncan's other fictional work, *Los cuatro espejos* adheres stylistically to the techniques of the Latin American "new novel," principally the nonlinear development of the narrative, the multiple narrative voices, and the use of flashbacks. The flashbacks in particular provide information about the protagonist's past as well as his relationships with other characters. Costa Rican critic Edwin Salas Zamora observes a correlation between the use of flashbacks and the nonlinear structure with the disconnected nature of memory: "These references to the past, especially the distant past, are present throughout the text. This characteristic produces a constant fragmentation that not only occurs with respect to the primary narrative thread, but also the details. This constant rupture of the linear structure is due to the irregular process of memory on the part of the characters" (Salas Zamora 1987, 382).[12] The flashbacks are essential for resolving Charles McForbes's identity crisis for they connect the incongruent experiences of his past and present.

Los cuatro espejos is also the first novel in which Duncan makes intertextual references to his own work. A portion of the novel takes place in Estrada, the town prominently featured in his first novel, *Hombres curtidos*. Jakel Duke, Clif Duke, his wife Clarita de Duke, Clovis, and the trouble-causing Bowman family, as well as other minor characters from *Hombres curtidos*, make appearances in *Los cuatro espejos*. Clif Duke and Charles McForbes are presented as childhood friends in the novel; Clarita de Duke, Clif's previously unnamed wife, is given more depth as a black woman who does not feel completely at ease or accepted in the rural town. Duncan's second novel also presents an intertextual reference to the author's collection of short stories, *Una canción en la madrugada*. In the narrative, the protagonist sits down to read a book written by a black Costa Rican author, and as he is reading, "Hierve . . . el agua sepultada en las venas de la tierra, y la tierra porosa, húmeda . . . y el viento hierve," readers familiar with Duncan's work recognize that McForbes is reading "Una carta," which appears in *Una canción en la madrugada*.

By grounding the novel in the historical and cultural reality of people of Afro–West Indian descent in Costa Rica, Duncan engages with his own theory of Afro-realism. For example, the author presents from a personal perspective the extensive labor of the Afro–West Indian settlers and their intimate bond with the land of the coastal province. The narrator describes the experiences of the Afro–West Indian immigrants and their descendants with the inhospitable land of the province:

> Because one had to have unshakable will or a congenital stubbornness in order to resist. Or perhaps an inherent cultural quality of the culture of a human group that after every flood, would begin to rebuild year after year. It was not easy to cultivate the land with vigor for eight months and then see all of that work destroyed a month before harvest due to the brutal advance of a torrent, rebellious like the nature of the lowlands that refused to define its course.
>
> *Porque había que tener una voluntad inquebrantable o una terquedad congénita, para resistir. O acaso una cualidad inherente a la cultura del grupo humano que después de cada llena, empezaba la reconstrucción año tras año, lustro tras lustro. No era fácil cultivar la tierra con ahínco durante ocho meses y ver el trabajo destruido un mes antes de la cosecha por el paso brutal de un torrente que, rebelde como la naturaleza del llano, se negaba a definir su curso.* (*LCE* 36)

Additionally, the Afro-realist tendency is portrayed in the belief in the supernatural present in some black communities throughout the Diaspora. These Afro-realist elements contribute to the tensions in Charles McForbes's psychological drama of identity as a result of dominant culture's labeling as superstitious the complex of African-derived spiritual beliefs. The power of popular belief systems such as obeah and communication with the dead are not intended to add the interest of the "magical real," but rather these elements are presented as a depiction of Duncan's concept of "ancestral community," elements that link Afro-descendants with the beliefs, myths, and history of their ancestors.

The alteration of chronological time, flashbacks, dream states juxtaposed with scenes from everyday life, episodes of the "marvelous real," multiple perspectives, and views from McForbes's psyche require the reader to become aware of the fragmentation of the narrative, a fragmentation that mirrors that of the protagonist and obliges the reader to put the narrative in order and context.[13]

Plot. The confused and disordered dreams of the protagonist, Charles McForbes, open the narrative of *Los cuatro espejos*. The protagonist's subconscious reveals a fear that he is losing his grip on reality, on his whole sense of being. McForbes feels that his body is displacing itself and in a sense "doubling," coming apart, or separating. He states, "My head was languishing outside of itself" ("Mi cabeza languidecía fuera de mi cabeza"; *LCE* 7). He feels a battle raging between sanity and insanity and between his life and death. The sleeper awakens several times from this crisis of the subconscious as his dreams continue and become increasingly more terrifying. McForbes attempts to dismiss the strange sensations he experiences by taking the approach that experience has taught him—allowing things to take care of themselves:

> I recovered control of my nerves. And I realized that I was dreaming, which gave me great relief. . . . Suddenly, I felt among the living and I could slowly abandon the dream. It was in every way the easiest thing to do and so I acted just as I had been taught in the capital: allow things to take care of themselves.
>
> There in the province I also saw that attitude and everyone considered it normal: the violent flow of the river and the capricious flooding of the lowlands.
>
> *Recuperé el dominio de mis nervios. Y me di cuenta de que estaba soñando, lo cual me produjo un enorme alivio. . . . Me sentí de pronto entre vivo, y me pude abandonar lentamente el sueño. Era de todos modos lo más fácil, y en eso actuaba como si me había enseñado en la capital: dejar que las cosas se resolviesen por sí mismas.*
>
> *Allá en el llano también ví ese comportamiento y todos lo consideraban normal: el discurrir violento del río de llanura, en la hondura caprichosa del llano.* (*LCE* 8)

The strategy of leaving issues to resolve themselves is one that contributes to McForbes's crisis. The increasingly chaotic and violent dreams prefigure the reality the protagonist is about to encounter, foreshadowing the psychological distress and dissonance that is to come:

> As the day was breaking, I dreamed that . . . I was hanging on the edge of a cliff, the same one that I saw before in another dream. Suspended, gasping for air, I felt my hands failing me and that my life was coming to an end. In an instant after that I was on the rocks below, my head shattered, my intestines exposed to the sun. I awoke sweating and shaken.
>
> *Clareando el día soñé que . . . yo estaba guindando la orilla del precipicio. Del precipicio ese que vi antes en otro sueño. Suspendido, tragando aire, sentí que mis manos me fallaban, que la vida llegaba a su fin. Un instante después estaba sobre las rocas, mi cabeza partida, mis intestinos exhibidos al sol.* Desperté sudando, conmovido. (*LCE* 9)

However, when the protagonist finally arises from the bed to put a halt to his subconscious adventures, he discovers that the reality he experiences is much more frightening than his dreams. As McForbes observes himself in the bathroom mirror, he notices that his appearance is not what he expects to see: "I then looked at myself in the mirror. A man with disheveled hair, dressed in blue pajamas, appeared before my eyes, but something was missing in the reflection." ("Entonces me mire el espejo. Un hombre de pelo desordenado, vestido de pijama azul, apareció frente a mis ojos. Algo le faltaba a la imagen." *LCE* 10). Charles McForbes cannot see his face in the mirror and sees only darkness where his face should appear.

The protagonist traces some of his distress back to a lecture of the previous night that he and Ester organized on racial minorities in Costa Rica. McForbes recalls the moment he entered the forum with his attractive wife. Radiating with an air of self-confidence and triumph, he appears to be at the summit of achievement and social standing, a long way from his humble origins as a cacao grower in Limón. With Ester on his arm he proudly displays the trappings of social position and popularity. McForbes states, "Ester and I sat down in front, right in front of everybody so that all interested parties couldn't help but see us." ("Ester y yo nos sentamos adelante, al puro frente de todos, para que ningún interesado se quedase sin vernos." *LCE* 11). McForbes fixates on the social and ethnic pedigree of his wife: "Grecian elegance . . . and a light Germanic strain. From a distinguished family, not rich, but descended from wealthy families with fertile pasts." ("elegancia griega . . . y un ligero rasgo germánico. De familia distinguida, no rica pero descendiente de ricas familias de fecundos pasados." *LCE* 10). McForbes also reflects on the material comforts he possesses—a new luxury car, a gardener—all symbols of his bourgeois achievements and all acquired through his marriage to Ester:

> It was a beautiful thing being Ester's husband after all. I'm not saying that she did me a favor by marrying me, no, not at all. But you can say that I have done well for myself with the marriage. . . . I was a Mr. Nobody, a simple man from the country and she was a Centeno.
>
> *Era bonito ser esposo de Ester después de todo. No llego a afirmar que me hizo un favor casándose conmigo, no, no es eso. Pero si puedo decir bien he ganado bastante con el matrimonio. . . . Y era un don nadie, un simple provinciano y ella era un Centeno.* (*LCE* 13–14).

Although McForbes complains that the behavior of the Central Valley elite is *cursi* (clichéd, corny), he embraces the superficial trappings of bourgeois life in the capital.

In spite of the appearance that he has fully integrated into the comfortable bliss of the Central Valley bourgeoisie, he is discomfited by the words of the lecturer that seem to contradict his reality. The conference on racial minorities in Costa Rica reverberates within him: "The alienation, marginalization, and extreme exploitation of which its victims are the blacks and Indians of this country, are not precisely an example of democracy. Their situation is desperate." ("La alienación y la marginalización, la explotación en grado sumo de que son víctimas los negros y los indígenas de ese país, no son precisamente un ejemplo de democracia. Su situación es desesperante." *LCE* 12). McForbes dismisses the lecturer's assessment of the condition of blacks and Indians in Costa Rica and also fails to see the racism he has internalized against his own ethnic group. For example, when talking about a black woman he remembers seeing at a function held in San José's renowned cultural institution La Casa Amarilla (the Yellow House), he comments that "the black woman was pretty in spite of her color." ("la negra era linda a pesar de su color." *LCE* 13). As he describes her body, particularly her waist and breasts, his reductionist gaze is no different from that of the Caribbean *negrista* poets whose verses relegated the black woman to body parts that indicate a sexual invitation. McForbes adds as an afterthought her possible intellect by adding, "And besides, she was a good conversationalist." ("Y además, era buena conversadora." *LCE* 13).

Haunted by the words of the lecturer about people of African descent in Costa Rica, his discomfort with his ethnic identity, and his inability to see his own face in the mirror, McForbes fears he is going blind. Without mentioning his plans to Ester, he leaves the house to see his friend, Dr. Pineres, an eye doctor, to remedy his problem. With this visit, the journey to recover his identity is initiated. He leaves his car and begins to walk. McForbes thinks about his sudden affliction, occasionally turning his interior monologue about his past into a conversation with the readers. McForbes passes the house of an acquaintance, who like McForbes, was once part of a gang, but became a social climber by acquiring increasing prestige through education, eventually joining the ranks of the middle class. However, it is also revealed that his social advancement was gained at the expense of others through betrayal. McForbes will soon learn that he too has paid a price for success, the denial of his ethnic and cultural roots. As he wanders the streets to seek a solution to his "blindness," McForbes begins to think about racism in society, an issue he is loathe to confront. He does not realize that the workers at a construction site are mocking him when they ask in English if he has a light for their cigarettes. McForbes grumbles with an ironic nationalistic twist that "we all have the gringo complex." ("todos tenemos complejo de gringos." *LCE* 19). He accuses the workers of pretending to be what they are not; however, the joke is on McFrobes. He seems to realize that his compatriots see him as a "foreigner" and as a black man from Limón, characteristics that imply that he is not part of the nation, and that he does not speak Spanish.

The issues of language, ethnic and national identity, and racism converge as he rides on the bus through the city and a woman stubbornly blocks the aisle after repeated requests for her to move toward the back to accommodate more passengers in the front. The driver, unable to get the woman to move, barks orders to the young black man standing next to her. He shouts, "Move up, darkie" (Córrase, Moreno) to the young man who asserts, "But where do you want me to go? . . . Are you afraid of the woman?" ("Pero ¿adónde quieres que me corra? . . . Que ¿le tienes miedo a la señora?" *LCE* 20). A Latino passenger is astonished that the black man speaks Spanish so well and asks if he is from Panama. The young man declares that he is Costa Rican from Limón, leaving the fellow passenger even more surprised. McForbes expresses his consternation at the exchange, making reference to the previous night's lecture:

> The guy had made one of those great logical conclusions that all Limonese because of their West Indian heritage, speak Spanish poorly. The words of the lecturer came back to my ears and this made me furious. If a Latino uses gender inaccurately, the audience understands it was an insignificant error. If a black commits the same error, it will provoke the ironic smile of the public.

> *El tipo había hecho una de esas grandes deducciones lógicas: todo limonense por ser de herencia antillana, habla mal el español. Las palabras del conferencista regresaron a mis oídos y eso me dio mucha rabia. Si una persona latina emplea mal el género, la audiencia comprende que fue un error sin importancia. Si un negro comete la misma falta, provocará la sonrisa irónica del público.* (*LCE* 20)

This incident also demonstrates that within McForbes is a latent awareness of black consciousness, although he puts distance between himself and the young man on the bus.

When McForbes finally arrives at the doctor's house, he receives an unexpected diagnosis. Pineres determines that McForbes is not going blind, but rather is suffering from a psychological disorder. The protagonist is bothered by his friend's opinion and goes to look at himself in the mirror for the second time. McForbes sees a minstrel-like caricature of his face and states, "In the bathroom I proved that I wasn't dreaming about the whole thing with the mirror. I couldn't see my face—I could see my eyes, yes, and if I opened my mouth, I could see my teeth, but not my face." ("En el baño comprobé que no había soñado lo del espejo: no veía mi rostro. Mis ojos sí y, al abrir la boca, los dientes. Pero el rostro no." *LCE* 21). Concerned about the mental stability of his friend, Pineres refers McForbes to a psychoanalyst, Dr. Díaz. McForbes meets Díaz and the two travel to the psychoanalyst's office in Díaz's car. In their brief encounter, McForbes becomes more sensitive toward matters of racial discrimination and is increasingly aware of Díaz's racism. A young white woman, "beautiful, almost naked" ("guapa, casi desnuda"), passes by, provoking the doctor to comment lasciviously, "Look at that bon-bon." ("Mira qué copa de helados." *LCE* 24). Moments later, Díaz has an entirely different reaction to a miniskirted black nanny who crosses the street holding the hand of the white child in her care. He abusively declares, "What nerve that black girl has. . . . They dress indecently as if they are in Limón. Only in Limón do people walk in the street like that." ("Qué descaro de negra. . . . Se visten a lo relajo como si estuvieran en Limón. Solo en Limón la gente caminan por las calles." *LCE* 24). Díaz's double standard considers the "almost naked" white woman as an object of beauty and sexual desire and attempts to "de-sexualize" the black nanny. Instead of being viewed as the hypersexual black woman (a common trope in Latin American literature), she is expected to adopt the nonsexual role of the "mammy" figure because she is the caretaker of a white child. The black nanny who Díaz presumes to be from Limón is not only a foreign object of contempt in the Central Valley, but also an object that needs to be under surveillance and control.

In spite of his Afro–West Indian roots and his awareness of the racial inequality that he witnesses, the protagonist remains distant from these incidents—

there is no sense of responsibility or affect. He stands on the sidelines during the incident on the bus when the young black man from Limón becomes the scapegoat for the mestizo woman blocking the aisle. He does not protest Díaz's racial bias, as if he has no part or personal stake in these matters. However, the words of the lecturer, the vision of Ester's white body, his violent nightmares, and the inability to see his reflection in the mirror eventually force McForbes to reexamine his own condition and position in Costa Rican society and the "different" treatment he and others of West Indian descent receive on the basis of color and origin.

McForbes consents to the psychoanalyst's exams, but he suddenly leaves the office and launches himself out into the streets of downtown San José. During this aimless wandering he begins to mediate the present and the past and to understand the imageless face he saw in the mirror earlier that morning. He purchases a mirror from a young street vendor in order to provide some answers to his dilemma. The initial happiness at setting eyes on an image quickly melts into shock and then horror when he sees the face of a black man staring back at him in the mirror. Instead of accepting the black face displayed in the mirror, McForbes believes his skin color has changed as a result of a chemical treatment:

> I had heard talk of some who managed to temporarily change the color of their skin, but those were experiments with chemicals. I had not undergone any chemical process, and because of that my sudden mutation seemed absurd.
>
> *Había oído hablar de algunos que lograron modificar temporalmente el color de su piel, pero fueron experimentos con productos químicos. Yo no me había sometido a proceso alguno, y por lo tanto, resultaba absurda mi repentina mutación.* (*LCE* 31).

His strong reaction to the black face in the mirror drives him to rant in the street like a madman and attack a street vendor. The racial epithets hurled by the onlookers indicate that his behavior now reflects the stereotyped expectations of his skin color as an enraged, violent, dangerous black man. He does not perform the role of the "good" negro, but rather takes on all of the negative signifiers of blackness and black masculinity. McForbes finds himself, like the black man on the bus earlier in the day, reduced to his color. This becomes even more apparent when he goes to a pharmacy for treatment after discovering he hurt his hand in the scuffle with the street vendor. At the pharmacy, a white woman is attended to first, although she entered the premises after him. He states, "I didn't know whether to attribute her privilege to her condition as a woman or to the color of her skin." ("no supe si atribuir su privilegio a su condición de mujer o al color de su piel." *LCE* 32).

The crisis of Charles McForbes continues as he wanders the streets of San José, questioning the black face he saw in the mirror. In a pivotal moment in the narration, the focus shifts from Charles's meanderings through the city to events from the protagonist's provincial past. The mud with its smell and the abundant vegetation depicted in this Limonese farming village where the character lived contrasts with the earlier scenes of the crowds, concrete, and asphalt of San José and his middle-class life with Ester Centeno. The retrospective returns to life before his settlement in the capital and marriage to his second wife. In this portion of the narrative, McForbes is a twenty-three-year-old Anglican preacher and cacao farmer in Estrada, a small town in Limón Province. His life with his black first wife, Lorena Sam, contrasts with the status and prestige he has gained in the capital through his marriage to his white second wife, Ester. The two lives, two wives, and two geographic locations present a clear picture of the causes of McForbes's crisis. His crisis occurs when he is unable to reconcile these disparate parts of his life and his identity.

Narrated in third person, the flashback revisits a critical moment for the protagonist when he discovers that Lorena is gravely ill. She has fallen victim to obeah by the jealous wife of McForbes's rival, Cristian Bowman.[14] McForbes has a presentiment that something destructive is about to occur, and he feels anxious and questions his life: "shit, why did I even bother having studied and returned bearing failure as a trophy right next to my diploma? And come back to swing a machete?" ("pucha carajo, total ¿para qué haber estudiado y regresar cargando el fracaso como trofeo a la par del título? Y volver a volar machete?" *LCE* 32–33). McForbes, an educated pastor, still must perform grueling agricultural work to survive.

When a neighbor informs him that Lorena is seriously ill, he hurries home from the cacao groves. The women who are caring for Lorena, including her best friend, Ruth, suspect that she has fallen victim to an act of obeah against her caused by Nabe Bowman, the wife of McForbes's rival and former friend, Cristian Bowman. Ruth, who like Lorena is the daughter of an Afro–West Indian obeah man, reveals that her friend was brazenly attacked by a *dopi*, a manifestation of an evil spirit that causes harm to the living, sent by Nabe's sorcery.[15] As youths growing up in Estrada, Lorena, Ruth, Charles, Clif, and Cristian were friends, but over the years Cristian's growing resentment toward Charles's education and his jealousy over the relationship between Charles and Lorena culminates in a brutal act of violence. Taking advantage of the trust developed during their childhood friendship, Cristian deceives Lorena by telling her that he and Charles have made amends and have called a truce in their personal war against each other. Under the premise of celebrating their renewed alliance, Bowman gains Lorena's confidence and then rapes her as a means to vengefully attack Charles McForbes. After the rape, Lorena gives birth to a child, and fearing that the child is the result of the sexual attack, the child is given to an orphanage. In spite of the vocal community outrage against Cristian Bowman, his wife, Nabe, denies that her husband is a rapist. Instead, Nabe sees Lorena as a seductress who willingly consented to have sex with Cristian and unleashes the power of the supernatural against Lorena. Although the community accepts a belief in obeah, for McForbes: "it was difficult to accept such a magical explanation after so many years of study." ("era duro aceptar una explicación tan mágica después de tantos estudios." *LCE* 41). His education in San José and his role as a local church pastor cause McForbes to reject "the magical response to a real event" ("una respuesta mágica a un hecho real"; *LCE* 41) and to seek a more concrete explanation for his wife's sudden illness. He finds an ally against folk beliefs and superstition in Clarita de Duke, a nurse and the wife of his neighbor, Clif Duke. Instead of herbal concoctions to heal Lorena, Clarita Duke puts her faith in modern medicine.

Nevertheless, there is an undeniable presence of the "marvelous real" or the spiritual dimensions of *afrorealismo*, the term Duncan coined to draw a parallel between the textual universe and the cultural reality, beliefs, and traditions of communities they represent.[16] The Afro–West Indian community depicted in *Los cuatro espejos*, in spite of "official" religious traditions like the Anglican Church, accepts that the natural and the supernatural planes are congruous and coexist in the daily lives of the inhabitants of Estrada. Witnesses from the community, including Ruth, see the "duppy," the white, malevolent spirit that attacks Lorena in plain sight and in the daylight for all to see. There are consultations with obeah men to cause harm to others, reverse hexes, and to create a spiritual defense against supernatural attacks. Cristian Bowman uses obeah against McForbes in order to destroy his crop yield. Lovers use obeah to attract and keep their partners. Individuals like Nabe use obeah because of misguided jealousy, with damaging results. In other examples of the coexistence of the natural and the supernatural, the dead reappear to give instructions to the living. During her illness McForbes's father, Pete McForbes, appears in Lorena's dreams to warn her that a spell has been cast against her. In one of his dreams, McForbes receives the winning numbers for the Panama lottery from Pete, an event that arouses more jealousy in Cristian Bowman. McForbes also speaks to apparitions of his father and Jakel Duke, who explain from beyond the cause of Lorena's illness.

Even when events occur that appear to have no scientific explanation, McForbes refuses to believe in the magical or marvelous real of his surroundings. When he sees a horse with two riders, one of whom has his face turned toward the animal's tail, the narrator questions whether he is being influenced by the commonly held superstitions of the community or if there is truth to their talk of obeah:

> There was something absurd in the scene. Perhaps it was the influence of the womenfolk's belief in magic. In any case, it ended up being an absurd experience. Was it real or imaginary experience? He was not capable of describing at this moment. But he was definitely convinced, having seen or imagined that pair of riders on the same horse. Total certainty did not ensure anything.
>
> *Había algo de absurdo en la escena. Tal vez era la influencia del pensamiento mágico de las vecinas. En todo caso, acababa de tener una experiencia absurda. ¿Experiencia real o imaginaria? No estaba en capacidad de definirlo en esos instantes. Pero de lo que sí estaba absolutamente convencido, era de haber visto o imaginado que un par de jinetes cabalgaban sobre el mismo caballo. Certeza total que no aseguraba nada.* (*LCE* 45)

His inability to determine with certainty whether the vision is something real or imaginary relates to the opposition Charles McForbes expresses toward the popular belief in obeah and his own powerlessness to change the conditions of his ailing wife. He repudiates the superstition and fatalism of the townspeople, but he does not know if science will be able to save her.

When the vision of the two riders on a horse appears for a second time, McForbes succumbs to folk traditions. He recalls instructions from his father, Pete McForbes, to make the sign of the lodge in times of need. Soon thereafter, with the sound of barking dogs invading the atmosphere, he sees Pete McForbes running from the unseen dogs followed by his friend Jakel Duke (Clif Duke's grandfather), even though both men are deceased. Their apparitions evoke fond memories of the two men and their friendship cemented by a passion for reading, rum, and discussions about their ancestry. Jakel was proud of his royal Ashanti roots, and Pete was proud of his Scottish blood, "and this infuriated Jakel, who on the contrary embraced his African purity." ("y eso enfurecía a Jakel, quien por el contrario se ufanaba de su pureza Africana." *LCE* 46).

This tumultuous time with Lorena's illness gives McForbes pause to think about the tensions between the official beliefs formed by formal education versus the popular folk beliefs of the culture in which he was born. These tensions between official/popular beliefs; Anglican Church/folk spirituality; religious dogma/human urges also appear in McForbes's struggles to distinguish the magical from the "real." He decides to follow the recommendation of Clarita de Duke and takes

Lorena to a specialist in San José for medical treatment, although he believes deep within that conventional medicine will not be able to help Lorena: "All of this would have been all right had the cause of Lorena's illness been physical. Before something natural, modern medicine, but Lorena's pain was not physical even though its manifestation was. ("Todo eso había estado bien si la causa de la enfermedad de Lorena fuese física. Ante algo natural, la medicina corriente. Pero la dolencia de Lorena no era física, aunque las consecuencias lo fuesen." *LCE* 47). The physician who attends to her is Dr. Lucas Centeno, the man who eventually would become Charles's second father-in-law. Centeno is a firmly cemented member of the Hispanic elite of the Central Valley and believes that the blacks of Limón are uneducated and ignorant because of their use of folk remedies and their beliefs in the supernatural, such as obeah.

Lorena spends one year in the hospital and McForbes, now twenty-four years old, rents a room in San José to be close to his wife as she agonizes in the hospital with a condition that no one can diagnose or cure. The couple faces financial hardship because they are unable to harvest the cacao on their small farm. In this section of the narrative, the storytelling of Lorena's death is crafted with an interweaving of suffering and meaning. During her lengthy stay in the hospital, Lorena laments over the child that was taken away from her, an experience she relates to the agony African women experienced during the transatlantic slave trade whose children were wrenched from them and sold. She also observes the death, dearth, indifference, and desperation that surround her in the public hospital. The apathetic and unresponsive hospital staff members place bureaucratic procedures over humane patient care, which leads to misdiagnosis in some of the youngest, poorest, and most innocent patients. This depiction presents an implicit criticism of the nationalized health system.[17]

This portion of the narrative that marks Lorena's agonizing death also marks the beginning of McForbes's transformation and reveals the circumstances surrounding the protagonist's settlement in the Central Valley. McForbes sells the farm and leaves his life as a pastor and small farmer in Limón behind, to make his way in the capital. He befriends Dr. Lucas Centeno, Lorena's attending physician, who takes special interest in McForbes's circumstances by offering him support for his studies at the university and a room in his home. McForbes becomes incorporated into the celebrated and elite Centeno family in spite of the fact that various members of the family express general disdain toward blacks. Centeno's daughter, Ester, and her cousin, Magdalena, despise blacks, as evidenced by their treatment of the family's gardener and the cruel taunting of a black schoolmate. Nevertheless, McForbes's presence in the household changes their attitude as both Magdalena and Ester fall in love with him and he marries Ester. In spite of the number of black patients he encountered and his acceptance of McForbes into his household, Centeno does not support the courtship of Ester and McForbes. He is displeased that his only biological child has chosen to marry a black man from Limón and blames himself for the deterioration of the family's aristocratic lineage:

> Yes, the family was glorious, and Lucas Centeno felt guilty for its decline because something bad was happening now. His only daughter, who for so many years he saw growing up, detesting blacks, was all of a sudden in love with a black man.
>
> Perhaps it was the Guanacastecan blood of his wife Aminga Vidaurre. Perhaps it was that—the black blood that was in her. Blood of a Castillian mulatta.
>
> *Sí, la familia era gloriosa, y Lucas Centeno se sentía culpable de su decadencia. Porque algo malo sucedía ahora. Su única hija, que por tantos años vio crecer detestando a los negros, estaba de pronto enamorada de un negro.*
>
> *Tal vez fue la sangre guanacasteca de su esposa Aminga Vidaurre. Tel* [sic] *vez fue eso: la sangre de negro que había en ella. Sangre de una Castilla mulata.* (*LCE* 74–75)

This commentary implicitly addresses the widely negated colonial origins of the darker complexioned residents of the Guanacaste Province in northwestern Costa Rica. Centeno wonders if an atavistic drive from the black blood of his wife is what pushes their daughter toward McForbes. The protagonist also comments that his father-in-law was relieved that he and Ester have no children, "saying to himself that it was better to have the definitive extinction of the family line rather than having the spoils passed into mulatto hands." ("diciéndose que era mejor la extinción definitiva de la familia a que sus despojos pasaran a manos mulatas." *LCE* 76).

The protagonist's first-person perspective, as well as the third-person narrator who relates the point of view of Centeno and his daughter Ester, reveal not only how Charles McForbes views himself but also how others view him. Centeno examines his son-in-law's rise in society as if he were a social experiment. When he learns from Ester that McForbes has consulted with a psychoanalyst, he urges Ester to think about her husband's past and a possible regression: "Ester, when you met Charles, who was he?" ("Ester, cuando conociste a Charles, ¿quién era?" *LCE* 99). Ester responds: "But Dad, he will always be a black man from Limón" ("Pero papá, sigue siendo un negro de Limón"; *LCE* 101), to which her father replies: "Precisely, that is what worries me." ("Y precisamente, eso es lo que me preocupa." *LCE* 101). He fears that his son-in-law has somehow reverted back to the "savagery" and the barbarism and superstition associated with the province of Limón and its Afro-Antillean culture.

In spite of his education, the geographic and cultural shift from the culture of his Afro–West Indian origins in Limón Province to the dominant Hispanic culture of the Central Valley leads McForbes to think of himself as a failure in his own eyes and in the eyes of others. In McForbes's eyes, his failure is rooted in his inability to escape his origins, "I was never able to rid myself of my condition as a Limonese in spite of it all." ("nunca me había podido quitar del todo mi condición de limonense, a pesar de todo." *LCE* 75). Even with his meteoric social rise, he is still the "foreigner," even though he wants to separate himself from his origins—a contributing factor to his own break with reality.

When McForbes permanently moves to San José and integrates himself into the bourgeois national culture, he imagines that he has transcended his ethnicity through his education, social relations, and marriage with a family of the traditional coffee elite. But in the eyes of Centeno, his father-in-law, he is "different" and not quite like "us." Centeno is unaware that Charles has made such a radical break from his past—a pastor who preached the black experience and who understood the Afro–West Indian culture of his forebears and the colonial heritage of color and caste—and has thus become unrecognizable to himself. He has not quite reached the extreme of Jose Antonio Pastrana in Afro-Ecuadorian writer Nelson Estupiñán Bass's brilliant novel *El último río* (Pastrana's Last River, 1987) who actually sees himself as a white man and comes to be viewed as white by others because of his antiblack actions and pronouncements. The dissonance between Charles's present situation in life and his humble origins is quite apparent.

The second part of *Los cuatro espejos* is narrated entirely from Charles McForbes's perspective and returns to his Orphic journey through the streets of San José. McForbes loses track of time and place as he meanders through the city at night. He still believes he is the victim of a cruel biological incident that has transformed him into a black man and fears if he goes home, Ester will find his color repulsive and deny that he is her husband. As he enters a bar, McForbes remembers Walker, a black schoolmate in San José, who suffered greatly because of his skin color. McForbes becomes more attuned to his recently "discovered" blackness, and he is aware of stereotypes, inequalities, and injustices in a racist society. While sitting in the bar, he observes the unfortunate circumstances of young, attractive, poor women who must display and sell their flesh to survive in an unjust world. One of the Nicaraguan dancers in the bar repeats a popular racial myth, "Blacks are hot-blooded and dance a lot." ("Los negros son ardientes y bailan mucho." *LCE* 119). Charles comments,

> I thought about my condition as a black man—suddenly discovered or imposed, unprovoked and shared with no one. Suddenly I woke up trapped in this skin, as if I had been born with it. Blacks are good dancers, they carry rhythm in their blood. And besides they are passionate and intelligent too. As if everyone was cut from the same mold, one by one, similar physically and morally with identical attributes as well as the same defects.
>
> *Pensé en mi condición de negro: condición descubierta o impuesta de pronto, no provocada, ni compartida con nadie. De pronto amanecí atrapado en esta piel, como si hubiese nacido en ella. Los negros son buenos bailarines, lo llevan en la sangre. Y además ardientes. Inteligentes también. Como si se hubiese hecho a todos en el mismo molde, uno por uno, parecidos física y moralmente, con idénticos atributos con los mismos defectos.* (*LCE* 119)

McForbes treats his blackness as if it were an aberration or a pathology, describing himself as a victim of this "condition." He also places an unbridgeable distance between himself and other blacks by decrying the tendency of the dominant culture to assume all members of a certain ethnic group behave in stereotyped ways. In spite of the encroachment of blackness, he maintains distance and disassociates himself from blacks and cultural associations with blackness when he uses the terms "them" and "the blacks" rather than "us" or "we." McForbes does not see himself as one who was born black. He is unaware of how he has acquired his dark skin and does not realize that it was always, already there.

As morning approaches, he considers going back to Díaz, the psychoanalyst, to commit himself to an institution. However, he just travels in circles through the city. He realizes "it is not the same being black as being a man because men are white." ("no es lo mismo ser negro que ser hombre. Porque los hombres son blancos." *LCE* 122). Soon after saying this, he finds himself in another bar, and instead of consulting a therapist, he decides to go to Limón by train. The train travel to Limón reminds the protagonist of moments with his marriage to Lorena, the obeah that was used against her, and the arduous train ride from Estrada to San José to take Lorena to the hospital. He encounters Clovis Lince on the train, someone from his past in Estrada, and someone who remembers the great harm Nabe and Cristian Bowman caused. At this moment during his voyage home, McForbes begins to accept the Afro-realist, popular spiritual beliefs in the supernatural:

> Lorena's death was unjust. She suffered that terrible sentence because a despicable man wanted to rape her, and his wife, his very obliging wife collected from the victim the sin of her husband. For that reason Lorena

> knew of her death before leaving Estrada—because it was something supernatural, revealed through supernatural means to all of us. But what happened is that I never accepted the reality of Pete's explanation. I preferred to cling to Clarita Duke's scientific claims. But it was not speculation because Lorena told Ruth to see her in San José because she would not be coming back to Estrada alive.
>
> *Lorena murió injustamente. Pasó por el tránsito de esa condenada manera porque a un desgraciado le dio la gana violarla y luego su esposa, su muy complaciente esposa cobró a la víctima el pecado del marido. Por eso fue que Lorena sabía de su muerte antes de salir de Estrada: porque fue una cosa sobrenatural, revelada por medios sobrenaturales a todos nosotros. Pero lo que sucede es que yo nunca acepté en realidad la explicación de Pete. Preferí agarrarme a las pretensiones científicas de doña Clarita de Duke. Y no son conjeturas: ella le dijo a Ruth que la fuera a ver a San José, porque al pueblo no volvería viva.* (*LCE* 127)

The thoughts of the unnatural causes of Lorena's death lead Clovis to curse Cristian Bowman and his malicious behavior. When Clovis states that Cristian's actions reflect poorly on blacks, "All of us black folk" (A todos nosotros: los negros), McForbes questions aloud "Us black folk?" (¿Nosotros los negros? *LCE* 128). McForbes understands that he is not going blind or going insane, but that he has entered a crisis of identity that he alone can resolve. He begins to develop a consciousness of ethnic and cultural difference and perceives himself as part of a group marked by difference. He is coming to terms with blackness:

> My travels through the city in the preceding hours suddenly seemed absurd. And the lecture I heard at the National Theater suddenly made sense. At what precise moment did I lose my own identity? What accumulation of dreams put me at odds with the culture suckled from the black breasts of my mother?
>
> *Mi paso por la ciudad durante las horas inmediatas anteriores, me pareció de pronto absurdo. Y la conferencia escuchada en el Teatro Nacional, de pronto me reveló su sentido pleno. ¿En qué momento preciso perdí mi propia identidad? ¿Qué cúmulo de sueños me pusieron en conflicto con la cultura mamada en los negruzcos pechos de mi madre?* (*LCE* 128)

His crisis is the result of denying and rejecting his ethnic and cultural heritage. His newly discovered insight, while leading him back to a consciousness of his identity and his origins, does not, however, completely alter his self-perception.

McForbes continues to struggle with his blackness. Looking at his brown skin, he says to his interlocutors, "You all can see my skin, shoot, it's not black. That is to say that if it weren't for my hair and my skin, I could pass anywhere as Latino." ("Ustedes pueden ver mi piel: pucha, no es negra. Es decir, si no fuera por mi pelo y mis facciones y podría pasar en cualquier parte como latino." *LCE* 128). Charles's self-assessment of the phenotypical markers of his ethnic classification raises questions about his ease of passing for Latino. He believes that his hair texture and facial features reveal his blackness and "give him away" as an Afro-descendant and that he does not have a clear and certain ability to pass.

McForbes continues to question himself, and "he soon realizes that he was born in the black town [of Estrada] and that he does not know what has happened to cause such a change in attitude" (Mosby 2003b, 142). This desire to escape his ethnic identity and cultural heritage has roots in messages McForbes received from his paternal family who distinguished themselves by touting their Scottish ancestry. The patriarch of the McForbes family in Jamaica, Saltiman McForbes, established himself among the caste of free people of color, mulattoes who rose above their enslaved brothers because of their lighter skin color, even though they were often begotten by the rape and sexual coercion of enslaved black women. Saltiman, Charles McForbes's grandfather, encouraged his sons to marry women who were white or light complexioned in order to distance themselves from their black origins. The protagonist's father, Pete, although he left the family fold in Jamaica, did not completely escape the values he inherited from Saltiman. Charles becomes aware of the impact of the family's denial of their blackness on his own dark body.

In Estrada, the village where McForbes spent the first twenty-three years of his life, he contemplates the connection between his black body and his relationships with Afro–West Indians and Latinos in his lifetime. McForbes thinks about Cristian Bowman, the black man responsible for Lorena's tragic death, and he ponders, "And perhaps that is why I fell in love with Ester's white skin, her bright blue eyes, her jovial spirit." ("Y acaso por eso me fui enamorando de la blanca piel de Ester, sus ojos azules, vivo, su espíritu jovial." *LCE* 133). He observes, "White were the hands that lulled me to sleep for many of my nights, black were the hands that tried to destroy me. Although . . . although neither Lorena nor Ruth were white. Shoot, nor Victoria. Damn, nor Clarita, nor Clif's way of thinking nor Jakel." ("Blancas eran las manos que arrullaron muchas de mis noches. Negras las manos que quisieron destruirme. Aunque . . . aunque . . . ni Lorena ni Ruth eran blancas. Pucha ni Victoria tampoco. Carajo, ni doña Clarita, ni el pensamiento de Clif, ni Jakel." *LCE* 133). He thinks about the contradictions and the role of skin color in his life. His life was ruthlessly altered by a black man who at one time was counted among his friends, but also in his past are other black men like Clif and his grandfather, Jakel, who were proud of their blackness and their cultural heritage and played positive roles in McForbes's life.

McForbes also contemplates the many women he has loved in his life, black and white. Deeply affected by Lorena's death, Charles resigned as an Anglican pastor. Heartbroken by his loss, he enters into simultaneous relationships with Ruth, Victoria, and Engracia in the period after Lorena's death and before he begins his relationship with Ester. He comforts his loss in the arms of Lorena's best friend, Ruth, and gives her the house he and Lorena shared when he decides to leave for San José. McForbes has a child with a young woman from Estrada named Victoria, to whom he leaves the profits from the sale of the farm. His only biological child grows up without having any contact with McForbes. While he is in San José, before his brief relationship with Magdalena and his courtship of Ester, he has an affair with Engracia, an older, married white woman he meets in San José. Engracia also becomes pregnant, but she terminates the pregnancy and eventually becomes Lucas Centeno's lover.

Charles McForbes is "[a] man who had abandoned his world and now was returning" (un hombre había abandonado su mundo y ahora regresaba; LCE 144). Now that he has returned for the first time since abandoning his home in Estrada, he searches for Victoria. She is now married to Alfred George, the new Anglican pastor who replaced McForbes and has become the father to the son McForbes abandoned. Returning to his old world, parts of his old self also surface. He assures George that he will not take Victoria away, but nevertheless he considers the possibility of divorcing Ester to win Victoria's affection. He calls on Ruth, discovers that she has a new male companion, but remains attached to Lorena's memory. McForbes and Ruth make love for one last time before the protagonist leaves for Limón and eventually San José. McForbes fully recognizes the crisis of identity he has suffered. He realizes at this late stage in his life that he has abandoned not only his town and its people but also his past and consequently himself: "a man leaves his world and returns to look for it and finds that the past has passed, trampling underfoot the best of desires." ("un hombre deja su mundo y regresa buscándolo y encuentra que el pasado ha pasado, atropellando los mejores anhelos." *LCE* 146). He now affirms his roots and his past, "They are my people; they are mine." ("Ellos son mi pueblo; son los míos." *LCE* 147). The protagonist claims his new sense of belonging by using "my" and "mine," no longer putting distance between himself and his ethnic and cultural origins.

From Puerto Limón, McForbes boards an airplane to make the return to his home in the Central Valley. He starts to read a book during the flight and ironically it is Quince Duncan's own *Una canción en la madrugada*. This mention of the author's first collection of short stories presents a playful self-referentiality and intertextuality characteristic of the new novel. After reading the book, McForbes satirically proclaims, "The truth is that the book seemed fitting for romantic women and compliant husbands." ("La verdad es que el libro me pareció digno de mujeres románticas y maridos conformes." *LCE* 150). The book by a fellow Limonense provokes him to think again about the past and to plan his next steps for his future. He continually muses about the need to escape the routine and boredom of his life, a tragic result of modernity, and he complains about his inability to find satisfaction. Although he has embarked on a great journey toward self-transformation, McForbes remains disquieted by what he has, and desires more. To break the routine he describes as a "vice," he considers asking Ester for a divorce even though he loves her. His ruminations are broken by a conversation with a fellow passenger on the flight to San José. While speaking with the young woman, McForbes discovers how to resolve his own feelings of racial doubleness by looking for humanity in others. He speaks to the girl about Limón, her studies, and the reasons for her travel to the capital: "Those simple things that transcend skin color and reveal to us the humanity in everyone." ("Esas cosas sencillas que vencen la piel, y nos revelan la humanidad de todos." *LCE* 153).

This incident gives McForbes an opportunity to reflect on "his struggle between two worlds—that of his black roots and the dominant culture of Costa Rica" (Mosby 2003b, 143). Charles describes his ethnic and cultural roots as "black wooly hair" and "heat," and the dominant Hispanic culture as, "hair the color of maize" and "cold." He searches for reconciliation in his "terrible and unattainable desire to possess both worlds without compromise." ("terrible e irrealizable deseo de poseer los dos mundos sin opción." *LCE* 153). Now that McForbes understands the basis of his identity crisis, he wonders if he will always be divided.

When he arrives back in San José, McForbes does not immediately head home. He accompanies the girl from the plane to her hotel and then checks himself into a cheap motel in order to continue retracing his history. He again walks through the city, recalling his days as a student and visiting "the places of poverty, the streets that one permanently carries within." ("los sitios de pobreza, las calles que uno lleva consigo irreversiblemente." *LCE* 154). His reengagement with San José differs from the connection he experienced in the previous hours in Estrada where he revisited the creeks, forests, and farms of his youth. The black and brown faces of the province contrast with "the white faces, [with] teeth of ivory shining in the evening cold [vespertine cold]." ("los rostros blancos, [con] dientes de marfil brillando en el frío vespertino." *LCE* 154). In the capital he retraces the paths traveled when he first arrived, passing by the city's major landmarks, but he finds that even San José is not the same place it was. He comments, "The haze had passed. I was now recovering the sharpness of things." ("El sopor había pasado. Estaba recuperando ya la nitidez de las cosas." *LCE* 155).

The protagonist eventually returns home and instead of finding his Ester waiting anxiously for him, he finds Manuela, the housekeeper. She tells him that Ester left to help Magdalena who is being blackmailed by Puma, a gang leader who threatens to reveal her drug use. McForbes leaves his home again in order to rescue Ester from the Puma's lair. Charles recalls his own dealings with Puma and his gang. As part of his initiation into the gang, he was stripped naked, tied at the hands and feet, and humiliated by "four enormous guys [who] reduced me to impotence." ("cuatro tipos enormes me redujeron a la impotencia." *LCE* 156). It is unclear whether McForbes was raped during his initiation, although he claims that his friend Luxe, who also joined the gang, was raped during his initiation and beaten for defending Charles. McForbes recalls being caught by the police during his initiation and jailed. He tried to be defiant and proud, but after intense interrogation gives the police information about El Puma and his gang and refers to the Centeno family—"una buena familia" (a good family)—to win his immediate release.

The last portion of the novel is perhaps weakened by the unnecessary inclusion of the Puma episode. Nevertheless, it continues the novel's theme of Charles's divided self as he attempts to negotiate his present and his past and resolve the contradictory aspects of his character. This episode also highlights the important issue of cultural reconciliation within the protagonist and the symbolic bringing together of Afro–Costa Rican cultural history with the Costa Rican nation. When McForbes rescues Ester from Puma, he sets his eyes upon her again after three days of separation. With his newfound sense of self, McForbes is surprised by the whiteness of Ester's body: "I looked at her again: her feet were white just like her breath and her kisses. Damn, she was very white." ("La volví a ver: blancos eran sus pies al igual que sus suspiros y sus besos. Pucha carajo, era bien blanca." *LCE* 163). Her white body, a symbol of the dominant Hispanic culture, is also a symbol of his displacement and unbelonging. His wife notices this gaze and responds intuitively, "If you have come for a divorce . . . forget it" ("Si venís por el divorcio . . . olvidate") and then assures him, "Charles . . . we are all chained. They are chains of God." ("Charles . . . todos estamos encadenados. Son cadenas de Dios." *LCE* 163). Ester's statement attempts to transcend the ethnic and cultural divide between them, referring to the tolerance, humanity, and self-acceptance that Charles seeks within himself as well as in society in general. Their bodies together offer the "new possibility of group formation" and the "symbolic joining of race, culture, sex, and locations" (Mosby 2003b, 144). Returning to the bathroom mirror where his odyssey began, Charles McForbes is finally able to see his face in the mirror and "[a] profound smile illuminated the color of my skin" (una sonrisa profunda iluminó el color de mi piel; *LCE* 163). He accepts his blackness, his racial and ethnic difference, and brings together his past and present selves. Although he may not be completely "at home" in the center of the nation,

McForbes is able to find self-acceptance through his physical and psychological journey.

Analysis: Passing and Double-Consciousness

Charles McForbes's desire to pass for "Latino" in the Central Valley and the crisis that emerges when he is unable to fully internalize that identity are features that permit us to consider *Los cuatro espejos* as a *passing* novel. Narratives of passing figure prominently in US African American literary history during the nineteenth and twentieth centuries in works by writers such as Jessie Fauset, Nella Larsen, George Schuyler, Pauline Hopkins, James Weldon Johnson, and Frances E. W. Harper. Racial, ethnic, and cultural borderlands are crossed when light-complexioned blacks attempt to pass for white in an effort to escape inequality and seek opportunities they would otherwise be denied. However, passing narratives that question the construction of the racial categories do not appear quite as often in Afro-Hispanic literature as in North American literature. Nor are they classified as a specific subgenre in contemporary Afro-Hispanic literature. This is perhaps because of the perceived fluidity of the racial borders in the Latin American cultural context. Passing functions differently in the United States than it does in Latin America. Whereas in the United States hypodescent has historically prevailed, where in "one drop" of black blood makes one black, in the Latin American context one drop of white blood certainly does not make one white, but also it does make one not black. Generally in Latin America, it is not just parentage that determines social race, but it is also the phenotype of the individual as well as his or her socioeconomic condition. In the US narratives, very light, "legally" black characters either unintentionally discover their black blood or opt to pass for white because of the rigid structure of the existing racial dichotomy that privileges whiteness. In a Latin American context, individuals exhibiting European phenotypes are already considered not black, but may make efforts similar to the African American narratives to negate their black roots.[18]

The "passing plot," according to Valerie Smith, "encompasses many different kinds of stories" and generally refers to "narratives that focus on the consequences of being genotypically black for a character or characters who pass for white, at least intermittently" (Smith 1994, 43). Although such characters appear in works by Afro-Hispanic writers, such as Max Ramírez and Antonio Angulo in *Juyungo* by Adalberto Ortiz, and Rebeca González in *Bajo la piel de los tambores* by Luz Argentina Chiriboga, both Ecuadorian authors, there are few narratives that exclusively focus on light-complexioned characters explicitly passing for white. There are, nevertheless, other elements that Afro-Hispanic novels share with the African American passing novels, particularly the consequences of passing that result in the characters' remaining in the white world, becoming reeducated, and returning "to the bosom of home and community to uplift the race," or receiving some form of punishment for their act of transgression (Smith 1994, 45). *El último río* (Pastrana's Last River, 1966) by Afro-Ecuadorian author Nelson Estúpiñan Bass provides one example of reeducation and return, and punishment. Unlike passing narratives from the United States, the protagonist is not a fair-skinned character whose racial ambiguity allows him or her to gain access to the privileges of the dominant ethnic group. It is the Latin American adage "el dinero blanquea" (money whitens) that operates in *El último río*, the prominent belief that nonwhite individuals who achieve financial success are able to "advance" in the color-class hierarchy toward whiteness. However, Edward Eric Telles observes that "whitening one's racial classification may be open to a person of mixed blood or appearance in some regions or contexts, but that a typically black person is classified as black no matter how wealthy he or she is," which is the situation of the novel's lead character (Telles 2004, 96).[19] The protagonist, José Pastrana, a black man from Esmeraldas, becomes so involved in gaining white privilege by accumulating wealth that he believes himself to be white, or as Richard Jackson calls the character, "a white black man." Prevailing antiblack racial ideologies push him to the point where he decides to turn away from his black origins and other blacks. He categorically rejects his black identity and his blackness, much to the dismay of the other black residents of the province, and becomes consumed by the desire for whiteness. Pastrana begins to accumulate wealth and power, following the Latin American model of "money whitens," and in his mind, he becomes a white man. His self-hatred is transformed into a hatred of all blacks to the extreme of "importing" whites to "improve the race." It is late in the narrative when Pastrana reconnects with his black consciousness and adjusts his antiblack position.

Richard Jackson notes, "Unlike Pastrana, however, who pretends he is white and convinces himself that he has convinced others of this pretense, in *Los cuatro espejos* Duncan's Black character really thinks he is White by virtue of marriage and position and by having adopted so well the values that go with both" (Jackson 1997, 77). McForbes's relationship with Ester facilitates his entry into the Central Valley elite, and he clearly acknowledges that his current status is the result of his marriage to Ester. He has lived among the nation's Latin bourgeoisie for a number of years, adapting to their idiosyncrasies and adopting many of their values to the point where he has actually become one of them in his mind, erasing his ethnolinguistic difference. However, the lecture on minorities in Costa Rica triggers Charles's repressed black past. After denying his ethnic and cultural roots for so long, he no longer has a sense of *who* he is, resulting in his being unable to see his image in the mirror. While "he forgets he is Black, . . . others do not" (Jackson 1997, 75). Others recognize his blackness—the people on the streets of

San José; his acquaintances in Limón; Pineres, the eye doctor; and Centeno, his father-in-law.

Interestingly, the character who does not fully see Charles McForbes's ethnic difference is his wife, Ester. Their romance begins after McForbes ends his brief affair with Magdalena, Ester's cousin. He becomes the savior of Ester's honor when he attacks her suitor, believing that she was about to be raped by the young man. Charles's actions are perhaps triggered by the haunting memories of the tragedy that befell Lorena and his inability to protect her from Cristian Bowman. Ester is rescued from sexual assault by the very figure she feared—a black man. Ester recalls her own feelings of prejudice against blacks as a child. The black gardener's "strangeness" and his difference came to signify the evilness of the "boogie man"—the malevolent product of the imagination who would steal misbehaving children. Magdalena and the maid would fill Ester's head with imaginary fears and then would tell her myths like, "Blacks don't bath or comb their hair" ("Los negros ni se bañan ni se peinan"; *LCE* 103), which fueled her fear and disdain. The irony is that it is a fellow member of the petite bourgeoisie who attempts to sexually attack her and not the stereotyped violent and hypersexualized figure of the black male. Instead, McForbes is her salvation from sexual violence and the protector of her sexual purity. This also marks a turning point for Ester in her attitude toward blacks. Charles becomes a man to her, more human and less Other. She does not see him as completely black—not black, not white, but something in between: "Charles is a strange being; neither white nor black. He is beyond those definitions, perhaps something satanic—a strange mix in any case that drives one mad." ("Charles es una persona extraña; no es ni negro, ni blanco. Está más allá de esas definiciones. Tal vez sea satánico: una mezcla extraña en todo caso, que la enloquece a una." *LCE* 111). Her father, on the other hand, in spite of his declaration that he has many Afro–Costa Rican patients, is not quite as ambiguous in his assessment of Charles's blackness. Luis Centeno declares to his daughter, "The simpleton has dedicated himself to one thing, and that is to be worthy of Ester Centeno." ("El muy simplón: se ha dedicado por completo a una sola cosa. Merecer a Ester Centeno." *LCE* 101). Centeno prefers the stereotyped image that blacks should be docile and smiling like the gardener, to know their place in society and to demonstrate their sense of belonging through hard work and not making trouble: "Hard working, passive, always smiling. I like those types of Negroes—always singing and dancing." ("Trabajador, pacífico, siempre sonriente. Me gustan los negros de ese tipo, siempre cantando y bailando." *LCE* 104). His daughter's marriage to McForbes is a source of disappointment and shame and makes him recall the African blood that flowed through his wife's Guanacastecan veins. In his eyes, McForbes will always be "a black man from Limón" and nothing more.

Nevertheless, in spite of the assessment by others, Charles McForbes sees himself as a class apart from other blacks, and because of his light skin color he is able to easily move into the dominant culture and pass for Latino. His social mobility eschews any relationship with his past as well as any feelings of obligation to his ethnic group. In many US narratives of passing, one of the central themes is that of racial responsibility. Julie Nerad states, "if one's family is African American, if one has any 'drop' of black blood, then one has the responsibility to the race and should proclaim oneself black" (Nerad 2003, 815). This idea is not exclusive to the United States. Within the context of the Anglophone Caribbean and the West Indian Diaspora in Central America, these ideas are clearly stated within the tenets of Garveyism, associated with the Universal Negro Improvement Association (UNIA), the pan-African movement of racial uplift and self-determination founded by Marcus Garvey of Jamaica. In the text, this is embodied in the presence of Jakel Duke, who is a proud "race man" exhibiting pride in his African Ashanti heritage as well as his black West Indian culture. Additionally, narratives of passing view characters who pass as betrayers who "depend . . . upon the association of blackness with self-denial and suffering, and of whiteness with selfishness and material comfort" (Smith 1994, 44). In the case of Charles McForbes, his self-denial facilitates his middle-class contentment and his "access" to privileges of whiteness in the dominant culture. He relishes the European beauty and elegance of his wife, the luxury of his automobile, and the dramatic entrance they make into the National Theater that captures the attention of the Central Valley political and social elite. However, that self-denial also opens the possibility for distress and crisis. If the passer does not continue to pass in the dominant culture, and if social mobility through passing is halted because of self-discovery or being discovered, the passer usually faces punishment and/or reeducation. McForbes's efforts to become Latino come to a standstill during his crisis of identity when he is unable to see his face in the mirror. The mirror is unable to reflect his image because the protagonist has distorted his own vision of his identity. Instead of presenting the true reflection of his character, what is projected is nothingness, and little by little, as McForbes rediscovers his identity and reconnects with his buried past, the remaining three mirrors gradually reflect a little more of his identity until his true self is reflected at the end of the novel.

The crisis that results when Charles McForbes denies his Afro–West Indian cultural heritage is what Martin-Ogunsola describes as an example of W. E. B. DuBois's conception of double consciousness. The two forces, his blackness and his Costa Ricanness, "warring in one dark body," are emphasized by the geographic dichotomy of San José and Limón. In the case of *Los cuatro espejos*, Charles McForbes's body shifts from black to nonblack as his geographic location changes from the West Indian cultural milieu associated with Limón to the Hispanic

Central Valley. These sites become "racially marked socioeconomic and cultural spaces" for the protagonist and he becomes "the allegorical representation of the tangential position of the white Central Valley (symbolized by San José) with the black Atlantic coast (symbolized by Estrada)" (Nerad 2003, 815; Martin-Ogunsola 2004, 90).

In Estrada, McForbes is a second-generation member of the Afro–West Indian community who holds a prominent role as a cacao farmer, but also is a formally educated man and Anglican pastor. He is aware of his community and its cultural practices, although he is not always accepting of the Afro-realist popular beliefs of the people. Although he is a black man of Afro–West Indian descent in a black town, the legacy passed on to Charles McForbes by his grandfather, Saltiman McForbes, plays a significant role in the self-perception and behavior that lead to the protagonist's crisis of identity. The name Saltiman appears as a hybrid of sorts—"Salti" bears similarity to the verb *saltar*, to leap over or skip, and the English word "man." The combination of the two indicates the patriarch's desire to leave the racial stigma of blackness behind by privileging the family's European heritage. Saltiman stresses with urgency the need for his progeny to conserve their light skin color and encourages his children to distinguish themselves through an elite education and marriage to people lighter than themselves, preferably whites. Saltiman McForbes instructs his children that they are a caste apart from the blacks and superior because of their skin color and Scottish blood: "At night he would gather his sons to remind them of what they were, 'You are not black, but neither are you white. You are mulattoes, people of color, never forget that. . . . You cannot expect much from blacks.'" ("Por las noches convocaba a sus hijos para recordarles lo que eran: 'ustedes no son negros, pero tampoco son blancos. Son gente de color, nunca se olviden de eso. . . . No se puede esperar mucho de los negros.'" *LCE* 130). He insists that the mulattoes or "gente de color" empower themselves to assert power over the blacks and gives his sons this mandate:

> I don't want any of you marrying a black woman. Look for a mulatta or an English woman. You must improve the race in order to escape from this shit hole that we're in. Blacks, from the time of Noah were condemned to suffer. They will always suffer, so distance yourselves as much from them as possible. You must whiten the family, that is the solution, you must improve the race.
>
> *No quiero a ninguno de ustedes casado con una negra. Búsquense una mulata o una inglesa. Hay que subir el color para escapar de esta cochinada en que estamos. El negro, desde Noé fue condenado a sufrir. Va a sufrir siempre: aléjense de ellos lo más posible. Hay que ir blanqueando, esa es la solución: hay que ir blanqueando.* (*LCE* 130)

When the family loses their inheritance from the fortune Saltiman amasses from his lumber company, Pete McForbes, Charles's father, "in a short time was just as poor as any Negro." ("al poco tiempo estaba tan pobre como cualquier negro." *LCE* 130). To seek his own fortune, Pete travels to Central America—never finding it in Panama or Costa Rica. He works hard to give Charles an opportunity to study in the capital and learn Spanish. In Limón, Charles revisits the history of the McForbes family in Jamaica and the circumstances that led to his father's arrival in Central America. In Limón, Charles reconnects with his blackness and with his heritage and once again learns the interrelationship between his color and ethnicity and his inherited history as a descendant of Afro–West Indians in Costa Rica. Charles is keenly aware of the transfer of values, although he ironically states, "My family never put on airs because they maintained all of their dreams except for one—the denial of our blackness" ("Mi familia, pues, no tuvo los aires pero conserve los sueños menos uno: el de negar nuestra negritude"; *LCE* 132). Through Jakel Duke, Clif Duke's grandfather, he sees a man who is proud of his African heritage and contemptuous of McForbes's European pretentions: "You are black and your grandfather Saltiman was a poor fool." ("Usted es negro. Papá Saltiman era un pobre tonto." *LCE* 132).

When he moves to San José after Lorena's death, McForbes begins to forge a new life and a new identity for himself. He earns a doctorate in English and becomes an integral member of the Centeno household. His marriage to Ester improves his ability to pass for Latino in the Central Valley. This strategy allows him to escape the conundrum of double consciousness and the burden of his black past. He sees no connection between himself and those who identify themselves as Afro–Costa Rican and feels no sense of racial obligation or interest in Garveyism. On the bus in San José, he sees no relationship between himself and a fellow black passenger also with Limonense origins whom the bus driver harasses as a scapegoat. He also internalizes the dominant culture's dualistic attitudes and its accompanying racial ideology. Black becomes a signifier of all things evil, corrupt, and malevolent, and McForbes sees "black as if it were a punishment" ("Negro, como si fuese un castigo"; *LCE* 119), referencing the Judeo-Christian curse of Ham. The words of an exotic dancer strike at his psyche: "I had a sister, evil as Satan with a black heart" ("Tenía una hermana. Una hermana mala como Satanás, con un corazón negro"; *LCE* 119), and he comments, "I thought, 'Black like my skin. Evil like my skin.'" ("Pensé: 'negro como mi piel. Malo como mi piel.'" *LCE* 119). Even though Charles is a light-complexioned black man, in Limón he viewed himself as an Afro-descendant. With his new life in the capital, he aligned himself with the dominant racial attitudes of the national culture.

His mind frequently returns to the lecture on minorities in Costa Rica, "Damned lecture. Just yesterday I was free, but we went to that damned talk. There was something not quite right about that talk." ("Maldita conferencia. Ayer no más era libre, pero fuimos a la maldita charla. Algo tenía de malo la tal charla." *LCE* 121). He curses the lecture that has been the catalyst for his Orphic journey within himself. It is not until he hears the lecture on minorities in Costa Rica that he begins to think of himself in connection with the blackness he has denied. At first he thinks he is going blind, but when he sees his eyes and mouth in the mirror, like the image of a blackface performer or the minstrel tradition in the United States, he knows his sight is not the problem (Martin-Ogunsola 1987, 10). Only when he buys a mirror from a street kid, a representation of the popular culture of the nation, does he begin to recognize his own blackness. The child sells him the third mirror in the text and in effect presents society's view of Charles, that of a black man of West Indian descent and not the Costa Rican of Spanish descent he desires to be. The popular class is not as polite as the bourgeois who allow him to pass, as the voices of the popular sector confirm: "Blackie, what happened to you?" ("Moreno, ¿qué te pasa?"), "Something happen to you Blackie?" ("¿Te pasa algo Moreno?"), "Blackie are you crazy?" ("Moreno, ¿estás loco?"), "Black SOB" ("Negro jijue"), "Wretched nigger" ("Negro desgraciado"), "That's it Cassius, hit 'em hard" ("Eso Casius, dele duro") (*LCE* 31). After seeing himself in the third mirror, McForbes begins slowly to understand the objectified status of blacks in Central American culture. He makes an analogy between blacks and inanimate objects, or dolls: "Perhaps the child will grow to love her doll. Perhaps she will come to love it as much as a person. But the doll will always be an object. Very much loved, but an eternally inanimate toy." ("Quizás una niña llega a querer a su muñeca. Tal vez llegue a querer tanto como una persona. Pero la muñeca será siempre un objeto. Muy querido, pero eternamente un juguete inanimado." *LCE* 120).

If Charles's punishment for passing is the psychic crisis he suffers, his reeducation begins on his journey to Limón. The moment Clovis Lince recognizes him and plaintively states, "We blacks," McForbes realizes he has been repressing his identity as Afro–Costa Rican. Although at times he continues to distance himself from darker-skinned blacks by maintaining his superiority in the color hierarchy, he nevertheless acknowledges that he is an Afro-descendant. He reconnects with the soil of Estrada and the people who were instrumental in his past. While he does not remain in the province like his friend Clif Duke, he understands his bond with the culture that nourished him for the better part of his life. As Nerad observes, "The reformed passer who returns to the black race recognizes the psychological dangers of racial deception. Her own insufficient moral and racial education is 'corrected' and then turned to the effort of educating others, usually toward the sociological ends of racial uplift" (Nerad 2003, 815). Charles McForbes's brief exchange with a young woman on the flight from Limón to San José puts him back in touch with his humanity, allowing him to transcend race without reverting to denial. However, with his reeducation and reconnection with his roots, he feels that he can no longer remain married to Ester. When she declares to him that divorce is out of the question and that they are linked by God, Ester is referring not only to their bonds of marriage, but also to their fundamental humanity. By remaining together, they symbolically connect the geographic and cultural divide between Limón and San José.

3
Novels of Samamfo

La paz del pueblo, *Kimbo*, and *A Message from Rosa*

For when you die and join your ancestors, I will raise up one of your descendants, one of your sons, and I will make his kingdom strong.
—1 Chronicles 17:11 (New Living Translation)

La paz del pueblo (1978), *Kimbo* (1989), and *A Message from Rosa / Un Mensaje de Rosa* (2007) have varied plots and themes, but these three texts share at the center of their narratives the Afro-realist concept of *samamfo*, which is characterized by ancestral voices, communication with the dead, and the connection to a cultural community. *Samamfo* is a term that Duncan borrows from the Ashanti religious belief, also called *samanfo*, honoring ancestral spirits and the belief in the simultaneous existence of the ancestral spirits of past, present, and future on the same temporal plane. Duncan uses *samamfo* to describe "the collective memory of the race which passes from generation to generation and which is active in the religious rites of the people in their struggles and in their experiences. It is the spirit of the ancestors who never abandon their descendants" (Ramsay 1994, 35). This African-derived belief system found its way to Jamaica through the transatlantic slave trade and traveled with its Afro–West Indian descendants throughout the Caribbean Diaspora. This belief system, known as Cumina or Kumina, connects descendants with ancestral spirits through drumming, counterclockwise dance, biblical verses, hymns, and possession, and also offers the practitioners the spiritual protection of their ancestors to provide guidance, to give advice, and to assist in acts of resistance. Spirit possession connects the deceased with the living and the unborn through the practice of dance and rituals. The ancestors also return during these rituals "to inspire resistance and rebellion, and to give religious sustenance, the ancestors return to dance with the living ancestors in order to inhabit their bodies and guide them to the afterlife" (Mosby 2003b, 154).[1]

The aforementioned spirit of rebellion and the invocation of ancestral spirits make a prominent mark in the three novels of *samamfo*. These texts present communities and individuals in highly tense situations, and the ancestral voices enter into the lives of the characters to provide guidance or support for acts of resistance. *La paz del pueblo* depicts a rural village in Limón Province that is consumed by political animosity and economic exploitation. *Kimbo* exposes the open wounds of Costa Rican society—the breach between the rhetoric of equality and democracy and the reality of racial injustice the title character experiences. *A Message from Rosa / Un mensaje de Rosa* is a novel of the African Diaspora that centers on the matriarch and patriarch of the mythical descendants of the Yayah who face extinction because they fear their descendants no longer remember them.

La paz del pueblo

This text is perhaps the most "West Indian" and stylistically complex of Duncan's novels. It is reminiscent of the short story "La Rebelión Pocomía" in the collection of the same name. The novel centers on a multiethnic and highly stratified agricultural community in Limón Province rife with social and economic tensions during the 1930s. The community is divided over issues of ethnicity, color, caste, class, and religion. These tensions reach a boiling point with the tragic death of Sitaira Kenton and the political martyrdom of her suitor, Pedro Dull. Of the many stories and themes that weave through Duncan's fourth novel, these two events form the dominant threads in the text.

The novel is centered on the family of Mariot Moody and Cornelio Kent, an Afro–West Indian couple with roots in Jamaica, and their only surviving child, the adolescent Sitaira. The family owns a small cacao farm, and their daughter, Sitaira, goes to the groves to harvest the fruit. Part of Sitaira's workday ritual is to bathe nude in the Pacuare River and connect intimately with her natural surroundings by stretching her naked body out in the sun. Sitaira has fallen in love with Pedro Dull, a young Jamaican-born man who has come to town to organize a Marcus Garvey–inspired labor movement for the workers exploited by the banana industry. However, the couple's happy union and the wish to continue the family's bloodline end unexpectedly when Cató Brown, a deranged man from an elite family, rapes and murders Sitaira. Cató's parents use their connections to manipulate the authorities and public opinion into accusing Pedro of the crime. Mr. Brown, the owner of one of the supplying plantations for the United Fruit Company targeted by Pedro's planned labor strike, not only wants to transfer the blame for Sitaira's death onto Pedro, but also wants him removed from the town to ensure that operations on his prosperous plantation proceed without disruptions from striking workers. Although he has the option to leave town, with the blessing of Sitaira's mother, to save himself, Pedro decides to lead a movement of economic and cultural resistance. In so doing, he calls upon the ancestral spirits of the religious cult of Cumina to assist him in this sacrificial endeavor.

Structure and Themes

La paz del pueblo is an intricate novel that interweaves the lives of characters in Costa Rica, Jamaica, and other parts of the Diaspora. Mariot Moody often repeats the phrase "life is a wheel," which reflects the cyclical nature of the novel, where actions repeat themselves in different times and locations. The white Jamaican grandmother, Elizabeth Moody, in her youth had the habit of walking through her father's plantation, enjoying nature, swimming in the river and sunbathing nude without inhibitions, to the dismay of the black servants Brown and Mamy. This same pattern is seen in her granddaughter, Sitaira, who in a different time and place walks through her parents' cacao grove on her way to work, enjoying nature, swimming in the river and sunbathing nude to the dismay of the town's gossips who find her behavior scandalous. Sitaira, like her grandmother Elizabeth, falls in love with an outsider with dire consequences.

Multiple voices and perspectives and temporal shifts are featured in the subsections of the eight chapters that comprise the novel. Even within a chapter's subsection there may be numerous voices, different time periods, and different locations. For example, the first chapter of the novel, which establishes the narrative rhythm of *La paz del pueblo*, begins with Pedro's melancholy lament near the Pacuare River after Sitaira's death. Within the same subsection we hear the voices of the gravediggers and Sitaira's mother. Chapters 1, 4, 7, and 8 are situated around the time of Sitaira's funeral and include flashbacks, memories, and dreams from the perspectives of Mariot, Pedro, and Cornelio, as well as dialogue of the townspeople. Chapters 3 and 5 center on the various accounts and perspectives of Sitaira's rape and murder. Chapters 2 and 6 take place in the remote past in Jamaica and reveal the tumultuous story of Mariot Moody's parents, Elizabeth and Josué, her own struggle to survive after the death of her mother, and her arrival in Costa Rica.

The novel contains the key elements of the new novel—multiple perspectives and narrative voices; nonlinear structure; dreams; interior monologues; flashbacks and flash-forwards; and intertextual references to poetry, songs, and biblical verses. There is no traditional protagonist. Martin-Ogunsola identifies Mariot Moody and Pedro Dull both as protagonists, or "cotagonists": "Because she gives voice to her female ancestors and progeny Mariot is not a secondary character, but emerges as a 'cotagonist' with Pedro" (Martin-Ogunsola 2004, 110). However, it may also be argued that the text has no protagonist or presents a collective of several protagonists. While the death and ghostly presence in the narrative of Sitaira motivate the actions and reflections of Mariot and Pedro, the silent but dominant presence of nature (rivers, rocks, vegetation) and the popular and contradictory voices of the pueblo also play leading roles in *La paz del pueblo*. Nature provides ominous auguries of events to come by changing the speed of the river or sending creatures like the owl or birds of prey as warnings. The river and the image of Sitaira that is incessantly associated with it are ever present in the text, as is the laughter of the deceased woman. Additionally, Pedro's association with nature, particularly rocks, along with numerous references to the jungle and groves that grow cacao and bananas, suggest that nature serves not only as background but is also an active character.[2]

Part of the richness of the text derives from the references to West Indian culture that attempt to capture life in Limón Province during the United Fruit Company's activities. Caribbean Afro-Christian religious sects like Cumina and Pocomania, as well as the traditional Anglican Church, play important roles in the life of the community. The practice of obeah, West Indian folk magic or sorcery, emerges as a means to resolve domestic problems or, in some cases, to harm a rival. The characters, following the Afro-realist heritage in the Americas, do not view the use of obeah, the apparition of the dead, or the visitation of ancestral spirits in dreams as unusual phenomena, but rather as part of inherited belief systems from the Diaspora. Another Afro–West Indian aspect in the novel is the emphasis that some characters place on skin color, which has roots in social hierarchies established during the colonial period of enslavement in the British West Indies. Although Been Brown is not considered the most cultured woman in the community, she occupies a place of privilege among the local West Indian elite because of her light skin color and her wealth. Her husband, Mr. Brown, owner of a banana plantation that provides supplies for United Fruit Company, is "quite black" but gains prestige for having married a woman of a lighter complexion. When rumors circulate about Sitaira's desire to marry Cató, the Browns' troubled son, there is much talk about how Cató should marry a woman with a lighter complexion to "improve" the family.

The West Indian folk speech and the literary oral tradition also add to the cultural depth of *La paz del pueblo*. Although the text is written in Spanish, the folk dialogue between the small-town characters captures the essence of popular speech and constitutes a kind of cultural resistance through language. The language used in the "folk talk" is not the official tongue of the country, but rather the specific speech of the ethnolinguistic enclave. The conversations between the townspeople, particularly the gossipy Mrs. Mantle and her daughter, "mimic the conversation of the Jamaican 'mouthamassy Liza' who cannot be trusted with secrets and spreads the business of others all over town" (Mosby 2003b, 159). The humor of these exchanges reveals not only a glimpse of the cultural life in the region before 1948 but also introduces the use of Limonese Creole words such as *paña* ("Spanish"), *bami* (bammy, bread made of yucca or cassava flour), and *dopi* (duppy, ghost or malign spirit). More importantly, the orally transmitted Anancy stories are interpolated within the frame of the novel and provide folksy illustrations of a speaker's viewpoint. In one example, the gossiping Mrs. Mantle tells her daughter an Anancy story about a sexual indiscretion involving Toucama's wife and her female "cousin." Mrs. Mantle uses this bawdy folktale to intensify her attack on Sitaira's family to illustrate that Cornelio has been made a cuckold.

Plot. The novel opens with Pedro wandering the lush landscape of Mariot and Cornelio's cacao farm after the death of Sitaira. He stands near the river where he bathed with his lover, remembering her beauty and laughter. As he contemplates his loss while drinking in the place where he and Sitaira shared many hours, a bird of prey looms overhead. The augers of death and misfortune are in the air as a conversation is overheard between two gravediggers who are preparing Sitaira's grave. Meanwhile, Mariot Moody mourns the loss of her daughter and last surviving child. She recalls their conversation about Pedro's love for her, but Mariot also felt a great inexplicable affection toward him. Upon first meeting Pedro, Mariot "felt suspicious toward this young man who appeared in town, saying that he had lived there as a child, but no one remembered him, and without warning or apparent motive fell in love with her daughter. Over time that suspicion turned into tenderness." ("sentía cierto recelo de este muchacho que apareció en el pueblo, diciendo que había vivido allí de niño, y nadie se acordaba de él, y sin aviso ni motivo aparente, había enamorado a su hija. Pero con el tiempo el recelo se fue volviendo ternura." *LP* 18). She had grand illusions for Sitaira and Pedro, envisioning her daughter's lover taking the place of her now-impotent husband as the head of the family. This emotional bond leads to rumors in the town that the mother brought Pedro into the household to be her own rather than her daughter's lover. In fact, Mariot was merely seeking the continuance of the family's ancestral line by having descendants who would remember her and Cornelio after their death, and therefore keep their spirits alive. Mariot was convinced that with the marriage of Sitaira and Pedro, "she would sit at the head of the town, and would get enormous pleasure from watching her grandchildren growing up, happy among the pastures, playing in the mud." ("sentaría cabeza en el pueblo, y que podría tener el enorme placer de ver a sus nietos creciendo felices entre el potrero revolcándose en el barro." *LP* 18). This dream has come to a tragic end, and Mariot and Pedro are left to grieve for Sitaira.

Both Mariot and Pedro see an apparition of the young woman swimming in the river, but say nothing to each other. Mariot, who is now alone with her invalid husband, prepares a rifle, gunpowder, and bullets to pass on to Pedro to take revenge on Cató Brown, the cause of their sadness. Pedro is unsure of his next step, but he remembers the words of his grandfather about the power of *samamfo*: "[Hell] is when everything ends—at the end, after final judgment. But for now no one dies, son. We simply return to samamfo" ("[El infierno] eso es cuando termine todo. Al final, después del juicio. Pero por ahora nadie se muere hijo: simplemente volvemos al samamfo"; *LP* 24). His grandfather continues to define *samamfo*: "You go back to the place of the ancestors, that's all. I don't care what the pastor has said to you. Preachers nowadays don't even read the bible and if they do read it they don't understand anything." ("Uno vuelve donde están los ancestros, eso es todo. Y no me importa lo que te haya dicho el pastor: los pastores de ahora ni siquiera leen la Biblia y si leen no entienden nada." *LP* 24). The Afro-realism aspect of the text recognizes the continuity of life beyond death as well as a popular belief system that contrasts with official religion.

Mariot, an adherent of *Cuminá* (Cumina) worries, "Who will I pass over your body, Cornelio, when you decide to leave? Who will inherit the strength, the destiny, the sorry and the glory of samamfo? Who will know now the secrets of our past? Who will make worthy on earth the rights of those who temporarily rest in the glory of the Lord?" ("¿A quién pasaré sobre tu cuerpo, Cornelio, cuando decidas alejarte? ¿Quién heredará la fuerza, el destino, la pena y la gloria del samamfo? ¿Quién sabría ahora los secretos de nuestro pasado; quién hará valer sobre la tierra los derechos de los que descansen temporalmente en la gloria del Señor?" *LP* 27).[3] The reverence and spiritual contact with the deceased ancestors is particularly important in Cumina rituals. Without their son or daughter alive to form families and produce progeny, Cornelio and Mariot's lineage dies; their ancestral line is broken. As Mariot dresses her mute, blind, incapacitated husband, he begins to weep, and she lashes out: "Yes, you have realized it. No one will be there to claim your legacy. Cumina is gone—we are alone." ("Sí, te has dado cuenta. Ya nadie habrá para recoger tu herencia. Cuminá se ha ido: estamos solos." *LP* 29). Their ancestral spirits will die because there is no one alive to remember them and to honor them as ancestors; nor will there be the spirits of the unborn to guide toward life.

The sadness of this couple, who realize the end of their ancestral line, shifts to the past where the novel reveals the family history of Mariot Moody. The narrative presents the point of view of Elizabeth Moody, the white daughter of Kingsman Moody, an English planter in postemancipation Jamaica. She and her twin sister, Margaret, go on an outing where their butler, Brown, introduces them to his nephew who is their new coachman. Josué, a free, French-speaking black man from Haiti, is noted for being "proud" (*orgulloso*), an undesirable trait in a servant. Hearing him speak French, Elizabeth comments to herself, "Those blacks—they put together words from the Europeans and make up their own language. They mock us." ("Esos negros: recogen palabras de los europeos y van armando su propio idioma. Se burlan de nosotros." *LP* 37). In spite of the education that has taught her to believe in the inherent inferiority of blacks, the "uppity" Josué intrigues her. Although Brown and Mamy try to prevent a sexual relationship from developing, Elizabeth crosses the lines of race and class and makes love with Josué. Their encounter is described as a natural occurrence that transcends the limits of humanly constructed barriers: "They recovered Adamic purity, sowing intemporal pollen in the flower. Willows and whispers of wind; the ring of bells, and a dream without time, without thistles. The two smelled of sweat." ("Recuperaron la pureza adámica, sembrando en la flor el polen intemporal. Sauces y murmullos de viento; campanadas, y el sueño sin tiempo, sin cardos. Los dos olorosos a sudor." *LP* 53).

Although Kingsman Moody and Mamy have an active sexual relationship, the relationship between Elizabeth and Josué is viewed as inappropriate. As the owner of the property and authority figure to all of those who reside at the plantation, Kingsman Moody exercises a considerable amount of power, which he uses to enter into a consensual, but unequal, relationship with Mamy. As the patriarch, Kingsman controls Mamy and his daughters; they are his property until they pass on to the hands of another white male figure. Elizabeth's relationship with Josué dismantles the established plantation order. The relationship with Josué violates her sexual and racial purity and makes marriage with an Englishman of her social rank impossible. After this forbidden relationship is discovered, the new Adam and Eve must be punished for transgressing the plantation's social and sexual order. They are thrown out of the Edenic paradise of Kingsman Moody's plantation for violating the unspoken rule that prohibits sex between a black man and a white woman. Elizabeth picks up her lover out of the mud and they flee with a barrage of insults behind them.

From Elizabeth's perspective, "The scene of the orchard ran through her veins, and suddenly the world became cold." ("Toda la escena del huerto corría por sus venas, y el mundo de pronto estaba lleno de frío." *LP* 53). The lovers are punished for what Anna Clark describes as a "twilight moment," "a metaphor for those sexual practices and desires that societies prohibit by law or custom, but that people pursue anyhow, whether in secret or as an open secret" (2005, 139). The couple is "exiled from the plantation and the lush, green fertile paradise of this isolated 'idyllic' space. Their bodies are transformed from the sweat and heat of the sexual act into coldness of the world outside of the plantation, much like the expulsion of Adam and Eve from Eden. Like the original couple, Elizabeth and Josué soon realize after violating the norms of the Garden that they are in the world outside its protection; they are alone, naked, and cold" (Mosby 2003b, 151).

The novel turns from the "disgrace" of Elizabeth Moody and Josué Prince (Mariot Moody's parents) to the rumors in the town about the beautiful Sitaira. The salacious gossip the mother-daughter dyad of Mrs. Mantle and her daughter share is interwoven with detailed descriptions of the hard-working young woman's daily routine as she prepares to go to harvest cacao from her family's farm. While the women of the town gossip, Sitaira carries her machete into the woods to collect the harvest. The townswomen accuse Sitaira of being an exhibitionist. We learn that Sitaira as a child would play in the woods and pastures and swim and bathe naked in the river, like her grandmother did in Jamaica. Sitaira was like the "men and women who had never heard about the Garden, free of original sin that society would later instill, living for life itself without a burdensome past nor a future that sows uncertainty in the mind." ("hombres y mujeres que no oyeron nunca la historia del huerto, libres del pecado original que luego la sociedad inculca, viviendo por la vida misma, sin pasado que pese ni futuro que siembre en las mentes la incertidumbre." *LP* 62). Like her grandmother who lived freely before her expulsion from the plantation, Sitaira was without shame and "had forgotten everything, including the shame of feeling shame." ("se había olvidado de todo, incluso de la vergüenza de sentir vergüenza." *LP* 62).

The only people to disturb Sitaira's relationship with the river and woods are Pedro Dull, who admires her beauty and shares her connection with nature, and Cató Brown, the disturbed son of a well-to-do West Indian plantation owner. Sitaira feels a romantic attraction to Pedro, with whom she eventually forms a relationship. Cató Brown watches her through the trees during her daily ritual and masturbates. Cató is enraged that Pedro has ruined his fantasy, and as he gazes at Pedro and Sitaira, Cató, El Loco (the Crazy One), experiences an irrational reaction:

> Pedro came, stealing the enchantment of his secret, prostituting it all; his happiness was turning into torment because of him—the one who fell in love with her and slept with her in the presence of the Crazy One, who was between the same thickets and there were times when he could have touched them by just extending his hands a little, and they never tired of making love, of saying sweet-nothings, of ruining the virginal purity with their crap.
>
> *Pedro vino, robando el encanto de su secreto, prostituyéndolo todos; la felicidad se fue volviendo tormento por culpa del maldito que la enamoraba y se acostaba con ella en presencia del Loco, entre los mismos matorrales, y hubo veces en que él los hubiera podido tocar con solo extender un poco las manos, y no se cansaban de hacerse el amor, de decirse estupideces, de romper la pureza virginal del mundo con sus porquerías.* (*LP* 83)

Cató, whose name derives from *catar* (to look at), obsesses about possessing Sitaira. He wants Pedro expelled from his personal Eden. While fantasizing about Sitaira in the cacao grove, his obsession gets the best of him and he loses control. He rapes then murders Sitaira. Although all signs point towards Cató's guilt, his mother, Mrs. Been Brown, one of the upstanding members of the community, protects her son and blames Mariot and Sitaira for driving Cató insane. She believes Sitaira wanted to marry into the well-to-do Brown family to improve her status by marrying the light-complexioned Cató.

On the day of Sitaira's funeral, the mourners retrace the final steps of the murdered young woman. The narrative interweaves a beautiful poetic litany with descriptions of the multiethnic procession and conversations from the pueblo. The conversation between the gravediggers reveals the historical difficulty for Afro–West Indians to prosper economically during the policies of León Cortés that prohibited blacks from working at United Fruit Company plantations on the Pacific. However, the calumnious voices of the town gossips stand out among the popular voices in the text. The voices of the gossiping pueblo disrupt the somber scene by adding humor and vividly portraying the popular discourse of West Indian culture. Gossiping townspeople, in addition to voicing public opinion, are also a mechanism of social control as they spread virulent condemnation of perceived violations of social norms. When the solemn marchers stop in front of the home of Mr. Pérez, who joins his family friends, Mariot and Cornelio, at the head of the line, the women begin to talk about the alleged affair between Mariot and Mr. Pérez that they claim produced Sitaira. They conduct their scandalous chatter with hypocritical glee. Referring to Pedro's absence from the funeral procession the gossips comment:

> "Where did so many people come from? Nobody cared about that woman."
> "Everyone has come just like us . . . well almost every one . . . as our Christian duty."
> "Almost everybody but not everybody."
> "Who's missing? Well, I mean anyone important."
> "The most important person."
> "Who? Hey . . . that's true."
> "I haven't seen him all day."
> "John Crow must have flown the coop."
> "Who knows! Best not to judge—he who judges will be judged."
> "Well, that part about 'will be judged.'"
> "Be quiet—the pastor is looking at us."
>
> *— ¿De dónde habrá salido tanta gente? Nadie quería a esta mujer.*
> *— Todos vienen como nosotros . . . casi todos . . . por un deber cristiano.*
> *— Casi todos, pero no todos.*

— *¿Quién falta? Quiero decir, así importante.*
— *El más importante.*
— *¿Quién? Hey . . . es verdad.*
— *No lo he visto en todo el día.*
— *¿Habrá volado el pajarito?*
— *¡Quién sabe! Mejor no juzgar: él que juzga será juzgado.*
— *Bueno, eso de que será juzgado.*
— *Callate: nos está mirando el Pastor.* (LP 73)

The ever-present vultures in *La paz del pueblo* are representations of the rapacious voices of people in the town who gossip about Sitaira and her family. Although there are many who grieve the young woman whose beauty was unmatched "from Kingston to Belize, from Bluefields to downtown Limón . . . not even Panama" ("desde Kingston hasta Belice, desde Bluefields hasta Limón centro . . . ni en Panamá"; *LP* 24), there are also townspeople who swirl over the decaying body of Sitaira like vultures, feeding their envy by tearing away her flesh, degrading her good looks, and feasting on humiliating rumors of sexual perversion and obeah. These voices not only attack Sitaira, Mariot, and Cornelio, but they also impugn Pedro who has now become the enemy in the eyes of the town's elite, particularly Mr. Brown, for his support for workers' rights.

Mr. Brown is the bastard son of a black Limonese woman and a "Scotsman" who Margaret Moody sent to retrieve her niece, Mariot Moody, who was in her care after the death of her parents Josué and Elizabeth. Mariot ran away from her abusive aunt who wanted to return her to Jamaica. Brown was poor, but was able to improve his social status because of his claim of Scottish blood and his marriage to the wealthy, light-skinned Been. He managed to build a successful business selling bananas to the United Fruit Company and has become a powerful force in the town. However, his workers are rising up against him and his policies. With the increased disharmony between management and the workers, there are fears of a possible repeat of the banana strike of 1934 that caused the loss of profit for the United Fruit Company and its independent growers like Mr. Brown. During a conversation with a Costa Rican employee, Mr. Brown complains, "The Company lost millions during that strike. The Company that has given so much to Costa Rica." ("La Compañía perdió millones en esa huelga. La Compañía que le ha dado tanto a Costa Rica." *LP* 89). Brown learns that the workers are on the verge of striking after rallying around Mr. López, a worker who was fired because he was disabled by the working conditions and for whom Mr. Brown refused to provide medical care. The workers are being led by Pedro who was cared for by Mr. López after his mother's death.

The Afro–West Indian elite of the town attempt to build momentum in their campaign against Pedro's growing labor movement. The Browns foster rumors that falsely accuse Pedro Dull of Sitaira's murder in order to remove suspicion from Cató. The Browns also encourage the Anglican pastor to use his pulpit to unite the congregation of the community's elite and middle class against the "dangerous" ideas of economic justice and better working conditions on the banana plantations that Pedro and his followers put forth. The pastor claims that "the peace of the town has been altered by people who aren't even from here. People who have come with ideas full of poison, to disturb the peace, to soil people's good name, to preach hate, not love." ("la paz de este pueblo ha sido alterada por personas que ni siquiera son de aquí. Personas que han venido con sus ideas cargadas de veneno, a mancillar la paz, a manchar el buen nombre de las personas, a predicar el odio y no el amor." *LP* 149). The "ideas full of poison" to which the pastor is referring are Marcus Garvey's ideas that advocated racial uplift and self-reliance for blacks of the African Diaspora and denounced the economic exploitation of workers, particularly black laborers. The pastor appeals to the bourgeois conformity of his congregation to dismiss the ideology of Garvey and the Universal Negro Improvement Association (UNIA) and support Mr. Brown's crusade against Pedro's appeal for workers rights:

> Last night I was listening to a talk by one of those Garveyites. Those crazy fools who believe we should return to Africa, to barbarism, to paganism. They were talking about the strike that, as I understand, affects the interests of a prominent member of this church, and I hoped to hear from among them some sort of protest of solidarity, some inclination toward justice. I thought to myself, although they are wrong, they are well intentioned. But no, everything I heard was of great African empires that only exist in their minds and the right that various people have to resist oppression, and above all the power blacks have to resist oppression by any means necessary. And I ask you, is that Christian?
>
> *Anoche estuve oyendo una charla de esos que siguen a Garvey. Esos locos que pretenden que volvamos al África, a la barbarie, al paganismo. Estaban hablando de la huelga que tengo entendido, afecta los intereses de un prominente miembro de esta iglesia, y yo esperaba oír de parte de ellos alguna manifestación de solidaridad, alguna inclinación hacia la justicia. Yo me dije que aunque equivocados, tienen buenas intenciones. Pero no: todo lo que oí fue de grandes imperios africanos que solo en la mente de ellos existen, y del derecho que tienen los pueblos a resistir la opresión, y sobre todo, el derecho que tienen los negros a resistir la opresión por cualquier medio que consideren adecuado.* (*LP* 149-50)

Brown uses this anti-Garvey momentum to foil the strike. In order to garner the support of the local government authorities, he lies to the political chief (*Jefe político*) about recent events. He calls Pedro a communist, implicates Pedro in the death of Sitaira, and claims that Pedro's use of obeah had something to do with the sudden muteness of Mrs. Mantle's daughter who, according to many witnesses, was nearly struck by lightning. Sensing the officer's hesitancy, Brown adds that Pedro is one of those Garveyites who wants to spread their message and form a new nation since, "It seems Jamaica is not enough for them any more." ("parece que ya no les basta Jamaica." *LP* 159).

Armed with the rifle Mariot gave him, Pedro weighs his options: travel to Panama to escape Brown's persecution and be viewed as a coward or continue to strike for workers' rights and risk his life. He decides to remain in the town but must first participate in a Cumina ritual with the venerable Shepherdess Mamá Bull—who also appears in "La Rebelión Pocomía." The ritual of drumming, dance, and song will allow the ancestors to possess his body and fortify his resistance: "Cumina in the histories of far off and unknown lands; in his warrior anguish, Cumina; in the myths of the world, of the world of all worlds, Cumina." ("Cuminá en las historias de patrias lejanas y desconocidas; en sus ansias guerreras, Cuminá; en los mitos de su mundo, del mundo de todos los mundos, Cuminá." *LP* 173). Pedro's mother did not share his belief in Cumina; she dismissed the cult as "foolishness" (*tonterías*), and she rejected her son's interest in his African roots and the Garvey movement. Pedro, however, for whom "the drums of samamfo reverberated in his ears like a dark echo" ("los tambores del samamfo resonaban en sus oídos como oscuro eco"; *LP* 177), requires the spiritual powers of the ancestors to continue the struggle on behalf of the workers and his own struggle to protect himself from Brown's deceit.

The political chief arrests Pedro and he offers no resistance. No one stands up for him or counters Cató's vicious accusations, although there are three witnesses who saw a deranged Cató riding away naked on horseback from the cacao groves. No one wants to contest Brown's political and economic power in the town. After Pedro's arrest, a blanket of silence covers the town, broken only by the arrival of the governor, who visits with the town's elite, including Brown. The arrival of the province's governor brings together the Anglican pastor and the Cumina priestess, Mamá Bull, who appear to get along well in a "surprising complicity" (Smart 1984, 55). Although one represents the officially sanctioned religion of the bourgeoisie and the other represents the Afro-Christian syncretic religious sect of the popular sector, they share some congregants and they also share a similar message. The pastor gives the people gathered at the reception for the governor "a sermon with strong reminiscences of the Biblical prophet Isaiah": "'From among my people, I will lift one up,' says the Lord, 'I will take away his heart of stone and give him one of flesh, and he will be the liberation of many and the glory of the people.'" ("De entre me pueblo levantaré uno—dice el Señor—le quitaré el corazón de piedra y le daré uno de carne, y será la liberación de muchos y la Gloria del pueblo." *LP* 184). The message baffles many in the pastor's presence, so they turn to Mamá Bull for clarification. After rubbing a stone that she has in her hands, she finally answers: "in the silence of midday was the answer, because one day Cumina would become incarnate in the people and it would be the people themselves, and the altars will run over." ("en el silencio del medio día estaba la respuesta, porque un día Cuminá se encarnaría en el pueblo y sería el pueblo mismo, y los altares saldrían sobrando." *LP* 184).

Even though the pastor and Mamá Bull come from different and competing traditions, the people interpret their message as pointing to Pedro for their terrestrial salvation. The references to the rock that appear in the pastor's message and the one Mamá Bull rubs in her hands symbolize Pedro, whose name is derived from the Greek word "petros" meaning rock. The people come together to support Pedro who in their eyes is the savior of the town's working people. The phrase that runs through Mariot's mind is one that is repeated throughout the text. "He is responsible for it all. For coming when no one called him, for staying too long when everyone expected him to leave." ("Él es responsable de todo. De haber venido cuando nadie lo estaba llamando, de estar, de permanecer demasiado tiempo cuando todos esperaban que se fuera." *LP* 19). While he could have easily slipped across the border into Panama, he chooses to stand with the people and in turn he becomes a symbol of resistance, solidarity, and *samamfo*, as he calls upon the ancestral spirits to guide his efforts. His return to the town and his arrest also imply sacrifice that leads Mariot to declare that "Pedro is a man." ("Pedro es hombre." *LP* 187). This prompts Mr. Pérez to support Pedro's defense, leaving the other men playing dominoes and drinking, "unable to look each other in the eyes." ("no podían mirarse en los ojos." *LP* 187). Pérez's intention to defend Pedro "symbolically joins the Afro–West Indian and the white and mestizo populations in the town in a common effort to exonerate their hero" (Mosby 2003b, 163). The spirit of Cumina dances "for the sake of peace" in the town, and in the distance everyone hears the laughter of a woman coming from the river. It is Sitaira's recognizable, ghostly laughter.

Pedro Dull's fate is uncertain at the end of the novel. However, it becomes clear that in spite of his imprisonment, he remains in a position of prestige and esteem for the working-class people of the town. He garners the assistance of people who will come to his defense because he is seen as "the man who will free his people from oppression" (Mosby 2003b, 163). Pedro unifies the popular sector of a town in turmoil over the exploitation of the banana workers and divided by culture, caste, class, and color. He is a rebellious figure, like the maroons who escaped slavery and who defied colonial order by providing refuge to other escaped slaves and by sabotaging the economic system that was based on their exploitation. By challenging authority, Pedro Dull is an antiheroic hero, inspired by the ancestral spirits, who sacrifices himself "for the sake of peace."[4]

Kimbo

According to critic Paulette Ramsay, in *Kimbo* (1989), "Duncan develops the idea of *samamfo* to the fullest" (1994, 35). The novel's title character is an Afro–Costa Rican who is faced with an impossible situation. He is accused of a crime that he did not commit, but there are several witnesses who identify him as the perpetrator of the kidnapping of a wealthy businessman. Kimbo feels he is battling an enemy much larger than himself because the witnesses are Latino and antiblack stereotypes and racism cloud the legal system. Instead of depending on the courts to provide him with a defense and exonerate him, Kimbo's fate lies with the ancestors. In *Kimbo* we witness the "spirit or power [of the dead ancestors] pervading the daily lives of the people so that they are always conscious of the dead and how the dead ancestors participate in their affairs" (Ramsay 1994, 35).

Structure and Themes

The novel is divided into four parts and includes a brief glossary of terms the author uses, mostly of Creole origin. Instead of a single narrator, the various chapters in the four sections of *Kimbo* are told by at least ten narrative voices that are primarily identified as "First Voice" (*Primera voz*), "Second Voice" (*Segunda voz*), and so forth. These voices present the various viewpoints on Kimbo's involvement in the kidnapping and represent witnesses testifying against the protagonist, his attorney, law clerks, Kimbo's prison cellmate, his wife, his girlfriend, family friends, a police officer, and the victim of the kidnapping, among others. In addition to the different narrative voices, there are chapters that feature a third-person-omniscient narrator who is able to convey the interior thoughts of the protagonist and sometimes shifts to second-person direct address to speak to Kimbo and the witnesses. The information many of the voices provide is contradictory, questionable, or the result of misinformation. Along with the questionable reliability of some of the narrative perspectives, the fragmentary style of the novel requires the reader to combine the different voices in order to form a larger, albeit still incomplete, picture of the life of the accused and the questions surrounding his trial. However, the element that distinguishes this text from other works by Duncan is that "in the structure of this work, the dead ancestors are given equal treatment with characters who are alive" (Ramsay 1994, 37). Voices of deceased ancestors and members of the community emerge in *Kimbo* to defend their progeny. The concept of *samamfo* reaches a new level in *Kimbo* because of the interaction between the living and the dead: "Throughout the work, the dead intermingle with the living, participating in all the discussions about Kimbo as if there were no difference between the living and the dead" (Ramsay 1994, 37).

Plot. An epigraph of "Metamorfosis de tu recuerdo" (Metamorphosis of your memory) by second-generation Afro–Costa Rican poet Eulalia Bernard appears at the beginning of the first part of *Kimbo*: "I remember you / so, dynamic, / so, beautiful / so, whole / and mighty. / I see you / now, weak; / now, deformed; / now, broken / and, meager." ("Te recuerdo / así, dinámico, / así, hermoso, / así, entero, / así, entero, / y, caudaloso. / Te veo / ahora, débil; / ahora, deforme; / ahora, partido / y, escaso." *KM* 11). The poem describes the decay of a male body that was once strong and whole that becomes in the eyes of the poetic voice weak, deformed, and fragmented. This is the condition of the protagonist the omniscient narrator describes when Kimbo enters the courtroom to face the witnesses who will give testimony against him. At the beginning of the novel, in spite of the title character's link to the Creole expression noted in the glossary, "kimbo off on me," which describes the akimbo stance of defiance when confronting a negative situation, the protagonist is anything but defiant.

Kimbo appears meek and submissive as he sits in the courtroom. He is on trial for participating in the kidnapping of Don Barrigón (Mr. Pot-Belly), though he has no memory of committing the crime and he appears to be the only person standing trial for the crime. Several witnesses are brought in to testify against him, and to Kimbo they appear to be credible people with no reason to lie: a teacher, a priest, a peasant famer. This places doubt in Kimbo's mind, and he believes he may be guilty. He shows his guilt by his body language—head hung low from the weight of being born black in a white-identified country. It is already a foregone conclusion that Kimbo will be found guilty when one sees the list of "upstanding" white citizens testifying against the stereotypical dangerous black male:

> In life the facts count for very little, Kimbo. The facts are irrelevant. What has the most weight, what will honestly determine your fate, Kimbo, is the opinion people have of the facts. . . . It is the opinion of those who don't even have a dog in the fight, those who decided to appear in court in order to become part of the consensus. All of them were going to construct the truth from the events, putting together the pieces of an enormous puzzle that when finally finished, will come out immaculate from the judge's mouth: guilty.
>
> *En la vida los hechos cuentan poco, Kimbo. Los hechos tienen poca relevancia. Lo de peso, lo que de veras [*sic*] definirá tu suerte, Kimbo, es la opinión que las*

> *personas tengan de los hechos. . . . Es la opinión de los que aún sin arte ni parte en el asunto, decidieron comparecer para ser partícipes del concenso [*sic*]. Todos ellos iban a construir la verdad de los sucesos, poniendo juntas las piezas de un enorme rompecabezas que luego, armado, saldría inmaculado por la boca del juez: culpable.* (*KM* 15)

Kimbo finds it difficult to raise his head and look his accusers in the eye because he already feels defeated by his life of struggle and poverty and by the circumstances in which he now finds himself.

What follows is a series of voices in support of and against Kimbo. Voices from *samamfo*, voices of the dead with roots in Kimbo's Limonese community—those who know his background, culture, and who witnessed his upbringing—give testimony occasionally in his favor but also casts his personality in a questionable light. The First Voice, narrated in first person, is the voice of someone from his community who knew him as a child and cannot imagine Kimbo with a machine gun in his hands. Kimbo is described as a submissive, obedient man and an avid reader who only showed rage when others broke the rules. The community supported Kimbo as a child, but the speaker says he was "submissive and rebellious at the same time." ("sumiso y rebelde a la vez." *KM* 17–18). When others transgress rules, Kimbo becomes "a snorting beast" ("una fiera bufante"; KM 17). Nevertheless, this member of the community doubts that Kimbo is a criminal and implores other voices from *samamfo* who knew him as a child to come forward: "Speak. Let all the voices shout their truth. ("Que hablan [*sic*], pues. Que griten su verdad todas las voces." *KM* 18).

The Second Voice to speak is that of Mrs. Rob speaking from the grave, a technique that resonates with Mexican writer Juan Rulfo's classic novel *Pedro Páramo* (1955). She says, "I remember him as tender. I never saw the snorting beast." ("Yo lo recuerdo tierno. Nunca vi la fiera que fufaba." *KM* 19). She also recalls how she would stop him on his way home from school to loan him books and to talk about what he had just finished reading. She saw a spark in him that she wanted to nurture with books, and he would devour the stories, fables, legends, and myths that he would later discuss with her. His community loved him, and she claims that he was a gifted singer and was destined to be the pride of his community. She strongly doubts his guilt and declares that Kimbo is a good boy and "this *I always maintained up until the day of my death*." ("eso *lo sostuve siempre hasta el día de mi muerte*." *KM* 20, emphasis in the original).

The Third Voice is Kimbo's defense attorney, who believes that Kimbo is innocent. He mentions that Kimbo was accused of kidnapping and terrorism by his wife, who after many years of separation decided to seek revenge and destroy Kimbo. The attorney notes that there was a marked change in Kimbo's personality before and after the court proceedings. The attorney is unaware of what caused his client to go from a self-confident man, convinced he would be released in a few hours, to a man "with his head hung low." ("con la cabeza agachada." *KM* 22). Kimbo believed that he would quickly be released because he was returning from a trip abroad when the crime occurred. However, the evidence exonerating him, including testimony from the taxi driver and records from the airline, became more difficult to piece together and fails to offset the parade of witnesses, casting accusatory fingers at Kimbo as a criminal:

> The press announced that one of the suspects, Kimbo, had been captured—and from that moment on, a mob. With the same face, they had seen him that same day, at the same time, in the same place. All of them the same. At the scene of the crime, machine gun in hand, threatening passersby, while he protected the getaway of his companions who gagged and blindfolded *the poor and innocent Mr. Barrigón* as one of them said, and they got into a blue car, a green car, a brown car, and the one who did all of this was him, the same one who is right there.
>
> *La prensa anunció que uno de los culpables, Kimbo, había sido capturado. Y desde ese minuto un tropel. Lo habían visto ese mismo día, a esa misma hora, en el mismo sitio, con la misma cara. Todo lo mismo. En el sitio de los hechos, ametralladora en mano, amenazando a los transeúntes, mientras protegía la fuga de sus compañeros que llevaban amordazado y vendado al pobre y al inocente señor don Barrigón como dijo uno de ellos, y lo montaron en un auto azul, en un auto verde, en un auto café, y el de todo eso fue él, el mismito que está allí.* (*KM* 23)

The supportive voices are countered by the Fourth Voice belonging to a bigoted, vulgar police officer who represents the authority of the dominant culture. He depicts a different perspective of Kimbo. The officer connects Kimbo to Don Barrigón through their business dealings, but there is skimpy evidence to connect Kimbo with the kidnapping. The police are facing pressure from the press, the public, and the president to produce a suspect. Although he states, "I am beginning to believe that truly this guy has nothing to do with the situation" ("estoy empezando a creer que de versa este muchacho no tiene nada que ver en el asunto"; *KM* 28–29), he nevertheless feels uneasy about Kimbo and feels that "he is hiding something. He has something on his conscience." ("algo está ocultando. Tiene algo en la conciencia." *KM* 28–29). Through insults, torture, and threats to gang rape his pregnant lover in front of him, the police officer extracts a flimsy confession from Kimbo and justifies his behavior by cloaking himself in the sacrosanct principles of democracy "so that the people may continue to be free." ("para que la gente pueda seguir siendo libre." *KM* 30).

The Fifth Voice is that of a legal clerk who works with the lawyer's girlfriend. He has a stifling and frustrating routine life, and he is tired of the rut of his family and work. His life consists of "crossing out and signing" ("tachar y firmar"; *KM* 33). As a bureaucrat shuffling papers from one hand to another, even he senses Kimbo's innocence. He makes comments about "the poor idiot and all of the idiot witnesses against him." ("el pobre loco y los testigos en su contra." *KM* 31).

One of the most interesting voices is the Sixth Voice, an old friend who knew the accused and his wife. The Sixth Voice is also the defense attorney's lover and the legal clerk's colleague. She claims that "I know she is guilty. But I also know that he is guilty as well." ("Yo sé que ella es culpable. Pero sé también que él es culpable." *KM* 36). The Sixth Voice states that during the court proceedings, Kimbo's estranged wife appeared in court unannounced in order to falsely testify against Kimbo, declaring that the plans to kidnap Don Barrigón "were very old plans that caused their separation." ("fueron planes muy viejos que incluso motivaron la separación." *KM* 36). The Sixth Voice describes this act as cruel and remembers the couple's bitter arguments, as well as their conceit. She was in an "uncomfortable position" as confidante to both Kimbo and his wife. She depicts a troubled marriage haunted by the word "sacrifice," which was the theme of many of the couple's arguments. The Sixth Voice recalls the words exchanged during the bitter argument, "She challenged him. 'For the first time in your life,' she said to him directly just like that, 'make a sacrifice for someone.'" ("Ella lo retó. 'Por primera vez en tu vida,' así le dijo así directamente, 'sacrifícate por alguien.'" *KM* 37). For this couple, sacrifice is a difficult concept because Kimbo was focused on building his career, and she felt eclipsed by his growing success: "'Because he has to shine like a king,' she told me once, 'so that he feels good. Shine yes, overshadowing the rest. It's not fair that I must make myself smaller for him to become magnified. He makes the decisions, I just give opinions. And the worst part is that the results aren't even apparent.'" ("'Porque él tiene que brillar como un rey,' me dijo ella una vez, 'para que se sienta bien, Brillar sí, opacando a los demás. Y yo debo achicarme, para que él se engrandezca y no es justo. El toma las decisiones, y yo solo opino. Y lo peor es que ni se ven los frutos.'" *KM* 39).

The Sixth Voice comments that in spite of all of their difficulties "they made it" through hard work and effort with a lovely house and car as proof of their success. This success has resulted in mutual estrangement, however. He was not a significant presence in the home and she lacked "a husband dedicated to her" ("un marido, dedicado a ella"; *KM* 41).

The Seventh Voice is that of a man from Limón who is imprisoned with Kimbo. The man is not of West Indian descent but insists that he knows the character of the Limonese people because he was born there. He says to an unresponsive Kimbo: "I know you well. Maybe not personally, but I was born in Limón around your people and I know how you people are." ("yo te conozco bien. Tal vez en lo personal no, pero nací en Limón entre tu gente y sé como son." *KM* 45). Having inherited the stereotypes and prejudices of the dominant culture, the man expects Kimbo to reflect the jovial stereotype of smiling, laughing, and singing Negroes that the nation associates with the black citizens of Limón. Listening to his cellmate, Kimbo sits quietly against the wall without responding to the man's incessant chattering and does not offer "confirmation of ancestral stereotypes" ("estereotipos ancestrales"; *KM* 45). Because Kimbo does not laugh, smile, or sing, the voice thinks he has the "Negro complex" ("el complejo de negro"; *KM* 47). He urges Kimbo to be a laughing, smiling *negro limonense*, "black man from Limón" and states:

> Why don't you burst out laughing?
>
> Your people know how to laugh during the worst moments. You got no right to put on that face—you're from Limón, you're black, you must've learnt how to laugh. Bust out laughing man—let it out.
>
> *¿Por qué vos no soltás la carcajada?*
>
> *Tu gente sabe reírse en los peores momentos. No hay derecho a que pongás esa cara: vos sos de Limón, sos negro, tenés que haber aprendido a reírte. Soltá la carcajada hombre: dejá salir la cosa.* (*KM* 47).

When Kimbo refuses to converse with his cellmate after the "encouragement" to imitate the stereotypes of his people, the Limonese cellmate accuses him of having a complex. The protagonist remains silent almost as if awaiting his own death. Indeed, the prison cell manifests signs that foreshadow an imminent death: a gust of cold wind, the cold light of indifference in Kimbo's eyes, the dark shadows of the cell, and the fetid smells. These circumstances indicate that the protagonist has already been entombed in the cold, rotting, darkness of the grave.

At the conclusion of the first part of *Kimbo*, the First Voice speaking from *samamfo* reappears. This voice represents Limón, and as the voice of the pueblo defends its native son: "We in the town do not believe it was him." ("Nosotros en el pueblo no creemos que fue él." *KM* 49). The First Voice expresses displeasure with Kimbo's wife and does not have faith in her declarations against him in spite of her beauty and education. The community noted her bad temper. The voice claims, "If they want to knock him down, it must be for something. And it is that this boy is already at the top and he's black and that bothers them. He's got brains." ("Y si lo quieren tumbar por algo será. Y es que ese muchacho está ya en la cumbre y es negro y eso les molesta. Tiene sesos." *KM* 49). The community prays for justice for Kimbo. The voice ends by declaring, "that boy is one of us, from our essence. That boy is us." ("ese muchacho es de nosotros, de nuestras entrañas. Ese muchacho somos nosotros." *KM* 49).

The second part of *Kimbo* opens with an epigraph from Costa Rican writer Carmen Naranjo: "Now they look for . . . a thinker so that they may deepen their roots into the land of thought and voices, all the voices, clear and light or passionate and violent or doubtful and anguished or firm and sharp." ("Ahora buscan . . . a un pensador para que ahonde sus raíces en la tierra del pensar y las voces, todas las voces, las claras y ligeras o las apasionadas y violentas o las dudosas y angustiadas o las firmes y agudas." *KM* 51). This quote addresses the voices that are present in the text—both the voices of *samamfo* and the accusatory voices of those who claim to be witnesses to Kimbo's alleged crime. The five chapters of the second part of the novel present "new" voices that were not heard in the first part of the novel, including the voices of the real kidnappers, Kimbo's lover, Don Barrigón, and his wife.

In the opening chapter of the second part of the novel, two co-conspirators are talking about the kidnapping of Don Barrigón as well as their pleasure at hearing that an innocent man is being tried for their crime. The men are part of a larger organization, the National Civic Defense Committee (Comité Nacional de Defensa Cívica), that masterminded the kidnapping of the businessman in order to extort money for their cause. One of the kidnappers expresses pity for the man accused of their crime, while the other is pleased at the turn of events. The former proposes a plan that will request that the authorities send Kimbo out of the country, which will free him but still provide cover for their group's crime because people will still think Kimbo is part of the kidnapping conspiracy. However, the second kidnapper is apprehensive about the idea: "Well . . . I don't know. It sounds good. It's just that this guy is a bad example: his own wife testifies against him. She herself condemned him. We cannot mix a guy like that up with our movement." ("Pues. no sé. Suena bien. Solo que el tipo ese es mal ejemplo: su propia mujer declara contra él. Ella mismo lo condena. No podríamos mezclar a un tipo así en nuestro movimiento." *KM* 55). The kidnapper believes his group cannot afford to associate their movement with the innocent Kimbo, but yet they continue to use his trial as a shield to protect their illegal activity.

In the second part we are privy to the thoughts of the victim of the kidnapping, Don Barrigón. Through an interior monologue we learn more about the crime that Kimbo is accused of committing. The terrorist organization that calls itself the National Civil Defense Committee has kidnapped Don Barrigón because he failed to give in to their demands for money. During his captivity he is to collect money from his family and businesses. He complains about his materialistic wife and son who are in Miami. Don Barrigón laments the changes that occurred in his young bride and doubts her fidelity, even doubting the paternity of their son. In spite of his captivity, Don Barrigón tries to see the positive in his captors by stating, "They're good boys—idealistic—they think the moon is made of cheese. That's all. And I can give the money that they're asking for." ("Son buenos muchachos: idealistas. Creen que la luna es de queso. Eso es todo. Y yo puedo dar la contribución que piden." *KM* 59). Apart from his wealth, he does not understand why he, a "peaceful, religious man" who has given to his community and country, is in this situation—held captive in a dark room by a group of terrorists.

The next "voice" we hear in part two of the novel is the point of view of Don Barrigón's wife. She returns from Miami after hearing about her husband's kidnapping, and more information is uncovered about her background and her marriage to Don Barrigón. She has two sisters, one called "la hermana cuerda" (the sane sister) and the other "la hermana loca" (the crazy sister), and she wonders whether she herself is sane or crazy. The family was profoundly affected by her only brother's suicide, which deepened the mental illness of her mother and sister and caused her family's dissolution. She feels as if she is in a family where the "normal ones leave, run away, or kill themselves" ("los normales se van, huyen, o se matan"; *KM* 67). She chooses to escape her unstable home environment by marrying her older, controlling suitor, Don Barrigón. After their marriage, she tells him she desires children. Knowing that he is sterile, he tells her that if after a year she is not pregnant, he will happily give her a divorce. Desperate to save her marriage, she has an affair. Hearing the demands of the kidnappers, she feels paralyzed, unsure of her next step since all of the property and money are in her husband's name, not hers.

At a local church service, a vigil is held to pray for the release of Don Barrigón. Throughout the chapter appear versions of the phrase, "the Spirit of God that resides in me and I sing like David." ("el Espíritu de Dios que mora en mi y yo canto como David." *KM* 71). This religious reference suggests psalms, or hymns attributed to the biblical David, as well as the legendary story of David's ability to drive out an evil spirit occupying King Saul's body with his musical ability. The ritual of the mass moves one of the congregants to approach the altar on his knees. This congregant, a poor peasant from Tres Ríos with a large family, confesses his sins to the officiating priest. He reveals that he gave false testimony implicating Kimbo in exchange for money. This causes the priest to question his own testimony as a witness. Although the peasant claims he does not know who committed the crime nor did he see it, the priest convinces himself otherwise, "He was sure that he saw him. It's true that all blacks look alike, but he was certain that he had seen him and the truth emerged from what everyone had seen." ("Estaba seguro de que él sí lo vio. Es verdad que todos los negros se parecen, pero estaba seguro de haberlo visto porque había otras personas que también lo habían visto y la verdad surgía de lo que habían visto todos." *KM* 73).

The next perspective, from Kimbo's lover, alternates between first and third person. When she receives word of Kimbo's arrest and news of the kidnapping she leaves the country house where she is staying and heads to San José with her sister. She is pregnant and distressed. The news about the kidnapping and arrest is all over San José to the point that it has become a "collective hysteria that has taken over the city" ("la histeria colectiva que se había apoderado de la ciudad"; *KM* 75). Rumors about the crime and its perpetrators spread throughout the city, some blaming the act on the communists and others blaming the kidnapping on a right-wing conspiracy. She goes to the doctor's office, the doctor is also a friend, but all he wants to talk about is the bikini he has found for her, and he is not concerned with her early contractions. He sends her away and she goes to visit Kimbo's attorney. On the second visit to the doctor, she and her sister confront a flawed medical system motivated by inhumane inflexibility and self-absorbed medical professionals. In spite of her cries of pain and efforts to get the attention of the medical staff, she loses the baby: "It was more than any woman could take: you, accused as a low criminal that kidnaps people in order to take their money; you, farmer, you with all of that rice in the warehouse, and all of those trips and all of that stuff about singing, and I have lost a child, a child begotten in my womb for you, a child that left my womb for you," ("Fue más de lo que hubiera podido resistir cualquiera: tú acusado como un vulgar delincuente que raptas a la gente para sacarles dinero; tú finquero, con todo ese arroz en las bodegas, y todos esos viajes, y todo ese historial de cantante, y yo he perdido un hijo, un hijo engendrado en mis entrañas por ti, un hijo que se fue de mis entrañas por ti," *KM* 80).

The third part of *Kimbo*, comprised of eight chapters and six voices, opens with two epigraphs: one from one of Duncan's short stories and another from Afro-Panamanian poet Gerardo Maloney. The quote from "Los mitos ancestrales" (Ancestral Myths) addresses betrayal: "The executioners are still here. They surround us and stare with accusing fingers. . . . If I die someone will be responsible for my death, someone will one day be confronted with rejection by his own people as punishment" (Duncan, *TBS* 285). The fragment of Maloney's poem is about the Yoruba deity Yemaya, the Great Mother, who suddenly arrives "as if to announce terrible things and nothing" ("como para anunciar / cosas terribles / y nada"; *KM* 83). Together the two epigraphs anticipate the commingling of the voices of the living and the dead to unveil the truth in Kimbo's defense as well as the appearance of strong female characters from the living and the ancestral spirits of *samamfo*.

In the first chapter of the third part of the novel, Kimbo and Don Barrigón are set to be on the same flight because Kimbo wants to prove his innocence to the man who was kidnapped by the terrorist group. Kimbo left the country as part of a deal between the real kidnappers and the court, but he returns because of the voice and vigilance of his dead mother from *samamfo* to prove his innocence. Kimbo's silence, which is not out of confusion or resignation, will be broken when he arrives at the airport. Waiting at the airport for the arrival of Kimbo and Don Barrigón are several women whose hopes, fears, and expectations during this crisis will be explored throughout the chapter. The first two women are Kimbo's wife and his lover. His wife's reflections reveal a tumultuous relationship characterized by jealousy, possessiveness, and hate. They spent the greater part of their courtship in separate areas—he was building his singing career in San José, and she was in the country. There was also a class distinction between them. To her, he was an unrefined country bumpkin. She describes him in the early stage of their relationship as "skinny, black, and ugly with unrefined manners, limited aspirations, and little experience" ("flaco y negro y feo como era, en sus modales poco refinados, y sus limitadísimas aspiraciones y poca experiencia"; *KM* 85). He struggled in the city "feeling humiliated because his girlfriend could dress better than he." ("sintiéndose humillado porque su novia podía vestir mejor que él." *KM* 88). Their love and passion became all-consuming to the point where there was little space for anyone else except themselves. They married not because of their intense love, but rather because of the dependence created by their world of two, in spite of their separation and violent love, a love that sometimes bordered on hate. Reflecting on Kimbo's incarceration, she knows he has a lover and states:

> It will hurt me to see him rot in jail, but it will have to be that way. I vowed that he will be mine or no one's. I vowed, without joining his fortune to mine, that he must return to the sewer. He'll go back to the slums and his children must hate him. I have vowed to make him surrender and I will make him answer to me on his knees, and I am going to screw him over so that no one knows any other story than the one that I am telling . . . and the kids will know the bad things about him and never the good.
>
> *Me dolerá verlo podrirse en la cárcel, pero no tendrá que ser así. He jurado que será mío o de nadie. He jurado que sin unir su suerte a la mía habrá de volver al caño. Volverá a los tugurios y sus hijos habrán de odiarle. He jurado doblegarlo y lo voy a hacer acudir a mi de rodillas, y lo voy a joder y a joder para que nadie sepa otra historia que la que yo cuento . . . y los niños sabrán lo malo de él y jamás lo bueno.* (*KM* 90–91)

The second woman present is Kimbo's lover, referred to as "the girl from the farm" ("la muchacha de la finca"), who was pregnant and recently lost the baby. In an interesting twist, we find out that during a visit to Kimbo in jail, the vulgar police officer who tortured Kimbo to extract a confession and threatened to rape his girlfriend is in fact the young woman's cousin. The third woman who appears among the awaiting members of the crowd is Don Barrigón's wife, who hopes this experience will bring about changes in her own and her husband's life. We learn that she feels she has not been able to realize her potential. Instead she has served Don Barrigón as a devoted wife, but more as a decoration than a meaningful partner. Don Barrigón is not the benevolent man he claims to be—he has used his influence with other members of the business community and the government to make deals for his own benefit. People hold him up to be a saint because he gives the impression that he is offering good prices out of the goodness of his heart, but his wife witnesses the influence peddling that has helped him maintain and increase his wealth. She is hoping the kidnapping will effect positive changes for both of them: "Yes, it is possible that the kidnapping could have no effect whatsoever and things could return as they once were, but that is doubtful." ("Sí, es posible que el secuestro no hubiera producido efecto alguno, y las aguas entonces volverían a su nivel. Pero era dudoso." *KM* 95). Don Barrigón's wife hopes to be able to recover her own identity and start anew when her husband returns from captivity. She resents being an "affluent beggar" ("mendiga acaudalada"; *KM* 97), having to beg and borrow money from friends, banks, and businesses because nothing is in her own name. Everything belongs to Don Barrigón—including her.

In the crush of the press and police gathered in the waiting area of the airport, two other women are present, but not visible. The fourth woman also waits for the arrival of the plane and is "beyond the eyes of the other three, with a serene blackness on her face" ("más allá de los ojos de las otras tres, con una serena negrura en su rostro"; *KM* 98). This fourth woman is a spiritual, not physical presence. Her voice, like her presence in the room, is "beyond all the other voices" (una voz que estaba más allá de todas las voces), and it is the voice of Kimbo's dead mother. Another figure from beyond appears, a fifth woman, "that suddenly emerged without being seen by anyone" ("que surgió de pronto sin ser vista por nadie"; *KM* 99). This woman "was of the same generation and the same time as the mother" ("era de la misma generación y del mismo tiempo que la madre"; *KM* 99). This figure is that of Mrs. Rob from Kimbo's childhood, who also claims Kimbo as a member of the community. She declares to his mother, "and I helped raise him. Our children were children of the community. Say, our son." ("y yo ayudé a criarlo. Nuestros hijos entonces eran hijos de la comunidad. Diga pues nuestro hijo." *KM* 99). Mrs. Rob joins Kimbo's mother as part of the chorus of ancestral voices who stand to defend and support Kimbo through the trial and false accusations.

Chaos erupts when Kimbo and Don Barrigón arrive to meet the crowd that has gathered. During the confusion Don Barrigón attacks a police officer and a scream is heard. Someone fires a shot and the minister of security pushes Kimbo.

After the pandemonium calms, Kimbo is dead, the victim of an unknown assassin. Through the voice of Kimbo's attorney we learn that his client's reticence was a strategy to protect himself, but he was in possession of more information than he felt he could reveal. The attorney believes his client was the victim of someone who wanted to keep him silent, the victim of someone who feared that when it was time for him to speak he would speak the truth. Kimbo becomes a sacrifice and a symbol.

According to the legal clerk, the shot that killed Kimbo came from the gun of a security official from inside the building, not outside as the press is reporting. The bureaucrat does not want to get involved, although he is a witness to the tumult that occurred moments before in the airport. He does not want to compromise himself or his work mate: "It was one of the big shots in security. I'm sure I saw him. He fired the shot. Now I hear on the radio that the shot came from outside the room through the window. I heard the announcer say they almost killed the very officer that I saw shooting. But it's not my business. . . . Now I'm going to shut up." ("Es uno de los jefes en la oficina de seguridad. Estoy seguro: yo lo vi. El disparó. Ahora oigo por la radio que el disparo vino de fuera de la sala, por una celosía. Oigo decir al locutor que casi matan precisamente al oficial que yo vi disparar. . . . Ahora me voy a callar." *KM* 108).

In the chapter, titled "El Testigo Principal" (The Main Witness), we hear the voice of the peasant from Tres Ríos who confesses to the priest that he gave false testimony against Kimbo under oath in exchange for money, but he also asks the priest not to say anything about his confession. He says, "Yes, it was me who sent him to death. I sent him to death. I didn't speak when I should have." ("Sí, fui yo quien lo mandé a matar. Yo lo mandé a matar. No hablé cuando tenía que decir mi propia palabra." *KM* 109). The guilt causes the peasant to assuage his culpability through alcohol. Ironically, instead of protecting and benefiting his family as he intended to do by participating in the conspiracy against Kimbo, his family is burdened with his alcoholism and the truth about his role in Kimbo's demise.

After hearing the peasant's confession, the priest reflects on his own complicity in the accusations against Kimbo. He joins the crowd at the airport because he "needed to get a good look at him. See him up close and make peace with my conscience." ("necesitaba verlo bien. Verlo de cerca. Quedar bien con mi conciencia." *KM* 111). He attempts to justify his actions by declaring, "God made all the blacks very, very similar I can't tell them apart very well. But I know I saw a black man, but I don't have any way of saying that it was precisely that black man. I didn't do it out of bad faith—I wanted to cooperate with the law," ("Dios hizo a todos los negros muy, muy parecidos. Yo no los distingo bien. Y lo que sí sé que vi fue un negro, pero no tengo forma de decir si fue precisamente este negro. Y no lo hizo por mala fe: quise cooperar con la ley," *KM* 111). The priest's comments highlight the pervasiveness of stereotypes about racial difference, and these imbedded notions come to the fore in the text. He is forced to rethink his role and his beliefs—eventually maybe his culture and his cultural complicity.

The last part of *Kimbo*, part 4, begins with epigraphs from the Afro-Colombian writer Manuel Zapata Olivella and Costa Rican writer and politician Abel Pacheco. Zapata Olivella's quote, "I feel that I have anchored in the harbor of my Ancestors" ("Siento que he fondeado en la rada de mis Ancestros"; *KM* 113), and the Abel Pacheco quote, "I have felt the oneness of men, that of the Gods as well as that Yemayá is María" ("Yo he sentido que los hombres son uno, que los dioses también, que Yemayá es María"; *KM* 115), combine the concepts of *samamfo* with the legacy of cultural contributions of the Diaspora. These quotes from a Colombian writer of African descent and a mestizo writer and politician who was born in the Central Valley and raised in Limón, foretell the tone and theme of the final portion of *Kimbo*. The ancestral spirits of *samamfo* advise and guide the protagonist in his self-defense and address the impact of Kimbo's life on others, his legacy.

In the first chapter of the fourth part of the novel, Kimbo hears the voices of the ancestors from "beyond." These voices of *samamfo* spiritually connect the unborn, the living, and the ancestors who have died. In Duncan's glossary, *samamfo* is defined as: "The values and traditions of a people are found in *samamfo*. It is the collective memory of the race/culture that is passed from generation to generation and is manifested in the religious-secular rites of the people, in their struggles, in their experiences. The ancestors have never abandoned their descendants" (*KM* 153). The voices of Kimbo's mother and Mrs. Rob communicate from this ancestral/spiritual space to support and defend their real and figurative son. Mrs. Rob uses an Anancy tale about using wit to overcome adversity. The Anancy story is about a rivalry between Bredda Tiger and Bredda Anancy that culminates in the triumph of the weaker Bredda Anancy over the Tiger.

Kimbo associates all of the witnesses who testified against him with Bredda Tiger: "they were the enemies who sprung forth from whence enemies always spring forth, they were the tigers and tigresses who had come out of the mountains." ("Eran los enemigos que brotaron de donde siempre brotan los enemigos, eran los tigres y las tigresas que habían salido del monte." *KM* 119). He realizes his options are to resign himself to fate and the accusations or "go back again to his age-old cry: I'm here, possessed by *samamfo*, shouting with the force of the wind that I am." ("volver de nuevo a su grito de antaño: heme aquí, poseído por samamfo, gritando con la fuerza del viento que soy." *KM* 118).

Mrs. Rob also shares with Kimbo another story that she calls ancient and global and part of their shared heritage; it guides her spiritual progeny through this difficult moment. She tells him the tale about the nephew of a king who was denied royal recognition and wealth and began stealing from nobles and other royalty. To avenge his disinherited family, he orchestrates robberies in his uncle's kingdom. The king presents his nephew with three tests, and if he completes them all, he will receive money; if he fails, he will be executed. The boy uses guile and trickery to achieve his goal, which maddens his uncle, the king, but makes the boy very wealthy. Mrs. Rob explains to young Kimbo that the story teaches a lesson that "one cannot conquer authority in a direct way that some people want. It's not possible to get strength from where you don't have it. That strength must come from *samamfo*, and that strength that comes from our heritage transcends all brute strength." ("no se puede vencer a la autoridad de esa manera directa en que quieren algunos. Que no es posible sacar fuerza de donde uno no tiene. Que la fuerza debe venir del samamfo, y que la fuerza que viene de nuestra herencia trasciende la fuerza de todos los brutos." *KM* 120). She warns him not to be blinded by religion, appearances, or promises. She is part of *samamfo* and her legacy continues by passing on to Kimbo these stories. She insists that he is not only the beloved child of his mother but also the child of the community and a "child of *samamfo*" by calling him "our beloved son." She says Kimbo can "cross to the other shore" ("ya puede pasar a la otra orilla"; *KM* 122), implying that Kimbo will join them in *samamfo*. With the guidance Mrs. Rob offers through the diasporic Anancy tales and timeless legends, he decides to follow the "rule of Anancy"—the small and weak must use their wit and intelligence to overcome larger, oppressive forces in order to survive. He remains silent and appears submissive, but when the appropriate moment arises, he will exact his revenge by using his seemingly weak position to reveal the falsity of the allegations against him.

Kimbo's spirit appears to his attorney, who takes a defensive position with his interlocutor, the doctor. He does not want to sound crazy as he describes "supernatural" phenomena of "ignorant blacks" that are beyond the realm of comprehension of the doctor's Western, linear mind. He explains the concept of *samamfo*—perhaps witnessing or sensing the presence of ancestors from beyond who have accompanied Kimbo. He insists, "The spirit of the people is something common to all of us. It lives in us, it gives us life. . . . I'll tell you one thing and I'll tell you willingly: four hundred years of common experience is more than folklore." ("El espíritu del pueblo es una cosa común. . . . Te digo una cosa, te lo digo con ganas: cuatro cientos años de experiencia común son más que folklore." *KM* 125). He further elaborates the Afro-realist connection between humanity, time, and the ancestors:

> They are four hundred years of common experience. Four hundred years in which we have had to learn many things: distance ourselves from the pain so that it doesn't destroy us. Keeping bitterness in check, above all, looking

for life in everything, to enjoy each moment as if our life would end there [in that moment]. I mean to say: it's a question of living today. And that is Samamfo. This is the rule for the living and the dead. Because the people survive. The rebellion of the people is always present. Because the astuteness of Bredda Anancy survives and prevails. Because we live for our grandparents, and for the grandparents of our grandparents. We live, we exist in their myths, in their history. And they live in us. They are incarnate in us, they become present everyday in our acts and for that reason I always tell you yesterday does not exist. Memories do not exist. Yesterday and today are the same: they are two moments of thought. One cannot divide them because then yesterday becomes a noxious illusion: those memories become idols and we consume them. But he who lives in *samamfo*, one who understands that life is a whole that flows, knows that time is an illusion. And those that were are.

Son cuatrocientos años de experiencia común. Cuatrocientos años en que hemos tenido que aprender muchas cosas: distanciarnos del dolor para que no nos consuma. Mantener a raya la amargura, buscar ante todo la vida, disfrutar de cada momento como si allí terminara nuestra vida. Quiero decir: es cuestión de vivir hoy. Y eso es Samamfo. Ese es el régimen de los vivos y de los muertos. Porque el pueblo sobrevive. La rebelión del pueblo sobrevive y está siempre presente. Porque la astucia del hermano Araña sobrevive y se impone. Porque nosotros vivimos por los abuelos, y por los abuelos de los abuelos. Vivimos, existimos en sus mitos, en su historia. Y ellos viven en nosotros. Se encarnan en nosotros, se actualizan todos los días en nuestros actos, y por eso es que siempre te digo que no existe el ayer. No existen los recuerdos. Ayer y hoy son lo mismo: son dos momentos del pensamiento. No se pueden dividir porque entonces el ayer se convierte en una ilusión nefasta: esos recuerdos se vuelven ídolos y nos consumen. Pero el que vive en el Samamfo, el que comprende que la vida es un todo que fluye, sabe que el tiempo es una ilusión. Y los que fueron son. (*KM* 126)

The Latino attorney understands the African-based system of *samamfo* and the African concept of time. According to Paulette Ramsay, "The *latino* lawyer seems to be employed by the author to explode the myth that blacks hold their beliefs in *Samamfo*, and by extension other aspects of the other African heritage because they are ignorant and primitive. The *latino* lawyer doubly validates this Afro-derived belief, since he is from the respected dominant race, as well as being highly educated" (Ramsay 1994, 38). From the perspective of the physician, the lawyer's discourse is nothing but "poetic license" since in his cultural frame the dead cannot come back. He expects those words to come from "one of those ignorant, backwater blacks" ("uno de esos negros ignorantes, del monte para adentro"; *KM* 133), but not someone as educated as the lawyer. He refuses to believe that a dead woman can convince her son to return to the country to tell the truth about the injustice committed against him. He insists that the attorney is losing his sanity because it is impossible for the dead to communicate with the living.

The attorney's girlfriend provides a more sympathetic ear than the physician. Initially she does not understand the concept of *samamfo*, but eventually she grasps the idea, particularly when her partner receives a letter from Kimbo that reads: "I am writing to you all because you are on a list of honest people that I made during this short exile. I have made seventy copies. What I am going to tell you is the truth." ("les escribo esta carta porque figuran en una lista de personas honestas que hice durante este corte exilio. He hecho setenta copias. Lo que voy a relatarles es la verdad." *KM* 134). This letter from Kimbo evokes surprise in the lawyer's girlfriend. She wonders, "Is this *samamfo*? Is it something like those that were are?" ("¿Es esto el samamfo? ¿Es así como los que fueron son?" *KM* 134).

Members of the press interview Kimbo's former cellmate; they also present the mate with a letter from Kimbo. The prisoner from Limón believes Kimbo remained silent because he had reason to do so. He announces: "I'm convinced that every word is true. I believe that this here paper don't have no lies." ("Lo que quiero declarar es poco: que estoy convencido de que cada palabra es verdad. Creo que el papel este no tiene ninguna mentira." *KM* 135). He believes what Kimbo states in his letter, and he also believes Kimbo knew his death was imminent. The prisoner again reiterates that he knows what the people are like in Limón—influenced by the Afro–West Indian culture. He lets out a laugh and explains, "no I'm not laughing at anybody: I'm from Limón and the Limonese, we know when to laugh because it is our way of letting things go." ("no me estoy burlando de nadie: yo soy de Limón, y los limonenses sabemos cuándo reír porque esa es nuestra manera de dejar salir la cosa." *KM* 136). In the room where the press interview is taking place, a warm breeze passes through. The intense rays of the setting sun and the bright lights of the cameras contrast with the cold wind and darkness of the cell Kimbo inhabited. As the Limonese prisoner gives the laughter of survival, he begins to cry and say, "its okay, paisano, you fucked all those sons of bitches" ("está bien, paisano, jodiste a todos estos hijos de puta"; *KM* 136).

Don Barrigón and his wife are also affected by their understanding of *samamfo* and Kimbo's letter from beyond. Don Barrigón blames Kimbo's return and subsequent assassination on the will of his dead mother: "That woman continued influencing him even after his death. I'm sure he returned to the country just to be faithful to his mother's teachings." ("Esa señora siguió influyendo en él aún después de muerta. Estoy seguro volvió al país solo per ser fiel a las enseñanzas de su madre." *KM* 141). He goes on to say, "She insisted all the time that her son go down what she called the 'path of righteousness.' Old ideas. They don't work in our times." ("Insistía todo el tiempo en que su hijo fuera por lo que ella llamó el camino recto. Ideas antiguas. No sirven para funcionar en nuestros días." *KM* 141). His wife asserts that Kimbo was an honorable man and insists that her husband say something on Kimbo's behalf since he is the sole person who could speak the truth. Don Barrigón is more concerned about making money than he is about rectifying the situation. When a letter arrives for Don Barrigón from Kimbo, it has damning information about Don Barrigón. His wife finally finds the courage to leave her marriage:

> Get your own jacket and go to hell. Go to hell Barrigón because you will have to make your own coffee from now on or pay someone to do it for you. Because I'm going to leave out that door tomorrow. Actually, I'm going to leave out that door right now. I swear on his life that this will be the last time I pass through this threshold.
>
> *Echá para tu saco vos y andate al carajo. Andate al carajo, Barrigón, porque tendrás que hacer tu propio café de ahora en adelante, o pagar para que te lo hagan. Porque yo voy a salir por esa puerta mañana. Es más, voy a salir por esa puerta ahora mismo. Y te lo juro por él, que ésta será la última vez que yo pase por este dintel.* (*KM* 144)

Kimbo's wife receives a letter from Kimbo in a chapter titled "La infidente" (The Disloyal One). She denounces Kimbo and his lover, the girl from the country. She says, "you dug your own grave" ("cavaste tu propia tumba"; *KM* 145). Although she claims that his shooting hurt her, the grief she experiences is more out of the inability to exact more harm, thus ending her possibilities for revenge: "But as soon as you were annihilated, I emerge victorious in everything. Everything was justified: the end of the marriage, the no holds barred fights that I subjected you to for all of these years, my image before my children, to whom I will explain that you were a dog that left them for another woman." ("Pero al caer vos liquidado yo surgía victoriosa en todo. Todo estaba justificado: el fin de nuestro matrimonio, la lucha sin cuartel a que te he sometido durante todos estos años, mi imagen frente a mis hijos, a quienes he explicado que eras un perro que los dejaste por otra mujer." *KM* 145). She also receives an accusatory letter from Kimbo from the grave that she promises to publicly dismiss as a hoax and a fraud in order to further damage Kimbo's reputation.

The novel interweaves the striking revelations of *samamfo* with the examination into Kimbo's death. There are conflicting accounts, misinformation, and uncooperative witnesses in the investigation. There is great mystery about the origin of the shots fired at the airport. The police officer angrily launches accusations against the reporters who have gathered for a briefing. The members of the press are investigating information they received that a member of the public fired a shot. He declares,

> No one on the police force fired a shot at him, nor do we have any motivation to do it, and there are no connections between that so called movement and us, because we all know where those scoundrels were trained, and everyone knows who we are, that we are loyal, very loyal to our country and to our families and to God and we have sworn to defend the honor of the Republic.
>
> *Nadie en la fuerza pública le disparó, ni teníamos motivo alguno para hacerlo, y no, no hay conexiones entre tal movimiento y nosotros, porque todos sabemos adonde se entrenan esos perros, y todos saben quiénes somos nosotros, que somos leales, muy leales a nuestra patria, y a nuestras familias y a Dios, y que hemos jurado defender el honor de la República.* (*KM* 128)

Those who have information about the trial, the shooting, and the death of Kimbo are afraid to come forward. The law clerk burns evidence that points toward Kimbo's innocence, and he refuses to reveal what he knows about the shooting.

With Kimbo now dead, the kidnappers disagree over their kidnapping strategy. The crueler of the two kidnappers says to the more pensive one that they followed his idea because the group feared he would talk to the press and the authorities about their plans. He blames the passive one's ideas for all the problems Kimbo's return from his exile abroad created. This forces the group to reveal the truth: "And we are going to have to go to the press and say that actually that dumbass had nothing to do with us because it is no longer useful for us to be associated with a dumbass like that who has all of a sudden become the hero of idiots, communists, and all of the traveling companions of all of those folks." ("Y vamos a tener que salir a la prensa y decir que en realidad el carajo ese no tuvo nada que ver con nosotros porque no nos conviene estar asociado con un carajo así que de pronto se ha convertido en un héroe de los idiotas, de los comunistas, y de todos los compañeros de viaje de esa gente." *KM* 138). The "bad" kidnapper threatens the "good one" with "you are going to be judged. . . . If you get out of this, go grow some potatoes. If you don't, well *adios*, darkie." ("Vas a ser juzgado. . . . Si salís bien librado de esta, dedicate a sembrar papas. Si no salís bien, pues adiós, morenito." *KM* 138). The kidnapper's statement to his accomplice suggests that he was the dark-skinned fellow the witnesses claimed they saw abducting the businessman.

The peasant farmer from Tres Ríos who claims to have seen Kimbo at the scene of the crime later recants his story. He returns to the church to meet with the priest. The peasant tells the priest that he received a letter from the dead Kimbo, as well as the priest. The peasant tries to get the priest to "confess" to his own complicity in Kimbo's death because of his false testimony. Apparently the taxi driver who transported Kimbo from the airport to his house confirmed Kimbo's alibi. So there is no way the priest or anyone else who testified against Kimbo could have possibly seen him. The peasant speaks of another truth, and that is one of race, color, and social status. He says to the priest: "I think what happened to that man could have happened to me. Because now I realize that in reality no one saw him there: they just saw a black man. That's all they say. . . . And I let myself be dragged into it like an idiot for a few pesos. I said stupid things and that could have happened to me and that worries me." ("yo pienso lo que le pasó a ese hombre me pudo haber pasado a mí. Porque ahora me doy cuenta que en realidad nadie lo vio allí: solo vieron un negro. Esos fue todo lo que vieron. Y yo me dejé llevar por mi lengua, por bocón. Y yo me he dejado llevar como un idiota y por querer unos pesos deje tonterías y eso me pudo haber pasado a mí, y eso me preocupa." *KM* 140). He urges the priest to step forward, but he is met with curses and is finally thrown out of the church.

The novel concludes with a chapter titled "Las dos mujeres" (The Two Women), which depicts the encounter between Don Barrigón's wife and Kimbo's lover at her country home. The conversation between the two women occurs during the setting of the sun, with dancing shadows and a refreshing breeze. The elements of nature that appear throughout this final chapter (the sunset, wind, light, and shadow) symbolize Kimbo's spirit and the concept of *samamfo*—that life is continuous and contiguous with the past, and that life and death are on the same plane. The lover will begin a new life without Kimbo and without their child. Don Barrigón's wife is looking for a new beginning and meaning for her life. She shares the letter she received from Kimbo with Kimbo's lover. The two women discuss Kimbo's life and murder. Neither believes the kidnappers ended his life. Neither utters the name of the assassin, but they confirm that his death was caused by many who were vocal and many who remained reticent. The novel closes with the two women looking out of the window while a fresh breeze blows through the country house. The "woman with elegant bearing" says to the "woman with calloused hands" that she is looking for work. Nothing more is said between the two women. The only action is that of Kimbo's lover moving a ringlet of hair so that it does not get blown by the passing wind. These two women, who are not of identifiable Afro ancestry, will pass on the knowledge and power of *samamfo*. They will remember Kimbo for his humanity and for his respect for the spiritual connection between the living and the dead and between the generations. They will maintain one of the key components of *samamfo*, which is keeping the memory of the departed alive. The two women are among those who believed in the protagonist and his innocence. They are loyal and the breeze that enters the room is the living spirit of Kimbo who lives on and watches over his "descendants'" *samamfo*.

A Message from Rosa / Un mensaje de Rosa

The concept of *samamfo* and *Afrorealismo* also frame the bilingual text *A Message from Rosa / Un mensaje de Rosa*. Subtitled "An African Diaspora Novel in Short Stories," the novel marks Duncan's first published work of fiction written in English. *A Message from Rosa* is made up of a collection of interconnected narratives and vignettes that are framed within the context of two African ancestors' long five-hundred-year wait to hear from their descendants who are dispersed all over the globe. This novel is an extension of Duncan's commitment to diffusing the history of the African Diaspora and the transatlantic slave trade. *A Message from Rosa* also follows the author's own notion of Afro-realism. He writes in the preface to *A Message from Rosa*:

> And, as our journey unfolded, stories told and retold by an infinite number of narrators: stories recreated, never the same, and yet always the same. Ancestral voices forever present and always alive, in our daily lives. A thousand readings of the same experience.
>
> They help us to resist, to keep, to survive. And they live on. They come back to us. They help us build the present. Afrorealism. Fragmentary consciousness reenacted. The building of a Universal Afro Identity. A new wholeness, a healing process. A call for diversity. All inclusive. All dignified. All recognized. (*MR* ix)[5]

This positioning of the African Diaspora stresses the paradox of the dispersal of Afro-descendant peoples that emphasizes the continuity of life and ancestral connections as well as the discontinuities of culture, experiences, and strategies of survival. Afro-realism takes shape not only by focusing on the themes of resistance to domination by African descendants in the Diaspora, but also through the notion of *samamfo*, the Ashanti-derived spiritual belief in the connection between the departed ancestors, the living, and the unborn. The two African ancestors, Aba and Ekwo, speak from the spirit of *samamfo* and yearn to hear from their descendants not only to learn of their fate, but also to require that the generations of their progeny remember them so that they will continue to survive and dwell in the spiritual realm and not fall into the abyss of being forgotten. As the two African ancestors, Aba and Ekwo, await word of the fate of their descendants, the novel crosses time and space—traversing oceans, political borders, cultures, and languages—to tell a story of the multiple experiences in different sites of the Diaspora in the Americas. Like Manuel Zapata Olivella's complex and masterful text, *Changó, el gran putas* (1983), *A Message from Rosa* fictionalizes historical events and characters and demonstrates the connectedness of Afro-descendants in the Diaspora through the drum beat of resistance and the depth of ancestral memory.

A Message from Rosa opens with a pair of elders of the fictional West African Yayah tribe. Aba, in particular, is growing tired and weary of the wait to hear from their descendants and to fulfill the promise that her tree, a gift from her father, will bloom on that auspicious day. As they wait for their descendants to return, the novel traces the intertribal wars and commercial slave hunting that led to enslavement and the dispersal to the Americas of some members of the Yayah, as well as their experiences in the New World over the next five centuries. The core trait the generations of descendants share is the resistance to subjugation through physical and cultural marronage, and the defense of their ethnic and cultural heritage as Afro-descendants. The Yayah offspring lead and participate in slave revolts to escape their enslavement. They establish maroon colonies to challenge the social and economic order of European domination. They join national struggles for independence from Europe. They initiate great social movements like Garveyism or the civil rights movement in the United States.

Structure and Themes

The text is perhaps the most linear of Duncan's fiction, in order to facilitate its pedagogical purpose of informing his readers about the trauma of the transatlantic slave trade, the history and legacy of resistance among the survivors of the devastating voyage, and the interconnectedness of the peoples of African descent in the Americas. *A Message from Rosa* is divided into three parts (Roots, The Middle Passage, The Diaspora) made up of chapters that portray the difficult and painful experiences of the dispersal of the Yayah tribe from West Africa to the New World. These subsections have multiple narrative perspectives and voices that sometimes present third-person-omniscient or first-person points of view, as well as multiple perspectives of a singular event, such as the capture of the Yayah that begins their enslavement in the Americas. Part 1 of the novel, set during the early period of the slave trade, is composed of five chapters and details the history of the Yayah, the invasion of their lands, and the enslavement of many members of their tribe. Part 2, with five chapters, takes place during the transatlantic slave trade and features strategies of resistance during the Middle Passage. The buying and selling of humans at slave markets in the Americas, slave rebellions, and maroon settlements unify the seventeen chapters of the third part of *A Message from Rosa*. Covering the sixteenth century from struggles of Iberian blacks to maintain their culture and dignity in the plantation system of Hispaniola, to the Haitian Revolution through the US civil rights movement of the twentieth century, the third part of the novel highlights political and social activism in the Diaspora. The author weaves the stories of nameless ancestors along with fictionalized representations of maroon leaders, such as Zumbi of Brazil, Benkos of Colombia/Venezuela, Nat Turner of the United States, Cudjoe of Jamaica; preachers of racial uplift like Marcus Garvey of Jamaica; and icons of the US civil rights movement, Martin Luther King and Rosa Parks. Rosa Parks is the only female descendant of Aba and Kwame mentioned by name.

Plot. The first part of *A Message from Rosa* takes place in the spiritual realm with two Yayah tribe ancestors, Aba, the female elder, and Kwame, the male elder. Aba is disappointed that a tree, carried to her from Timbuktu as a gift from her father, has not bloomed as promised. Kwame narrates, "She yawns daily with nostalgia, hoping to see her father's words coming true. She lives her life hoping to see if her people have kept or recovered the supreme dignity of the Samamfo that is, if they keep the Ancestral Spirit alive, renewing the clans of our nation. She went about wondering if they had chosen to build their homes like ours, and if they chose to return, would they be alive like people should be, or simply subsisting with a hollow mask of vitality" (*MR* 5). The tree she has guarded and protected for years symbolizes ancestral roots and the knowledge of cultural history. Aba must keep watch over the tree until it blooms. However, after waiting for many centuries, she claims that she is tired and wants to sleep. When an ancestor is not remembered and she decides to go to sleep, it implies the death of her spirit and the descent into nothingness, the realm of the forgotten and the end of their lineage.

Kwame is affected by her wish because he has accompanied her across time and knows this will mark the end of the Yayah: "You're simply going to toss everything into the ditch and lie down to sleep. And so you're going to let the laugh of the hyena take possession over our nation and wipe out our memories, leaving no trace of us, not even of the last of us" (*MR* 6). These two elders, Aba and Kwame, are the last to know the history of the Yayah, and they are keepers of this collective memory. Kwame manages to convince Aba to wait a month before descending into the "Valley of Forgetfulness" (el Valle del Olvido) and they wait for their descendants to present a sign of remembrance and for the sacred tree to bloom.

Aba reflects on the changes that have occurred among the Yayah, as well as the threats to their culture. The Yayahs have been under a constant state of siege—in Africa and in the Diaspora. They have been attacked by a rival nomadic tribe, the Fulahghi, who captured and enslaved members of the Yayah and then sold them to their European allies. The female elder observes the tumultuous state of their history and their condition: "For never before in the history of mankind has there been a war so cruel, so ruthless, and so senseless. In all these years, there has never been a single moment of peace. Not a single day without some sort of action, some sort of blow, inflicted as a reminder of our subordination, or our captivity. Our pride does not allow us to admit it. . . . Our history, no matter how glorious, has not been registered in books and the vigor of our drums and the clear sound of our poets thrive on the border of death" (*MR* 10). For Aba and Kwame, this history, one that does not appear in books, is the history of the capture, enslavement, and dispersal of the members of their tribe—their voyage from Africa to the Americas.

Various members of the two elders' families tell their story of the Fulahghi raid on their village, the confusion as the Yayah tribe members defend their village, and the terrible aftermath of the battle with their rivals. While Kwame and Aba defend their home, their children and grandchildren are captured. Aba finds solace in her tree, which symbolizes survival, the cycles of life, and family lineage. Aba's tree remains a constant reminder of their tribe and represents their resilience. Meanwhile, Aba and Kwame's son hopes that he will be able to negotiate with the Fulahghi before the captive Yayah reach the coast. He has heard rumors of men with white skin buying slaves, but believes that escape is possible. However, once the captured Yayah reach the coast, they are met with fetid smells, poor food, and abusive treatment. Aba and Kwame's son swears that he will defend his people at all costs and curses his Fulahghi captors for their collaboration with the Europeans in the enslavement of his tribe.

The system of slavery practiced by the Yayah, in contrast with the Europeans, is made markedly clear through the voice of Aba and Kwame's grandchild. The child at first thinks he will become the slave of the king, which is a privilege among the Yayah. However, his optimism dissolves as the Europeans violently inspect him and other slaves like animals. They are traded to the whites in exchange for objects like bronze, glass, and mirrors. The Yayah child is transported with others to the slave ship. He states: "Later we were forced around the Tree of Forgetfulness and into the boats; forced to become the outcast, the helpless, the useless, meat for the White men" (*MR* 26). He calls upon the powers of *samamfo* by seeking the help of the ancestors and draws upon the millenary resistance of the Yayah. He declares, "I will not be a slave!" and leaps from the boat and into the sea—preferring to end his own life rather than be a captive (*MR* 26).

In the chapters titled "First Route of the Body" and "Second Route of the Body," which open the second part of *A Message from Rosa*, the black female body becomes a site of resistance. Both chapters are told from the point of view of an unnamed Yayah woman on a slave ship en route to the Americas, but each chapter offers an alternate ending. The horrific smells, base conditions, and the decomposing cadaver next to her bring attention to her own body and the bodies of others in the hull of the ship. She focuses on the very human level of her existence, stripped of the comfortable parameters of her tribe and her culture. She takes notice of bodily functions, smells, sounds, and fluids. Outside of the order, mediation, and control of Yayah society, all she is left with is her body. On board the ship she witnesses bodies that are dominated, raped, subjugated for the pleasure of their European captors, and bodies in need. The Yayah woman sees the cruelty the Europeans inflict on each other, as well as their brutality toward the slaves, and she wonders what will happen to her. The inhumane conditions make her long for better times as she turns to her Islamic faith and thoughts of her family's traditions. The memories of the past are brought to an abrupt end when she is "examined" and then raped by the captain. She contemplates killing him in his drunken state. In the "First Route of the Body," the female subject chooses murder, and in the "Second Route of the Body," she makes a very different choice to survive.

Similarly, the following two chapters, "The First Route to Mutiny" and the "Second Route to Mutiny" introduce a rebellion planned by members of the Yayah with other tribes on board a slave ship. The various options presented by the slaves include suicide as a way to return to the ancestors without the humiliation of being held captive, turn the ship around to return to their homeland in Africa, or establish themselves as a new people in a new home, free of European subjugation. They decide to rebel, but a betrayal foils the plan, resulting in the deaths of many of the African mutineers. The story of the insurrection is told through dialogue among the slaves and from the perspective of the third-person narrator. The same act of slave resistance is told by a third-person-omniscient narrator from the perspective of the mutiny leader in "Second Route to Mutiny." The latter chapter gives additional detail of the uprising that results in the death of the ship's captain, the capture of the European crewmembers, and the Africans gaining control of the ship. Land is spotted and they plan to go ashore, an implication that they will join a place in the history of African resistance in the Americas by becoming maroons.

Another voice that appears in the second part of the narrative is the voice of a mulatto slave trader from Cape Verde who almost finds himself enslaved. The unnamed mulatto entered into an arrangement with Orwell Boxman, an English pirate, agreeing to give him five slaves; however, he reneges on the deal, keeping the pirate's money. When Boxman encounters the mulatto, he is willing to forgive his debt if he helps him raid a Portuguese slave ship that is in port. The brown-skinned trader sees this as an opportunity to not only have his debt forgiven but also to have an opportunity to make even more money by selling the information to the Portuguese port authorities. After the successful siege of the ship, the mulatto fears for his safety. Although the young man claims he is not black but brown, the lighter shade of his skin will not prevent the Portuguese from selling him as a slave in Brazil or the West Indies if his collaboration with the English pirates is discovered.

The mulatto manages to escape the Portuguese armada by sea and realizes that he cannot return to his home in Cape Verde. He must continue on to the Americas with the captured slave ship, and he questions how he will be treated there as a "half-breed." He is told contradictory information by others: "A boy like you could live like a King in Saint Domingue. You could be an official in the army if you were in Brazil," as well as "Behave yourself, boy. In the West Indies you would be no more that [*sic*] a houseboy" (*MR* 53). The racial reality of the Americas presents a risk to the freedom he enjoyed in his homeland. As a strategy of survival, he plays Anancy in an effort to use information he learned about a planned conspiracy among the captured crew to take over Bowman's ship. The astute young man takes the information of the plot and notes the names of the conspirators, manipulates the black supervisors aboard against the conspiracy, and informs Captain Bowman, thus assuring his loyalty. The captain swiftly carries out justice against the conspirators and allows more leisure time to be given to the slaves to ensure their cooperation. The unregistered pirate ship with its illegal cargo arrives in Cuba, known to turn a blind eye to the unlawful shipment of slaves. The pirates sell the slaves with altered paperwork to make the sale appear legal, and the mulatto decides to capitalize on his skills and remain in Havana to work for the captain general of the colony. He states of his new career: "I took advantage of my knowledge of Africa, the Portuguese pirates, and my light skin, to open my way in Havana" (*MR* 56).

In part 3 of the novel, "Diaspora," we learn that the unnamed mulatto lives with a *parda*, a brown-skinned woman; however, his mother-in-law voices her opposition to the union. She claims to be a descendant of the Spanish Moors and Juan de Valladolid, a black servant of the Catholic kings, Ferdinand and Isabella, whom they named the *juez* (judge) or *alcalde* (mayor) of the black population in Andalucía. She shares with her daughter stories about Africans on the continent, including stories of her ancestral connection to the legendary King Mansa Musa of Mali and about blacks in Europe before the slave trade. She contests the notion that all culture was erased by sharing her history and memories with her daughter. The *parda* woman also criticizes her son-in-law for his association with pirates and declares that a pirate is not good enough for her daughter and their distinguished family line: "We have been the relatives of kings and queens. We have been loyal to Spain. I never imagined my daughter married to an African Portuguese pirate, with those devilish green cat-eyes" (*MR* 67).

The *parda* woman came to the Americas as a free woman and like many had a dream that her family's hard work would benefit future generations in spite of the fear of slavery. Although she is aware of the cruelty of Caribbean slavery and recognizes that the Spanish do not obey any of the laws established to protect the slaves, she at one time believed, "if we had to be enslaved, that would be just a temporary inconvenience" (*MR* 67). With the passage of time and her growing resentment toward the American-born Spanish Creoles, who are not like the Spaniards on the peninsula, and the rights being taken away from *pardos ladinos* (Catholic blacks from Spain) because of the arrival of *bozales*, or "saltwater Negroes," recently arrived from Africa and threats made by maroons, escaped slaves, she desires to return to their "homeland" in Spain. However, she needs the permission of the governor to make the voyage. She wants her pirate son-in-law to speak with the colonial official to grant permission to return to Granada.

In "Scataration," the narrator that tells of the capture of a young boy named Newlife and others in his village in Africa by European slave catchers and continues the story of mutinous Africans in "Santos del Congo" (Saints of the Congo). The newly freed Africans from different tribes and practitioners of different religions arrive in Mesoamerica. In honor of their arrival as free people, the Africans of all nations pour libation at a tree on the beach where they landed ashore. Years later, in the chapter titled "Yangá, "we find that this foundational tree has now become a central gathering place and part of the home of Yangá, the leader of a community of maroons near Veracruz, Mexico.[6] From their *palenque*, or settlement, they attacked Spanish colonists and impeded the flow of their trade; however, the maroons have decided to propose a peace treaty with the Spanish crown. Yangá, who was called Newlife as a child, remembers the chaos of the raid on his village and the separation from his parents. After running away, he joins the maroon village that is made up of indigenous peoples, Africans, and *zambos* (mixed-race African and indigenous). His arrival to the settlement becomes the fulfillment of prophecy, and the community renames him Yangá. Yangá negotiates with the Spanish to establish the town of San Lorenzo de los Negros and agrees not to attack the Spanish colonists or impede their trade. This treaty, like many involving maroon settlements, also includes compromises and collusion with the colonial authorities, including the return of any escaped slaves who enter the maroon community in exchange for peace.

The story of black resistance continues with "Juan Bautista's Story," told from the perspective of a female narrator who encounters an unusual stranger named Juan Bautista Congo, the grandson of Yayahs. He tells the narrator and her mother that his people escaped from slavery in Coro, Venezuela, where they established a maroon settlement. Juan Bautista shares the story of maroon struggles of resistance with the blacks and Indians in the narrator's village. He explains that Spanish forces destroyed his peoples' settlement and killed the maroon colony's leaders—but they did not kill their spirit of resistance. The ancestral spirits of the murdered king and queen led a slave rebellion on Margarita Island and inspired others to escape Spanish slavery and form their own maroon communities. In spite of the Spaniards' insistence that King Miguel and Queen Huida are dead, the people still continued to communicate with the spirits of their deceased leaders who encouraged them to rebel against Spanish authority and live as free people in their own settlement.[7]

The spirit of King Miguel becomes reincarnated in the body of a boy named Domingo Biyojo who is the slave of Pedro de la Granda. The young Domingo is accused of theft and is punished by his master. His uncle is a slave carpenter who offers to pay his master the one peso fine to have Domingo become his helper. The master accepts the money from Domingo's uncle, but does not release Domingo to his uncle's care. This event raises the boy's consciousness of the Spanish colonist's dependence on slave labor. He thinks: "Life would certainly be tasteless in this country if they had not been able to benefit from the skills of the Africans and their descendants" (*MR* 92). Inspired by the exploitation and violent physical abuse he witnesses, Domingo organizes a rebellion and assumes the name King Benkos.[8] The narrator affirms: "He was confirmed heir of the Old African Kingdoms by the council, and given a new name: King Benkos" (*MR* 93). Benkos establishes his *palenque*, periodically raiding and attacking Spanish settlements in order to protect their freedom. After thirteen years, the Spaniards allow the residents of the maroon colony to remain free and give them the right to wear Spanish-style clothing. However, the Spanish representatives break their agreement, accuse Benkos of conspiracy, and then execute the maroon leader.

Following the tradition of his Yayah ancestors, Juan Bautista Congo continues spreading the news of palenques and King Miguel and King Benkos's maroon resistance to other black communities throughout the Americas. In Brazil, he influences a slave named Antonio who is servant of a priest. Padre Elias warns the boy not to take part in anything involving Juan Bautista Congo, claiming that his activities are primitive and not Christian. While attending to the priest, Antonio overhears a conversation between his master and Don João about the maroon settlement of Palmares and its leader Zumbi, a former companion of Antonio. The two Portuguese colonists express regret for reaching an agreement with the *quilombo*'s predecessor, Ganga Zumba, and lament their part in educating Zumbi. Before becoming a maroon, Zumbi was called Francisco and wanted to become a priest after receiving his education. The religious orders rejected him because of the color of his skin. Angered by the racism he encountered, Zumbi joins Ganga Zumba in the Palmares *quilombo*. He asks a young Antonio to join him, but his friend chooses to remain in his enslaved condition with his mother. Hearing information that could be beneficial to Zumbi and the defense of his maroon settlement, Antonio writes a letter and passes it on to another slave named Felicio, despite his wife's warning to not participate in anything that might jeopardize his safety and service to the priest. Felicio is caught with the letter, but Antonio manages to save Felicio and himself because he is perceived to be a loyal servant of Elias, and also illiterate. Antonio learns of another plan to attack the Palmares maroons, this one by the multiethnic forces of Domingos Jorge Velho. He writes another letter to Zumbi through Felicio, which is also intercepted. Antonio realizes that it will not take long for them to discover that he can read and write and that he is the author of the two letters destined for the maroon leader. To cover his escape to Palmares, he asks his wife to cause a commotion, saying that people from Palmares kidnapped him and forced him to write the letter. Antonio promises to send for the family to join him in Palmares as soon as it is safe.

The narratives of maroon settlements in Latin America and the Caribbean are linked with the spirit of black resistance to oppression in North America. In a chapter titled "Nat," the novel addresses the slave rebellion of Nat Turner. The lay preacher has a vision of his grandmother that quickly transforms into reliving her experience in the Middle Passage. She is the voice that appeared in "The Second Route of the Body," the slave woman who was raped by the ship's captain. The vision presents the memory of her ordeal on the ship next to the decomposing cadaver. Nat experiences everything she thought, heard, felt, smelled, and witnessed, and this awakens the desire to rebel against the oppressive conditions of slavery, a rebelliousness that was passed on to him by his grandfather, Juan Bautista. Nat, "the Great Messenger consecrated by God in order to liberate the Black slaves of the region" (*MR* 118), uses the power of God and the ancestors to attack his owners, the Travis family. A more widespread attack is halted when Jim, a slave who was in the household, found the bodies of the white family and let his white half-brother, Captain Harris of the militia, know what had occurred. During the hunt for Nat and his co-conspirators, Jim refused to participate, resulting in his own death. Jim declares to Captain Harris, "Me save you life . . . but sah, me not able to help you kill off my people, sah, after all, sah, all them want is freedom" (*MR* 119).

Madison, a participant in the rebellion, flees the county to save his own life. He thinks about how the authorities may have captured, tortured, humiliated, and killed his leader, Nat Turner. Although he is wounded, he continues on to Canada to find his freedom. While in Canada, Madison is assisted by people of many ethnicities and decides to take the risk to return to Virginia to bring his family to freedom. Madison arrives in Virginia, but he and his wife are captured en route to Canada and sold to different owners. Madison's wife, realizing that she may never see her husband again, begins to plant the seeds of rebellion in other slaves by spreading the message about Nat Turner and his rebellion. She finds herself on a ship in the Caribbean, and her message inspires action among the blacks to rebel against their imposed condition. An enslaved woman on board defends her body against the sexual violence of a crewmember by killing him. Taking his keys, she passes them on to other slaves who free themselves from the shackles that bind them. In an act that echoes an earlier recounting of a slave mutiny, the slaves take control of the ship and demand to make port in English territory where the slave trade was prohibited. When the slaves disembark, Madison discovers that he and his wife were aboard the same vessel.

The social conditions leading to the Haitian Revolution become the backdrop for "Ladies in Bed." This chapter is told from the perspective of Mathilda, an octoroon woman from a wealthy family who awaits the return of her beau, Jacques, from his studies in France. When Jacques returns to the colony, he marries a white French woman instead of Mathilda. Against her better judgment, Mathilda enters into an illicit romance with Jacques. She and Jacques's wife become pregnant at the same time. In order to improve appearances, Jacques arranges for his quadroon cousin, Gerard, to marry Mathilda in exchange for land; however, her family opposes the union because they desire to "improve the race" by marrying their daughter to a Frenchman.

Gerard begins to accept the ideas of a mulatto rights movement in Haiti, and as he becomes more militant, it becomes clear that he must end his marriage of convenience with Mathilda, particularly since news has spread about the arrangement. Jacques vehemently opposes rights for people of African descent, calling mulattoes "bastards, good for nothing, and traitors" (*MR* 136). Mathilda is wounded by his words against his own blood. When a mulatto rebellion breaks out, Gerard and his co-conspirators are captured by the French, tortured, and executed. In spite of reprisals by the French against free and enslaved blacks and mulattoes, a second uprising occurs among the slaves led by Buckman. The insurgent slaves begin killing the white colonists and setting free any blacks and mulattoes they find in bondage. The word "advanced" is repeated several times, accumulating resonance as the masses gather to ferociously destroy the oppressive colonial order in the name of freedom. The rebellious groups of blacks join forces with the mulattoes, and together they outnumber the French. A religious figure named Pierre-Baptiste, whom the slaves call "Father Yayah," instructs the black leader, Toussaint L'Overture, on how to command his army and lead his new nation.

From the events and personages of the Haitian Revolution, *A Message from Rosa* abruptly shifts to "maroon" figures and leaders of black movements of the nineteenth and twentieth centuries who are connected with the fictional Yayah peoples. The Afro-Cuban matron, Mariana Grajales, mother of the mulatto independence leader Antonio Maceo, is featured for her revolutionary inspiration for Afro-descendant freedom in the Americas. The Jamaican-born founder of the

Universal Negro Improvement Association (UNIA), Marcus Garvey, is featured as a Yayah descendant who is spurred by racism and the economic exploitation experienced by African descendants on the United Fruit Company plantations in Central America to create his movement of racial uplift. The narrative presents a vignette about the childhood of US civil rights leader Martin Luther King Jr. and his mother. The fictionalized young Martin questions the racial barriers and limitations imposed upon them by racist practices as the pair cross from the "white" section of the city to the "black" section of town where they reside. Although his mother insists that he control his urge to use the bathroom until they reach the black neighborhood, his need is so great he runs into a whites-only hotel, much to his mother's dismay. When he is chased away by vile insults, the journey home sparks more questions in the young Martin and a disquieting impulse for justice.

The chapter that follows the episode with the young Martin Luther King Jr. is followed by an incident that takes place in Europe. Telling his family's story, the narrator reveals that in Nazi Germany, Abby, the biracial child of a German mother and an African Yayah father, witnesses some of the brutal policies and practices of the Third Reich. She witnesses Jewish neighbors being forcibly removed from their homes and "disappeared." The racist rhetoric of the government places a wedge between the young woman and her best friend when she learns that she is not invited to her wedding because of her race. The Nazis launch a forced sterilization campaign for "undesirables" that includes peoples of African descent like Abby. The narrative takes a positive turn when years later Abby and her French African husband are expecting their first child and they discover that the operation never occurred thanks to her childhood friend Peter.

In the chapter titled "Rosa," the narrative moves back to the Americas with the fictionalization of the famous act of resistance by Rosa Parks on the evening of December 1, 1955. Parks refused to give in to the demands of bus driver James I. Blake, who ordered her to give up her seat on the bus to accommodate the white men who were standing. Present on the bus that famous evening is Sam, a black man who is an alcoholic vagrant who prefers to drink than to work. When Parks declines to leave her seat, Sam wants to tell her to just move to the back of the bus and not cause a disturbance. He goes to the pastor's house after witnessing Parks's humiliating arrest to tell him what he has just witnessed. The following Sunday, a sober Sam, who becomes active in the Montgomery bus boycott, attends church to hear the sermon of the young pastor, Martin Luther King Jr.

The last chapter of the novel, also titled "A Message from Rosa," reconnects the interwoven lives of the characters featured in the individual chapters to the original characters, Aba and Kwame. Aba, the maternal head of the Yayahs, still languishes with fatigue and frustration because the tree given to her by her father has yet to blossom as promised. She wonders what has happened to her sixteen children and the others from her village who the Europeans kidnapped and enslaved. Aba fears that she and Kwame may be the last of the Yayah, "The end of history. Because it is true, the tree never flourished. Her father's premonition—that blooming would signal better times, while serving as fuel to survival, had had no other practical consequence" (*MR* 176). She and Kwame wait to see if their descendants have paid attention to their ancestral memory and the spirit of *samamfo*. Kwame meditates: "All we wanted to know was whether or not the Ancestral Spirit of our clans had survived, creating new life in our Nation. It would have been nice to find out if they had kept our Spirit alive, building their homes as we did, living as living people should, without a mask to disguise emptiness" (*MR* 176). Kwame feels that this moment may mark the end of their lineage because their descendants have not affirmed their existence through active remembrance and return. He and Aba prepare themselves to go to sleep for eternity and enter oblivion where there will be no memory of them left on earth. Their intentions are interrupted by a young girl who arrives at the door of their home to deliver the message, "Miss Rosa asked me to tell Mama Aba that she will never again sit at the back of the bus" and that she and others came with the "African Diaspora League" (*MR* 176). Her startling arrival and announcement take Aba and Kwame by surprise and is followed by the sudden appearance of several children in the couple's yard who are all asking for Mamá Aba and passing on the same message from Rosa in different languages. Kwame and Aba's great-granddaughter, Aba Nzinga, lets out a shout, which was "an ancestral bellow, shaking the earth and imposing immediate silence" (*MR* 177). They are still remembered by their progeny, and neither their family lineage nor the spirit of the Yayah has died. With the arrival of all of these remembrances from their descendants, the tree that was long bare blooms as promised with a pledge for the continuance of the ancestral spirit of the Yayah and their spirit of resistance. The children of the Diaspora who have come with a message from Rosa surround the blooming tree, and Kwame observes, "As they gathered under the shadow of the blooming tree, I could see on their faces a million Yayah smiles" (*MR* 178). Across different epochs and geographic spaces the ancestors and the descendants unite at the tree of life to commemorate the essence of *samamfo* and the Yayahs' survival.

The Insurgent Power of the Spiritual: Afro-Realism, *Samamfo,* and Resistance

The three texts *La paz del pueblo*, *Kimbo*, and *A Message from Rosa / Un mensaje de Rosa* address many of the six elements of Afro-realism that Duncan outlines in his treatise, "Afro-realismo: Una dimension nueva de la literature latinoamericana": the restoration of the Afro-American voice through the use of Africanisms;

the vindication of the African symbolic memory; the informed restructuring of the historical memory of the African Diaspora; the reaffirmation of the concept of ancestral community; the adoption of an intrinsic perspective; the search and declaration of a black identity (n.p.). The three works also incorporate elements of orality into the multiperspective narratives, folklore, blackness as an identity, and African or Afro-Caribbean cultural traditions, as well as the concept of the Diaspora. However, all of these elements are linked by the interconnected core notions of spiritual and cultural resistance.

Paulette Ramsay describes the African-derived elements, manifestations of resistance and cultural marronage, as textual representations of literary marronage: "Cultural marronage has been used to describe the psychological level on which the African slaves resisted slavery through the preservation of the cultural forms which they brought with them to the New World" (1994, 32). In the context of literary marronage, works by some black writers present "the affirmation of their blackness and links with Africa through the highlighting of different aspects of the African heritage," which "demonstrates an important posture of resistance and defiance" (Ramsay 1994, 32). In the case of *La paz del pueblo*, *Kimbo*, and *A Message from Rosa*, the Ashanti-derived spiritual concept of *samamfo* is the source of resistance portrayed in these works. This idea falls within the realm of Afro-realism that, according to the author, "achieves an Africanizing subversion of language that falls back on mythical references that are up until now unpublished or marginal, such as Muntu, Samamfo, Ebiyiye, the vindication of the gods like Yemayá and the incorporation of elements of coastal English Creole" ("El Afro-realismo," 7). This statement emphasizes the important role of literary marronage, demonstrating that literature can be a means to explore the presence of religion and spirituality as representations of diasporic resistance.

Considering these notions of *samamfo* and resistance in *La paz del pueblo*, *Kimbo*, and *A Message from Rosa*, Duncan's work may be viewed not only as a Latin American literary counternarrative that addresses the voicelessness and invisibility of blackness in canonical texts, but also as part of the tradition of writing resistance in Caribbean literature. Duncan's work depicts the lives of Afro–West Indian immigrants and their descendants in Central America, the island nations of the Caribbean, and the role both locations have in the wider vision of the Diaspora. Central to these representations of spaces and cultures in *La paz del pueblo*, *Kimbo*, and *A Message from Rosa* is the insurgent power of the spiritual.

Spirituality is one of the central cultural features of universal humanity, but it is a particularly defining characteristic in the African Diaspora because of religious and spiritual traditions that have been at the heart of resistance movements against oppression. According to Ramsay, "It was to the religious beliefs and practises that the survival of the African slaves was most attributed, with the consequence that religion has been established as the most dominant component of the African heritage in the New World" (1994, 33). Revolts and other acts of resistance by enslaved Africans and their descendants were often spiritual or religious in nature, such as the slave rebellion in Haiti that was inspired by Boukman's voudou rites, the role of church deacon Paul Bogle in Jamaica's Morant Bay Rebellion, Nat Turner's religious visions that led to the insurrection in rural Virginia, and the spiritual leadership that guided the US civil rights movement. In Duncan's texts, *La paz del pueblo*, *Kimbo*, and *A Message from Rosa*, the spiritual and ancestral connection of *samamfo* is particularly notable because it extends the theme of resistance of Afro-descendants against systems of oppression through the representation of a diasporic adaptation of an African cosmological principle. By the use of this Afro-realist concept not only as a religious expression but also an expression of resistance, Duncan contributes to the rethinking of Diaspora as a fact that is not just historical but spiritual as well. With this conceptualization and application of *samamfo* in Duncan's work, there is an implicit notion that communication with the departed ancestors motivates the living to defy race-based and class-based systems of oppression.

In *La paz del pueblo*, *samamfo* is that ancestral element that Pedro Dull calls upon to resist the exploitation of workers by the banana company and challenge the false accusations against him. Pedro, who appears as a "forceful representative of the Afro-American revolutionary religious tradition" and as a messiah leading his people, symbolizes the Afrocentric mission of Marcus Garvey's Universal Negro Improvement Association to rise up against the forces of oppression. It is at this point in the narrative where Ian Smart observes the following:

> The pace of the final movement picks up, when the author reveals the true source of the strength with which Pedro resists oppression. . . . Pedro is a practitioner of the Pukumina religion (*pocomía*). He has been initiated into it by the same Mamá Bull who appears in the title story of the collection *La rebelión pocomía y otros relatos*. His very participation in the ritual represents an important step on the road to revolution, for he does it against the wishes of his mother, impelled by his evocation to service and conquering his own initial resistance to the call of *Cuminá*. . . . Under *Cuminá*'s influence his revolutionary consciousness develops; he sees the glories of the African past; he sees the need for justice in the neocolonial present. (Smart 1984, 54–55)

The elaborate and rhythmical religious rituals of *cuminá* (Kumina) "bring down" the spirits in order to guide the congregants whose bodies receive them during spiritual possession. The ancestral power of *cuminá* is also an expression of *sa-*

mamfo, whereby the ancestral spirits make contact with their living descendants. This ancestral power also is the source from which Pedro Dull draws his plans to organize a strike against the banana company and is the source of his resistance.

Kimbo heeds the advice of the ancestral voices that not only defend him against the false accusations about his involvement with the kidnapping of Don Barrigón but also guide him to face his accusers and reveal the truth about his innocence. The spiritual voices of the dead speaking from the realm of *samamfo* "intermingle with the living, participating in all discussions about Kimbo as if there were no difference between the living and the dead" (Ramsay 1994, 34). The ancestral voices of his mother and Mrs. Rob influence Kimbo's decision to return from the exile arranged for him by the kidnappers and explain his innocence and also influence members of the dominant culture—Kimbo's lawyer, his girlfriend, and Don Barrigón's unnamed wife—to believe in the power of the ancestral spirits of *samamfo*. The fact that the nonblack characters understand and accept the notion of communication with one's ancestors demonstrates that "the author seems to hint that belief in the ancestors is not an exclusively black belief, and should, therefore, not be so readily debased by non-blacks" (Ramsay 1994, 38).

In Duncan's *A Message from Rosa / Un mensaje de Rosa*, the elder ancestral spirits Aba and Kwame of the fictional Yayah are at the center of the redemptive return of their diasporic descendants. The progeny of the Yayah are also witnesses and participants in movements of resistance throughout the African Diaspora. *A Message from Rosa* reconfigures the Diaspora by looking at the mythical accomplishments of the ancestors of the Yayahs and demonstrates that wherever Afro-descendants are subjugated, they carry with them the spirit of their ancestral past and the spirit of resistance. The central focus on Africa and the ancestors, Aba and Kwame, is momentarily displaced by the Diaspora, which with its shifting chronologies and spaces, becomes the focus of the novel until the Diaspora "remembers" the ancestral spirits of *samamfo* and reconnects the Diaspora to its African origins.

The three texts recover the ancestral voice to address injustice in *La paz del pueblo* and *Kimbo*, and to reconfigure the idea of history in *A Message from Rosa*, by framing the fictionalized vignettes of historic acts of black resistance around the ancestral backdrop of the spiritual realm. Additionally, by making these ancestral voices heard in the three "novels of *samamfo*," the spiritual ancestors are given textual representation, an important component of Afro-realism. *Samamfo* provides a stable continuity within cultural ruptures, uprootedness, upheaval, and dispersal of peoples of African descent across the globe as a direct or indirect result of the transatlantic slave trade and European colonial projects in Africa and the Americas. Its power of resistance demonstrates that in the Americas in particular, the desire for freedom persisted among Afro-descendants who had an enormous capacity to challenge their circumstances. This resistance, which draws upon the ancestral power of *samamfo* in *La paz del pueblo*, *Kimbo,* and *A Message from Rosa*, also reveals that resistance is constructed as a fundamental expression of diasporic identity. Out of the complex and heterogeneous cultural groups who were enslaved by the Europeans and transported across the Atlantic emerge similar patterns of resistance to oppression through revolts, marronage, or the recreation and adaptation of African practices and traditions in a new environment. Whether individual or collective, Africans and their descendants used resistance to dismantle a system that was imposed upon them.

Duncan's use of the African-derived concept of *samamfo* corresponds with his own theory of Afro-realism, which serves as both cultural and literary marronage in accord with Ramsay's study. With the continuity of the living and the dead with *samamfo*, the lived experience of the departed spirits guides and protects their descendants in a collective ancestral continuum. *La paz del pueblo*, *Kimbo*, and *A Message from Rosa*, through this inclusion, not only centers on the denigrated culture of Afro-descendants in the Americas and the Diaspora, but also the texts themselves challenge the representation of blackness and Afro–West Indian culture in Costa Rican national literature. Other works by Duncan, such as "La Rebelión Pocomía," "Dos caminos," and his two earlier novels, *Hombres curtidos* and *Los cuatro espejos*, portray cultural aspects of both popular folk spirituality and official religious denominations. For example, in *Los cuatro espejos*, Charles McForbes's duality is expressed in what Ian Smart calls syncretism. As an Anglican pastor he is, "an upholder of the principles of the prestige European religion" but he also represents the Afro–West Indian folk spirituality of the community (Smart 1984, 53). Although it is not obvious, it may have been the ancestral calling of Clif Duke's grandfather from *samamfo* that brings the protagonist from his comfortable home in the Central Valley back to his origins in Limón Province in order to vindicate his deceased ancestor. While Afro-realist spirituality is found in all of Duncan's work, *La paz del pueblo*, *Kimbo,* and *A Message from Rosa* in particular expand the realm of the spiritual by putting the concept of *samamfo* at the center of texts' narrative discourses in order to emphasize the redemptive power of resistance gained through the insurgent power of the spiritual.

4
Dismantling the Myths
Final de calle and *El trepasolo*

Y no puedes hallar la calle que da a tu casa
—(And you can't find the street that leads you home; *Final de calle*)

The novel *Final de calle* (Dead-End Street, 1979 [1981]) and Duncan's only published dramatic text *El trepasolo* (The Lone Climber, 1993) present serious critiques of Costa Rican society by dismantling some of the myths of the nation. These two works, separated by almost fifteen years, are joined together in this study because they mark a departure from the author's previous work. Rather than center on the descendants of West Indians in Costa Rica, these works are both historical and cultural studies of Costa Rican society. They address themes of national identity and culture, particularly the myths of egalitarianism and democracy. *Final de calle* contends with the specific issues of democracy and the power of political fractions after the 1948 civil war and presents a "vision from below" that counters official versions of the conflict and its repercussions in Costa Rican society. *El trepasolo* portrays a more general examination of the subject of class mobility by unveiling the fallacy of social equality. Duncan offers a critical gaze at Costa Rica, exposing some of the fissures in the national discourse of equality and democracy.

Final de calle

In the 2004 presentation of Duncan's *Cuentos escogidos*, Costa Rican literary critic Albino Chacón calls *Final de calle* (1979 [1981]) "his [Duncan's] best known work . . . his book that is most reflective of the Central Valley and therefore the book that most clearly departs from the series of Afro-Caribbean literature" (Chacón 2006, n.p.). This is, however, one of Duncan's least studied works by scholars outside of Costa Rica. Although *Hombres curtidos*, *Los cuatro espejos*, and *La paz del pueblo* were lauded by critics and scholars, Chacón's assertion that *Final de calle* is Duncan's "best known work" perhaps holds true for Costa Rican national letters because it is the only novel in Duncan's oeuvre that does not have an explicit Afro–Costa Rican theme, nor does it feature the life and culture of Limón. It is the novel that Duncan submitted anonymously to disprove critics' charges that his writing had little aesthetic merit and was published simply because he is black. The novel was sent to the Editorial Costa Rica and won the esteemed Aquileo J. Echevarría National Prize in 1978.

Of the novels Duncan had published with the Editorial Costa Rica between the beginning of his career and the twenty-fifth anniversary of the publishing house (*Los cuatro espejos*, *La paz del pueblo*, *Final de calle*, *Kimbo*), *Final de calle* was selected for reprinting as part of its special commemorative collection of the texts that best represent the history of the press and national literature. Duncan admits that he was perplexed by the choice, since he is known for his treatment of Afro–Costa Rican themes in his work. Nevertheless, he was told by Costa Rican critic Víctor Julio Peralta that "*Final de calle* is more *ours* " ("*Final de calle* es más *nuestro*; Duncan 2004, "Afrorealista Manifesto" n.p., my emphasis). Although the text proved that an Afro–Costa Rican can write on issues of national history, it also demonstrates that the literary establishment in Costa Rica, exemplified by the venerated Editorial Costa Rica, does not see the themes of Afro–Costa Rican culture as part of "lo nuestro" ("that which is ours").

Final de calle takes up the topic of the aftereffects of the 1948 civil war, a defining moment in Costa Rica's contemporary history, from the point of view of its participants on both sides of the conflict. It is a novel published almost thirty years after the nation's civil war and is among the few novels of the time that deals with the conflict. The author's note at the beginning of the novel addresses some of the wounds the bloody conflict left: "*Final de calle* is above all a novel. It attempts to remain faithful to the events as they were told by its protagonists from the popular sector" (*FC* ix). In his efforts to "remain faithful to the events" and portray the popular voice, he also depicts "a people's history" or an intrahistory of the conflict and its aftermath. Intrahistory ("intrahistoria") is a term derived from the work of Spanish writer and philosopher Miguel de Unamuno (1864–1936) and describes the history of ordinary people, the soul of a nation, who do not appear in the official chronicles of great events. This is also very similar to the concept of "history from below," which seeks to center the story of the common women and men who typically occupy the margins of histories focused on the individual deeds of "great men." The characters presented in the novel are portrayed as everyday people—*liberacionistas-figueristas* (supporters of José María Figueres) and *calderonistas* (supporters of Rafael Angel Calderón Guardia)—and their reaction to the major historical episodes in the nation. The renowned Costa

Rican playwright Alberto Cañas comments in a review of the novel in the University of Costa Rica journal, *Káñina*, that "this novel by Quince Duncan is the most serious attempt made at this moment to bring the Costa Rican Revolution of 1948 to the field of literature" (Cañas 1981, 131). Cañas states that in 1979, Costa Ricans put some distance between themselves and the war, and he observes, "Perhaps this is because of a curious timidity worthy of study: each one of us is committed to the facts, participated in them, kept them near, and then not dare to write what could have been a passionate chronicle or a subjective approach to the events" (1981, 131).

The Historical Context of *Final de calle*

There are many complex factors leading to the eruption of the nation's civil war. Social, economic, and political tensions between the nation's Europeanized elite, composed of coffee-producing families and the merchant class, and the lower middle and working classes translated into limited social mobility and an increasing gap between the "haves" and "have-nots." These tensions were heightened in the aftermath of the 1929 crash of the stock market in the United States, which resonated in Costa Rica. As a nation dependent upon the export of coffee and bananas to the United States, the country's economy faced difficulties for much of the 1930s. However, beginning in 1940, "despite declining State revenues, an ambitious program of Social Reform was undertaken by the government of Rafael Ángel Calderón Guardia (1940–44)" (Molina and Palmer 2004, 88). Calderón Guardia was a physician and a devout Catholic who eschewed the secularism of his predecessors. He gained support for his ambitious social welfare and labor reform not only from the church, but also from the Partido Vanguardia Popular (Popular Vanguard Party), the nation's communist party. He added to the country's constitution the "Social Guarantees" (las Garantías Sociales), a collection of fifteen social entitlements that included social security and protections for rural and urban laborers.

As the popularity of the Social Guarantees grew among peasants and urban workers, the elite grew increasingly hostile toward the reforms, the involvement of the church in affairs of the state, and the troubling involvement of the communists. Calderón Guardia's successor, Teodoro Picado (1944–48), also encountered resistance by anti-Calderón forces through the opposition's accusations of electoral fraud and corruption. The opposition accused Picado's government of being a puppet of Calderón, who was said to be controlling the executive branch and the reform program from behind the scenes. Pressure from the opposition forced changes in Picado's government: "Picado's administration brought the social reforms to an end, split with the Communists and attempted to provide the opposition with guarantees in the new electoral code of 1946. But it was to no avail" (Molina and Palmer 2004, 91).

In 1948 the conservative candidate Otilio Ulate Blanco, who was supported by middle-class intellectuals of the Partido Social Demócrata (Social Democrat Party) and the oligarchy, defeated Calderón Guardia's attempt to run for a second presidential term. However, *calderonistas* (Calderón's supporters) in the legislature rejected the outcome and annulled the results in order to prevent Ulate from assuming the presidency. When negotiations failed between Calderón and Ulate, "a renegade member of the elite called José Figueres rose up in arms. The Civil War had begun" (Molina and Palmer 2004, 91). The conflict lasted a total of forty-four days with over two thousand casualties and ended with the political triumph of Figueres's National Liberation Army (Ejército de Liberación Nacional). Figueres, who had once been forced into exile by Calderón for protesting the government's policies, instead of turning the presidency over to Ulate, led an eighteen-month-long governing junta. The restructuring that took place under Figueres's junta included notable acts such as the abolition of the army, outlawing the Communist Party, the enfranchisement of women and Costa Rican–born blacks of West Indian descent, the establishment of a civil service system, the creation of schools, the nationalization of banks and utility companies, the construction of a national infrastructure, and the drafting of a new constitution. Figueres and his followers founded the National Liberation Party (Partido Liberación Nacional, PLN) in 1951, which would dominate much of the nation's post-1948 political landscape, "maintaining control of the state apparatus" (Villalobos 1982, 54).

Final de calle opens in the early 1970s, over twenty years after the revolution of 1948, but makes numerous references to the events surrounding the civil war and its aftermath through flashbacks. With more than twenty years between the beginning scene of the novel and the war, the political culture of the nation has been dominated by the PLN—fourteen years in the presidency and over twenty in the legislature. In spite of revolutionary reform, the novel reveals cracks in the promises of progress the civil war hoped to bring. The problems the rebel forces promised to eradicate and the reforms that were ushered in by the Second Republic eventually reveal that the same issues of nepotism, paternalism, patronization, bureaucracy, corruption, and the suppression of oppositional voices resurface in the democratic programs and progress pushed forward by the party that triumphed over the *calderonistas*. They condemned Calderón's alliance with the communists, who put forward the Garantías Sociales among other issues. Interestingly, the new governing junta after the civil war maintained those same reforms but rid the government of the dangers of communism by outlawing the Popular Vanguard Party. Ileana Villalobos concludes in her study that the power of the oligarchy remained the same before and after the war—changing allegiances and accommodating reforms, but maintaining the same political and economic power they have always had. She states:

> The model of development imposed by National Liberation (*Liberación Nacional*), that up until the moment the novel takes place had controlled the executive power for fourteen years and had always dominated the Congress, allowed for the continuing dominance of the oligarchy, however under new conditions. For example, by not abolishing the Social Guarantees of the Calderón government obligated the oligarchy to accept them. The party consolidated its influence in the middle class, allowed reforms to attenuate the exploitation of the popular sector, nationalized banking that facilitated the redistribution of credit, a relative purging of the electoral process that acquires autonomy relative to the government, etc. Facing the reality of two armed forces with the triumphant Liberationist Army and the defeated government military, Figueres abolished the army in Costa Rica, which reduced the possibility of the oligarchy turning back the process. (Villalobos 1982, 54).

Through Carlos López, the principal character in the novel, these contradictions of the revolution are explored. His personal political differences with the government for which he fought and the sacrifices he made for the Liberationist cause frame the novel. The same discord and tension open and close the novel, leading to the literal and figurative "dead-end street" of the title. The political friction that serves as a prelude to the 1948 war created a conflict that sharply divides not only the country but also Carlos and his father. This legacy causes great consternation in Carlos, who wonders if his participation in the conflict was worth it when his own son, Daniel, is erroneously depicted as a communist and an enemy of the state for exercising the democratic right to protest and free expression for which his father fought during the war.

Structure and Themes

In addition to featuring the intrahistorical perspectives of the people who participated in the civil war of 1948, the novel's stylistic features—the characteristic short sentences and fragments, flashbacks, self-questioning, descriptive passages, and rhythmic stops—lend credence to the interrogation of the political outcomes of the war and its reforms. The nine chapters of the novel, mostly in first person, alternate "between participatory (past) and interpretive (present) modes" (Martin-Ogunsola 2004, 142). The novel also features temporal shifts between Carlos López's dilemma in the early 1970s and memories of his revolutionary activities in 1948. *Final de calle* also contains shifts in narrative perspectives and memories of the conflict from the viewpoint of other characters. Martin-Ogunsola comments that "the framework for the novel, which consists of chapters 1, 2, 3 and 9, shows the interaction between Carlos and various officials," while "in chapters 4, 6, and 8—the inner core of the novel—Don Caliche recounts his role in the struggle to Doña Carmen" (Martin-Ogunsola 2004, 142). The remaining chapters, 5 and 7, present the perspective of Don Euclides Herrera, the aging oligarch "which interweaves with the external framework and inner core of the work" (Martin-Ogunsola 2004, 142). Although Carlos López dominates the novel's discourse, the voices of his father, Don Caliche, his father's third wife, Doña Carmen, and the aging oligarch Euclides Herrera reflect the complexity of not only the armed conflict but also the conditions that led to the rebellion and the reverberations of the war on the national psyche. Additionally, these multiple voices support the cyclical structure of the novel that reveals that the *calderonistas*, who were on the losing side of the war, feel the same way about the opposition as those in power, the *liberacionistas-figueristas*, once felt about the Calderón government. But the oligarchy and the tendencies of the political elite remain unchanged. The myriad of voices highlights the circularity of the political and social climate and the fragile illusion of democracy for those segments of the population left out of the nation's progress.

Plot. Businessman Carlos López, the novel's protagonist, turns on his car radio and hears two alarming pieces of news: there has been a clash between the police and "communist agitators" in Alajuela, and his son, Daniel López, is one of the protesters hospitalized from the confrontation. Ironically, this occurs on April 11, Juan Santamaría Day. This holiday commemorates the death of a young hero-soldier from Alajuela who in 1856 participated in the military conflict against the invading forces of the American mercenary, William Walker, and his eventual defeat at the Battle of Rivas. The elite class of Costa Rica "diffused a republican national identity based on the war of 1856–1857 and the sacrifice of Santamaría" (Molina and Palmer 2004, 67). On this day, important to Costa Rican national identity and democratic values, Daniel and his classmates are protesting the high cost of living and government corruption, including the sale of protected land for private development to foreign investors. The students are brutally attacked by plainclothes public security officers authorized by the government. In the hospital with missing teeth and broken ribs, Daniel dispels the news report that the group was communist and insists that it was nothing more than an effort by two student groups to restore the patriotic meaning of the holiday. Daniel states, "The national holiday has lost its meaning . . . they celebrate it with marches of the US Marines and Juan gave his life in the battle against William Walker, filibuster who was a member of the US Marines" (*FC* 3). Daniel also reveals that he and his fellow students were attacked by the Comandante, "Commander," dressed in civilian clothes who gave orders for other plainclothes officers to attack the crowd. Upon hearing this news and knowing that his comrade-in-arms, Salchicha Gutiérrez, is the country's security minister, Carlos feels a sense of betrayal:

> We had fought for a country free of people like Tavíos [a communist figure], and after all of these years I was not about to let us fall into the same situation that with so much energy we had condemned, fought, and eradicated until we created a new order for which many had sacrificed their lives.
>
> *Habíamos luchado por un país libre de Tavíos, y yo no estaba dispuesto a que, a la vuelta de los años fuésemos a caer en lo mismo que, con tanta energía habíamos condenado, combatido, y erradicado, hasta crear un orden nuevo por el cual muchos habían, de paso, dado sus vidas.* (*FC* 4)

Carlos López had participated in the armed struggle of 1948 on the side of the opposition Liberation forces against Calderón and Picado. At the time of the war, they had hoped to bring about economic reform and social advancement, including restoration of the democratic values the opposition felt were ignored by a government that was increasingly intolerant of oppositional voices. López begins to question the postwar Second Republic that was supposed to eradicate violations of human rights such as the violence Daniel and the other students encounter.

While the father expresses his doubts about the lofty goals of social democratic reform promised by the *liberacionistas* and the government he put his life at risk to form, his son, Daniel, painfully asks if the student protest was really an act of communist agitation:

> Pa . . . Is that communism? I mean, going around with signs against Vesco, corruption, the high cost of living, in defense of the Isla del Caño, denouncing the human rights violations in Nicaragua . . . Pa, is that communism?
>
> *—Papá . . . ¿Es eso comunismo? Quiero decir, eso de ir con pancartas contra Vesco, la corrupción, el alto costo de la vida, en defensa de la Isla del Caño, denunciando las violaciones de los derechos humanos en Nicaragua . . . eso . . . papá . . . ¿es comunismo?* (*FC* 4)

López has no response for his son and leaves the hospital "with his heart in the shape of a fist and his mind dazed in profound indignation." ("con el corazón hecho un puño y la mente aturdida en una profunda indignación." *FC* 4).

Carlos is troubled by what happened to Daniel and goes to meet with one of his old comrade-in-arms, Fermín Solano, who is the president's chief of staff. The pomp and circumstance of official meetings and flowery language is juxtaposed with the agony Carlos López experiences in his attempts to clear his son's name. They accuse his son of possessing marijuana in addition to being a communist agitator. He is still troubled by the words "agitator," remembering a time in the not too distant past when he, Fermín Solano, Salchicha Gutiérrez, and Don Pepe (José María Figueres) were also called agitators. The judicial system they fought to reform dispenses not justice but a labyrinthine bureaucracy that serves the interests of the governing politicians, not the citizens. The courts will not provide the solution for López and his son. Instead of receiving punishment for attacking his son and damaging his reputation by calling him a pot-smoking communist, the Comandante is merely transferred to another post. Fermín Solano and the Comandante Salchicha Gutiérrez were his old comrades-in-arms, but now these reformers who were so eager to forge a new society have embraced the status quo. The two men are "Ex-terrorists who now speak against terrorism" ("Son exterroristas que hablan ahora contra el terrorismo"; *FC* 47). Carlos López, expecting more respect and support from those with whom he shared the trenches and the dream of building a second republic under the social democratic banner of the *liberacionistas*, is in disbelief:

> And suddenly I had to ask the question—was this the same Fermín Solano? Was this the same man who crossed the mountain slopes that morning with me so that we could meet up with the rebels, to launch the battle for the Second Republic? The very same Fermín Solano!
>
> *Y de pronto hice la pregunta: ¿era el mismo Fermín Solano? ¿Era el mismo que cruzó conmigo los cerros aquella mañana para reunirnos con los alzados, para emprender la lucha por la Segunda República? ¡El mismo Fermín Solano!* (*FC* 8)

The war that he, Solano, and Gutiérrez participated in stimulates a flashback to 1948 as he remembers his attempt to leave his father, Don Caliche, and his stepmother, Doña Tomasa, who were both *calderonistas*. Don Caliche was a baker and a yucca grower who had political dealings with men of a similar mind, but more powerful and blue-blooded than Don Caliche. A life-altering schism occurs between father and son when the young Carlos López decides to join the rebel army and secretly goes to receive a recommendation letter from a local *liberacionista* destined for Don Pepe Figueres of the opposition Liberationist forces. Carlos's father, an ardent supporter of Calderón Guardia, discovers him. This discovery prompts an avalanche of insults and threats: "You're going off with those insurgents, right?" ("¿Te ibas con los sediciosos, no?" *FC* 11). He calls his son "a bastard" and a "bad son" for his political dissention. His father is a *mariachi*, the name given to supporters of President Calderón Guardia and his Social Guarantees, and Carlos has decided to throw his support to the National Liberation Army (Ejército de Liberación Nacional), the rebel troops led by José María Figueres, called "Don Pepe" by many. He crosses the mountains and joins with Fermín Solano, Salchicha Gutiérrez, and others who will fight with José María Figueres.

Remembering the idealistic goals he and his comrades once had as they fought against the corruption of the Calderón and Picado governments, he refuses to pay bribes to bureaucrats in order to restore his son's name. He reflects, "I crossed the mountains in order to end with arbitrariness and corruption, and I swore, I swore to Fermín Solano that I would make sure that they punish the Commander." ("Crucé los cerros para terminar con la arbitrariedad y la corrupción, y juré, le juré a Fermín Solano que haría que castigasen al Comandante." *FC* 12). López then confronts his former comrade, Salchicha Gutiérrez, who is now minister of security for the *liberacionista* government. As he faces his former comrade-in-arms, the one with whom he fought for democracy and a progressive nation, López defends his son against the accusations that he is a pot-smoking communist. Gutiérrez is only concerned about suppressing any problem of potential insurrection originating among the youth, who according to him, are not like they were in the past and says "they are the devil" ("son el Diablo") with drugs on one side and communism on the other (*FC* 13). Gutiérrez wants to maintain and protect the order of the government from the subversive voices of university students. Ironically, this is the government that in its glorious past based itself on the idealistic principles of young intellectuals who wanted to effect change and who were once seen by their opponents as subversives attempting to disrupt the *calderonista* order. Those revolutionary principles, once held with zeal by those who fought against the establishment, have now been forgotten by those who have assumed power, like Solano and Gutiérrez. Unsettled by his comrade's reactionary statements that reflect the perversion of revolutionary zeal, Carlos López repeats the phrase "because I had crossed the hills" ("porque yo había cruzado los cerros"), recalling a bygone era.

Daniel is released from the hospital and encourages his father not to take action because he believes it is pointless to fight against the force of an oligarchy that is bigger and more powerful than any ideals López once had in 1948. Daniel says to his father:

> Pa . . . what I'm going through is nothing. Two less teeth, a broken rib, and the absurd accusation that I'm a pothead. Everything is normal. It's part

> of the growing militarization of the country and it's a result of the influence that the dominant groups exercise in our country—the burgeoning international fascists.
>
> *Papá . . . lo mío no es nada. Dos dientes menos, una costilla fracturada, y la absurda acusación de que soy mariguana. Todo es normal. Forma parte de la creciente militarización del país. Y es producto de la influencia que ejerce sobre sectores dominantes de nuestro país la escalada fascista internacional.* (*FC* 19)

Hearing this from his son's mouth, over twenty years after López almost died for a democratic civil society, his frustration with the PLN government mounts. He does not want Daniel to resign himself to a fatalistic belief that there is nothing he can do to clear his name or vindicate the great injustice done to him and the other students protesting on Juan Santamaría Day.

The fourth chapter of the novel shifts the narrative perspective and is told from the point of view of Doña Carmen and Don Caliche. Carlos pays a visit to the home he once shared with his father and stepmother Doña Tomasa, Don Caliche's second wife. Doña Carmen, Don Caliche's third wife, was active in politics in the days before the revolution. Her deceased first husband, Salamón, a communist, and Don Caliche were good friends and supporters of Calderón and the Social Guarantees. Her insight reveals that Don Caliche suffered greatly at the hands of the opposition forces that Carlos joined. They tried to burn the bakery, the source of his livelihood, and made other threats. Nevertheless, she encourages Carlos and his father to reconcile.

After twenty years of estrangement, a desperate Carlos López communicates with his father, Don Caliche, to deliver the news of Daniel's beating and to enlist his help to clear Daniel's name. The elder López contacts an old political acquaintance, Euclides Herrera, a wealthy landowner whose family owns a newspaper. Carlos hopes that Don Caliche will be able to intervene on behalf of his grandson and persuade Don Euclides to publish an article that will defend Daniel and criticize the government's missteps with the student protestors. Don Caliche and the oligarch were *calderonista* political comrades, and now Carlos must turn to his political rivals in order to restore his son's honor. The political division of father and son is also emblematic of the rupture that occurred within the nation as lines of class allegiance were drawn. Don Caliche comments, when his son joined the Liberation Army, that he will never understand how "a son of workers, grandson of workers, destined to be the father of workers and grandfather of workers, was not on the side of workers." ("un hijo de trabajadores, nieto de trabajadores, destinado sin duda a ser padre de trabajadores y abuelo de trabajadores, no estaba al lado de los obreros." *FC* 48). In spite of the political rifts that alienated Carlos and Don Caliche, Carlos now needs his father's support to restore Daniel's innocence and his rights as a citizen of the nation that father and son both fought to protect, though from different sides of the political spectrum.

This newly formed father-son alliance kindles memories of the events leading up to the civil war. Don Caliche reflects on the political past that has contributed to the present. He recalls the Huelga de los Brazos Caídos (Strike of the Fallen Arms), a general sit-down strike supported by Otilio Ulate and his social democrat followers designed to pressure *calderonista* business owners. Don Caliche was shocked to read an appeal for the strike in the newspaper:

> His skin became goose pimpled when he read the devastating sentence from Don Otilio, so close to the nearing election: "If someone is *calderonista*, do not buy from them . . . do not sell to them."
>
> *Su piel se le puso de gallina al leer la lapidaria sentencia de don Otilio, tan cercana al proceso electoral que se avecinaba: si es calderonista, no le compre . . . no le venda.* (*FC* 44)

Although this strike was intended to present a social and economic blow to business owners, it had a chilling effect on small proprietors, like Don Caliche, who could not weather the loss of sales as could the wealthy *calderonistas*, like his comrade Don Euclides. Additionally, people who did not want to participate in the divisive political theater were unwittingly drawn into the fray by the strike. Those who had no political allegiance to the *calderonistas* or the *liberacionista* opposition stayed away from shops out of fear of repercussions of appearing to support Calderón by shopping. Many were afraid to make purchases, and many small business owners not affiliated with the political battle also closed their doors to their businesses out of fear. Don Caliche realizes the significant financial ramifications the strike will have not only on his financial well-being but on his patrons as well. He says to himself, "If we don't close . . . at the end of the strike we are not going to have a single customer" ("Si no cerramos . . . al final de la Huelga no vamos a tener ni un solo cliente"; *FC* 44), and he is struck by the contradictory actions of the owner of the corner store, who is a member of the Social Democrat opposition and political supporter of the strike. He has closed the front door of his business but continues to sell from the back. Don Caliche resents the strike:

> Don Caliche maintained that it was not a strike, while he looked at the baked loaves that had been on the shelves since early morning, it is the folly of three rich men. A stoppage of bankers and owners of big department stores.

> *Don Caliche sostenía que no era una huelga, mientras miraba el pan horneado desde buena mañana que permanecía en la estantería sin consumo, es una majadería de tres adinerados. Un paro de banqueros y dueños de grandes almacenes.* (*FC* 43)

A matter of class loyalty and politics divides Carlos and his father, Don Caliche. Although it appears to be a division between the workers and devout Catholics in support of Calderón and the wealthy who support the opposition, the oligarchy participated on both sides of the conflict.

Even Carlos López, after joining the *liberacionistas*, expresses his doubts about the class divisions of the two political bands. As a son of a farmer and small business owner, he muses at a meeting of Social Democrats: "The room was filled with middle-class dandies: a nucleus of young professionals, students, university professors" ("La sala estaba llena de 'glostoras': núcleo de profesionales jóvenes, estudiantes, profesores universitarios"), and says to himself, "I tried to be a dandy" ("Quisiste ser glostora"; *FC* 21). The term *glostora* is derived from the brand name of a hair gel marketed to men that featured elegantly coiffed and dressed men in its advertisements. The term also signifies one who uses lofty, bourgeois language that is beyond the comprehension of the common worker. Don Caliche is upset that after all he taught Carlos about life before Calderón's reforms (minimum wage, social welfare, education) that he chose to follow a different political path. Don Caliche feared the *liberacionistas* would not only end the corruption present in the president's administration, but also inadvertently deal a devastating blow to Calderón's reforms that benefited the poor. He tries to expel Carlos not only from the home but also from his concept of the nation. Because Carlos does not support the presidency of Calderón or Picado, he joins the "fatherless," illegitimate, and godless band of rebels.

Don Caliche also questions his own role in the political events around 1948. The elder López participates in a raid to catch suspected members of the opposition who conspire against the government. He captures Tuerto Solano, the brother of Carlos's comrade Fermín Solano, but also feels awkward about the situation:

> Don Caliche felt in that moment and later he would remember the sensation of the deep pain of his people burning in his veins. Why would a rural family be on the side of the rich? And why would he, the son of a farmer, grandson of a farmer, nothing more than a bread maker and descendant of rural settlers, be sent here to capture one of his own? He could not make them understand that the government, beyond its faults, was a good government; he could not because he himself did not have a clear picture.

> *Don Caliche sintió entonces y luego recordaría la sensación del dolor profundo de su pueblo ardiendo en sus venas. ¿Por qué una familia campesina estaba con la causa de los ricos? ¿Y por qué él, hijo de campesino, nieto de campesino, panadero no más, descendiente de colonos campesinos, era enviado a detener a uno de los suyos? No, no podía hacerles comprender que el gobierno, por encima de sus errores era un gobierno bueno; no podía, porque él mismo no tenía claro el cuadro.* (*FC* 55)

The portrait of Carlos trying to fit in among the educated bourgeois of the social democratic *glostoras* ("dandies") and that of his father questioning his complicity in government actions against those of his same class portrays the political and social intricacy of the 1948 civil war and its aftermath. Don Caliche doubts the sincerity of his government's support for the poor when poor people are fighting the oligarchy's war on opposite sides. Twenty years after the conflict, his son, Carlos, distrusts the government for which he fought that is now showing signs of complacency, corruption, incompetence, and the persistent and invisible power of the oligarchy.

The fifth chapter of *Final de calle* introduces the perspective of Euclides Herrera, an aging oligarch and former *calderonista*, who reflects on the past and future of his family and nation. His son, Frenillo, now manages the newspaper his father owns and is part of a new political generation. Don Euclides represents the traditional sector of Costa Rica with important last names and historic bloodlines: "Marín, Escalante, Guardia, and Tinoco. Those were the last names of those who forged the Republic, the names that made history." ("Marín y Escalante, Guardía y Tinoco. Eran los apellidos de los que forjaron la República, los nombres que habían hecho historia." *FC* 71). His ancestors and others of their class created the "European national culture" ("la cultura nacional-europea") that provides the base for Costa Rican "exceptionalism" that "has one foot in the country, collecting its fruits; the other in Paris with the mind wandering through the Champs-Élysées." ("Un pie en el campo, recogiendo de la tierra sus frutos; el otro en París, la mente vagando por los Campos Elísesos." *FC* 71). He remembers the great names of the past attached to the men who founded the republic based on lofty ideals and European philosophies. Looking back, Don Euclides yearns for the glorious past of the oligarchy.

The narrative then returns to Don Caliche's perspective on the war, recounting battles against the rebel forces of the National Liberation Army (*liberacionista*) under the leadership of Figueres. The war, although long passed, appears increasingly absurd to him. While he still identifies with the *mariachis* and still calls his son a bastard, he must come back to the present day to help his grandson Daniel, who was attacked by "ex-combatants in the name of who knows what" ("los excombatientes en nombre de no sé que"; *FC* 93). Carmen urges Don Caliche to put aside his differences for the moment and not to show the twenty years of hostility he has held against his son. In spite of Doña Carmen's pleas, Don Caliche finds it hard to forgive his son for the price he paid during the war. He lost his livelihood and family and the *liberacionistas* destroyed businesses, ruthlessly searched the houses of their opponents, and contributed to the death of his second wife. Don Caliche "has been defeated on all fronts and only the affection of Carmen seems to keep him alive" (Villalobos 1982, 60).

In the seventh chapter, the novel shifts to Don Euclides, who remembers the negotiations between presidential candidate Ulate (the opposition) and President Picado (*calderonistas*) when the election results were annulled. During a walk with his nurse, the doorplate bearing the name of Nino Menezes, a member of the national legislature, triggers memories of historical events. Menezes urged Picado not to give in to the demands and threats of the opposition, and Figueres's troops later killed the politician. Euclides is stunned to learn that the descendants of Menezes are *figueristas*, followers of the National Liberation Party (PLN). He yearns for the security of status that the past offered and is baffled to find that many of the traditional oligarchic families have joined the PLN, which controls the current government: "they're all Figueristas" ("todos son Figueristas"; *FC* 120). He comments on the past as he reminisces about the era before the war when he was a member of the elite:

> You have your memories of glorious times when upstanding men governed and honor had another meaning and was understood in politics, and the people were simple, and you didn't have the diabolical television that adorns your living room, and you had time to sleep with the housekeeper and go to the German Club with your wife.
>
> *Tienes tus remembranzas de tiempos gloriosos en que gobernaban hombres de bien, y el honor tenía otro sentido, y entendía la política, y el pueblo era más sencillo, y no tenías el diabólico televisor que hay adorna tu sala, y tenías tiempo para acostarte con la empleada, y acompañar a tu mujer al Club Alemán.* (*FC* 120)

Times have changed for Don Euclides and his class. He does not understand the political ambiguity and paradigm shifts that have occurred. When he expresses his desire to support his comrade, Don Caliche, by publishing Daniel's view of events on Juan Santamaría day in the newspaper, Don Euclides is dismayed by his son's reaction. Frenillo becomes part of a new elite class and the "representative of a pragmatic, executive, and managerial bourgeois" (Villalobos 1982, 60). His financial management of the newspaper involves dealings with the PLN and his father's former enemies—namely, Fermín Solano. Don Euclides is even more disquieted by the inability and unwillingness of Frenillo to publish Don Caliche's grandson's travails precisely because of those business dealings with government functionaries. The *enredos* (entanglements) with different sectors that troubled the Calderón government surface again under a different guise. Frenillo and those in his class position are in a "place of privilege in the emergent new order" (Villalobos 1982, 60); they share power with the enemies of their fathers and are reluctant to give it up. Don Euclides is a reminder of another time when, "They were different men, although they have the same last names." ("Eran otros hombres, aunque tuvieran los mismos nombres." *FC* 127). The changes are too much for Don Euclides to comprehend, which is a common thread uniting all of the characters of the novel. He decides to pass power on to Frenillo and instructs his son to call the lawyer and give him control of all of his business holdings: "I don't understand anything" ("No entiendo nada"; *FC* 127). In spite of Don Euclides's failure to comprehend the political changes that have occurred, his son, Frenillo, is very much connected to the need to preserve class interests. The only characters who maintain the same level of prosperity before and after the war are members of the Herrera family, who manage to maintain their financial position by aligning with both the *calderonistas* and the *figueristas/liberacionistas* (Villalobos 1982, 60).

The voice that appears after the narration of the aging oligarch is that of Doña Carmen, who represents the viewpoint of the pueblo (people) in language peppered with colloquial expressions. While Don Euclides represents the fiction of the *leyenda blanca* of Costa Rica's Europeanized national self-image, "the voice of Doña Carmen emerges from down under" as a subversive counterdiscourse (Martin-Ogunsola 2004, 143). Her body, which she describes as chocolate in comparison to that of her deceased first husband, problematizes the myth that Costa Rica was founded by white, Spanish, peace-loving peasants with a predilection for egalitarianism and democracy. Doña Carmen remembers the contrast between her skin color and her first husband's: "His skin was like cream and mine like chocolate" ("como cremita la piel de él, como chocolate el mío"; *FC* 129). She also expresses incomprehension over changing circumstances as she contemplates how Gustavo, the owner of the corner store, and former friend, has become an enemy. Earlier in the novel she interrogates her first husband's support of Calderón. Salamón was a communist and she questioned the involvement of Nicaragua's dictator, Somoza, on the side of Calderón who received troops from the country's neighbor to the north. Doña Carmen is a simple and illiterate woman who often self-deprecatingly says that she is stupid (*tonta*). However, from her lowly position, she speaks wisdom through "common sense, experience, and traditional wisdom" (Martin-Ogunsola 2004, 149).

In the last chapter of *Final de calle*, the novel is brought full circle. Carlos López reflects on the state that has emerged out of great struggle and affirms that his participation in the revolution was worth it. He asks Daniel's friends to join his efforts to sue the government and get justice for those innocent youth accused of being pot-smoking communists. However, he finds that the PLN-controlled government bureaucracy reaches into all areas of their lives, and "rocking the boat," threatens their personal lives. Elías is supportive but fearful of losing his scholarship to the state-run university. Nor does he want to jeopardize his family's opportunity to get better housing. Another boy, Franco, is also supportive but is afraid of losing his government job: "we public employees cannot get involved in politics and in a certain way what happened in Alajuela was political." ("los empleados públicos no podemos meternos en la política y en cierta forma eso de Alajuela era política." *FC* 135). The last boy, Tony, an Afro–Costa Rican, refuses to participate in spite of the blows he received because he does not want to cause harm to the political party that granted blacks the vote, and the party that his father, a former fighter in the war, helped to found. Daniel urges his father to give up the struggle to clear his name, but Don Carlos is struggling with his sacrifices to build a just government: "because I crossed the mountains so that you could be strong. . . . I crossed the mountains, dying, and watching my comrades die in their youth; I'm a bastard to my father, cursed by him." ("porque yo había cruzado los cerros para que vos fueras valiente. . . . Había cruzado los cerros, muriendo y viendo morir a mis compañeros de infancia; bastardo yo para mi padre, maldito por él." *FC* 136). Don Carlos discovers the futility of fighting his government when his son reveals that the state-funded physicians make no mention of the teeth that were knocked out or the ribs broken in the riot on Juan Santamaría Day. The Herrera family newspaper labels Daniel and his companions "communist agitators" and publishes the government's version of the protests because of the financial relationship between Frenillo Herrera and Fermín Solano, the president's chief of staff. The government has closed ranks to protect itself like the *liberacionista* army during the civil war.

Carlos wanders the streets thinking about what has happened and the promises the revolution hoped to deliver to this growing democracy. He questions himself, his decisions, and his role in the events that leave him now unable to protect his son and their family's name. He encounters difficulties finding his way home. He encircles aimlessly the rotunda near his house and then finds himself facing the wall between his property and the rotunda behind him. He has the option to scale the wall or find another path. He finds himself paralyzed at a dead-end street, a metaphor for the current political situation:

> Don Carlos finds himself in a world with no exit. The governing sector of *liberacionismo* is consolidated into power. Carlos's comrades-in-arms of yesterday are today's owners of large extensions of land, and controllers of the state apparatus. They have allied themselves with the oligarchy, like the Herreras, who if they do not dominate, evidently control to a certain point. Their relationship with power is such that they defend themselves amongst themselves, including resorting to lies and defamation against the son of an old comrade. To them, traditional values like *padrinazgo* (patronage) and truth are secondary. The only punishment that Don Carlos finally gains is the temporary transfer of the Comandante. (Villalobos 1982, 59)

Villalobos sees two possibilities for the protagonist: "return to the hills" to rebel against "the established order that he himself helped to create or admit that it is not worth it and accept the present situation" (Villalobos 1982, 58). It is ambiguous which path Carlos will adopt, if any.

The crisis that Carlos López faces at the end of the novel is the same dilemma he faces at the beginning—he has neither found justice for his son nor made an absolute determination of how to diminish the decadence of the PLN's well-cemented power. The protagonist's predicament in *Final de calle* reveals serious fractures in the government's post-1948 myth of progressive democracy and questions the construction of a national identity. Above all, the novel interrogates the official version of events by focusing on the intrahistorical perspective, or a "view from down under," as Martin-Ogunsola observes, of the people who participated in the complex and complicated struggle to form Costa Rica's Second Republic.

Analysis: Text as Intrahistory

According to Dellita Martin-Ogunsola, "*Dead End Street* [*Final de calle*] (1979) explores the implications of Costa Rica's one-sided perspective of history and articulates some unresolved sociopolitical issues that resurfaced in the aftermath of the 1948 civil war. Because that event was a watershed in the country's history, Duncan utilizes it to scrutinize and challenge the traditional notions of self, community, and polity" (Martin-Ogunsola 2004, 140). The one-sided history of the official discourse of the nation is challenged through the use of intrahistory in the narrative. Intrahistory concerns itself with lives of the everyday people and their participation, point of view, and reaction to the historical moment in which they live. When this perspective appears in literature, it often portrays the vision of those marginalized, neglected, or made invisible by the official discourse. Intrahistory presents the experience of the common person instead of heroic figures or events in the nation's official history. This point of view, rather, depicts the struggles of the ordinary people and their role in the formation of history.

Final de calle also unravels the carefully constructed image of the PLN and its role in postwar politics and society. As Ileana Villalobos states, the novel presents a "'disenchanted perspective' as a critical attitude toward the national reality in which ideological positions are questioned, adopting an attitude of attack, protest, criticism, and lack of trust in relation to the established order without presenting a way out or putting into doubt all of the proposed outcomes" (Villalobos 1982, 53). The novel makes an effort to present a counternarrative to the official history of the events of the war that have been defined by the founders of the Second Republic and members of the PLN. As Villalobos asserts, "*Final de calle* establishes itself against the official version of the historical events of Costa Rica in the 1940s . . . contrasting the historical project of the National Liberation Party (PLN) in relation to the initial objectives of the group that justified the ideological level of the 1948 Civil War" (1982, 53).

When the novel opens in the 1970s, there is great frustration with the PLN government when expectations of the reforms were not implemented or did not provide expected results (Brenes Molina 2003, 51). In spite of the incredible gains and the establishment of important social, educational, and cultural institutions, accusations of corruption and using political position to accommodate self-interests tarnished these accomplishments. Also as Villalobos comments, "For the first time since the Civil War, the defeated sectors dare to speak en masse, and publicly question the official version of the war" (1982, 55). By presenting the disillusioned viewpoint of Carlos López and his son Daniel, as well as forefronting the lingering questions in the minds of former *calderonistas*, the novel contests the narrative of progress and democracy official history presents. The inclusion of the popular perspective allows Doña Carmen and Don Caliche to recall political events from the *calderonista* perspective. They mention names like León Cortés and Otilio Ulate, as well as Calderón Guardia's strange alliance of stalwart Catholics and the Vanguardia Popular, Costa Rica's Communist Party, but it is their involvement and reaction to the events that is significant. They both discuss the complex and complicated events and political figures from the point of view of the people. Their re-visioning of Costa Rican history from a popular perspective is differentiated from that of the official version and fills in the ellipses left by the official version of the story. Martin-Ogunsola notes that Doña Carmen's inclusion in the narrative is particularly important because as a dark-skinned woman "her perspective is not found in any written accounts. Because history is written primarily by the conquerors, it had been difficult to perceive alternative points of view until the recovery and rescue of dissenting texts in the late twentieth century" (Martin-Ogunsola 2004, 156).

The family of Don Caliche and Carlos López illustrates the divide the civil war created between *calderonista* father and his *liberacionista* son, showing how the popular sector was divided with "some on the side of the government and others with the opposition. One side fought to defend the Social Guarantees that the opposition was supposedly going to suppress and the other in order to gain political and economic reform" (Martin-Ogunsola 2004, 156). Even within the ranks of the *liberacionista* opposition that later formed the government, there are expressions of frustration and disillusionment brought on by the failed democracy demonstrated by the mistreatment of Carlos's son, Daniel, and his classmates. Fitting with the theme of the novel, Carlos López, a supporter of the PLN and a former combatant in the Liberation Army, displays the "perspective of disenchantment" shared with many other *liberacionistas* of the time. Those who supported PLN begin to question their party and its failure to adhere to its principles and goals. Carlos López witnesses the public's distrust in the government, politicians who use their positions for personal gain, the hypocrisy of reformers, and the futility of the legal system. The protagonist is frustrated by the corruption, greed, and complacency of the government he sacrificed himself to construct.

Final de calle also challenges the official history of the war, which has been portrayed as the confrontation between two bands, the followers of Calderón Guardia and the followers of Ulate and Figueres. Villalobos clearly states: "*Final de calle* establishes itself against this version and seeks to demonstrate that in the background of what occurred was a battle in which the dominant economic sector did not divide, but rather worked on both sides to defend their own interests. The main objective of this sector, according to the novel, was to take the Popular Vanguard Party out of the political arena and succeed in the abolishment of the social laws promulgated by the Calderón government" (Villalobos 1982, 56). The novel illustrates that not only did the oligarchy maintain control of economic and political power by forming alliances with the *calderonistas* and the *liberacionistas*, but also that although this sector managed to remain in the background, it nevertheless dominated all the while.

In addition to questioning the war and its political outcomes through intrahistory, the text also interrogates the manipulation of events and the invention/creation of history by those in power whose vision of that same history differs from participants who are not its major protagonists. The dilemma that Carlos López faces at the beginning of the novel sets up the competing visions of history revealed by the perspective of Fermín Solano and Salchicha Gutiérrez, committed to protecting the image of the government, and the popular vision represented by Daniel. These dual points of view between the official and popular versions of events are related to the theme of intrahistory and are an attempt to give voice and space to points of view that would otherwise be obfuscated by the dominant discourse. Additionally, the official history is being shaped by those who manipulate the facts and written records, as in Daniel's case. The press is not independent of the government and therefore does not challenge its actions or explore its corruption because the very same owners of the press are entangled in deals with the politicians. When Fermín Herrera refuses to respect his father's request to help Don Caliche's grandson, it proves that the ruling classes are not loyal to political principles but rather economic interests. This also is demonstrated in the changing allegiances of the Menezes family, whose progenitor was a staunch Calderón supporter killed by followers of Figueres, who are now *liberacionistas*.

It is important to note that this supposedly "raceless" novel does insert Afrorealism into the narrative. The understated references to color and ethnicity contest one of the fictions of the official historical discourse of the nation, the *leyenda blanca*, the myth that Costa Rica is a homogenous nation founded by white Spanish Catholic peasants who did not enslave the Indians or blacks, thus producing an egalitarian and democratic society. Martin-Ogunsola comments that Duncan "demythologizes the white legend by juxtaposing various oral/unofficial and written/official perspectives of history and by subtly recasting Costa Rica's national identity in terms of its racially and ethnically diverse population" (2004, 140). For example, the historical Juan Santamaría, also referred to as "El Erizo" (the curly-haired one), was a mulatto with roots in the province of Guanacaste, a cattle-producing region that had a significant slave population during colonial times. During one of the flashbacks, Carlos remembers asking his father about the policy adopted by León Cortés in the 1930s to prohibit Afro–West Indian workers from accompanying the United Fruit Company from its operations in Limón to the Pacific coast. In this conversation Carlos is troubled to learn that all of the blacks already working there were fired, and he responds to Don Caliche's dismissive response with, "I'm not making up things Pa, they're injustices." ("No son inventos, papá: son injusticias." *FC* 22). Don Caliche accuses the black workers of stealing Costa Rican jobs. Here in the narrative, Carlos is demonstrating his awareness of racial inclusion and exclusion that justifies his alliance with the *liberacionistas*. Additionally, the implication that Doña Carmen has dark skin reveals the hidden colonial history of blackness in Costa Rica. The active but marginalized participation of not only Daniel's black classmate Tony in the protest in Alajuela on Juan Santamaría Day, and the reference to his father's participation in the conflict of 1948, also dispels the commonly held notion that Afro–Costa Ricans did not participate in the war.

This novel, which was chosen as a representative text of Costa Rica's finest narrative fiction, is a serious work that addresses the complexities of history and identity in Costa Rica. Duncan unveils hidden truths in this fictional account of the 1948 civil war. As Dellita Martin-Ogunsola states, "The anguish expressed by the ex-guerilla protagonist, Carlos López, echoes that of a nation that refuses to look at the discrepancies between its fantasy and its reality, and such blindness leads inevitably to a *final de calle*, or a dead-end street" (2004, 161). The intrahistory presented by the popular sector of the participants pulls back the cover that has obfuscated the multiple voices of the numerous classes and ethnicities that form the nation and challenges long-held myths that render these differences invisible. At the end of *Final de calle*, the nation faces a dead end like the protagonist, and it must decide how to reconcile these differences to make the figurative return home or mount a political revolution.

El trepasolo

The goal of dismantling the national myth of egalitarianism and democracy has a dramatic and tragic end in *El trepasolo*, Quince Duncan's only dramatic text.[1] It appeared in 1993 as part of the collection *Teatro para el teatro*. The issue of class and social injustice forms the principal theme of the dramatic text. The middle and upper classes fight to maintain their position and privileges and actively discourage the efforts of the *trepasolo*, or social climber, to improve his circumstances. The social criticism present in *El trepasolo* is a part of the critical process of questioning national myths and decolonization. Diana Taylor and other scholars of Latin American theater have affirmed that in the latter part of the twentieth century, "Latin American theatre has turned its power of investigation on itself, both to examine the role of cultural domination and to reshape itself into an instrument of decolonization" (1991, 1). Taylor identifies the years between 1965 and 1970 as significant moments in the theater of crisis, which is marked as a period of decolonization and transformation. It is "a 'turning point' between death and regeneration" that takes "into account both the *objective* systemic shifts or ruptures (revolution, military takeovers, wars, and civil wars) that affect the nature of society as a whole and the *subjective*, personal experience" (1991, 6). As part of this process, a society must confront its material conditions, social inequalities, and national myths. Through the dramatic text, Duncan conveys that the bourgeois establishment is neither inclusive nor just. *El trepasolo* presents troubling issues of class, inequality, power, and domination and criticizes the systems and institutions that perpetuate socioeconomic schisms in favor of the dominant class.

The theater of crisis seeks to "bring previously marginalized realities into focus" and "incorporates . . . the stories and voices of the victims and the downtrodden that have systematically been left out of official and cultural history" (Taylor 1991, 7). As such, social criticism is implicit in *El trepasolo* and demonstrates that in the prevailing ideologies of the Americas, the hemisphere is still in the process of decolonization. The unequal legacy of the dance of the colonizer and the colonized in the twentieth century is reflected in the power relationships constructed on a racialized social hierarchy and caste/class systems. Although *El trepasolo* does not coincide with the years Taylor assigns to the "theatre of crisis"—1965 to 1970, because Duncan's work occurs after the political upheaval in Central America—the work may be designated as such because it shares characteristics with other dramatic texts and it questions the ideologies of caste and class.

According to Terry Eagleton, ideology "signifies the way men live out their roles in class-society, the values, ideas, and images which tie them to their social functions and so prevent them from a true knowledge of society as a whole" (1976, 16–17). At its core, the theater of crisis is characterized by the use of oppositional forces to raise the level of consciousness in order to urge its members to question social constructs and institutions by exposing "the integrating theatricality of their social setting, the political shams and the rhetoric of legitimating that authority figures use to pacify the public and maintain illusions of justice and social well-being" (Taylor 1991, 20). This uncovers systems and institutions that perpetuate inequality in favor of the dominant class.

Instead of the traditional three acts, *El trepasolo* is divided into seven short acts that take place over several days in the modern living and dining rooms of businessman Don Emilio. The drama presumably takes place in an upper-middle-class neighborhood in the Central Valley where universal expectations are placed on class roles and social order. The tasteful luxurious furnishings with various electronic devices along with the imported whisky bottles, the servants, and decor items purchased from overseas travel indicate that the home belongs to a family of economic means. While recuperating at home after an unspecified illness and drinking coffee, Don Emilio is suddenly interrupted when his guard brings in a disheveled man at gunpoint. The guard tells his patron that he caught the stranger entering the vacant house next door with a small child. The shabbily dressed man, Carlos Morado, suggestive of the word *morar* (to inhabit or reside), claims he is the new owner of the house. Morado's unkempt, shabby appearance, his brusque and unrefined mannerisms, and his popular speech characterize him as working class and signify that he is better suited to work for the owner of the house rather than be the owner of property in an upper-middle-class area. Don Emilio believes that Morado is crazy at best and a criminal and corruptor of children at worst. Amid accusations of illegal entry, theft, and the corruption of a minor, the police take Carlos Morado away, but it is revealed that this man, a newspaper vendor, is not only the legitimate owner of the house, but he also has paid for the property, valued at over two million pesos, in cash. This prompts Don Emilio, who is concerned about his own financial well-being due to sizeable debt and building equity in his home, to begin his campaign to remove Carlos Morado from the house and use potential profits from the seizure and sale of the neighboring house to pay his own high-interest loan. Because Morado does not have the "look" or appropriate background of someone who belongs in the neighborhood, this allows Don Emilio to enlist the support of all the resources available to him as a member of the upper middle class—his personal contacts with the police, his friendship with a lawyer, knowledge of acquaintances at the municipality's assessor's office, the intimidation of his employees, and his relationship with an aspiring local politician—in order to protect his financial and class interests.

Don Emilio praises the engineer Lucas Sanch, a neighbor and aspiring politician with his own business, for pulling himself up by his bootstraps through education and hard work: "You see, people progress. The truth is that this is a country that gives opportunities to everyone." ("ya ve, la gente progresa. La verdad es que este es un país que le da oportunidad a todos." *TR* 32). He then actively campaigns to deny Carlos Morado's desires for economic progress and opportunity. Sanch has gained bourgeois acceptance by following the approved path of education and taking on the superficial trappings of the bourgeoisie—a late model car, European suits, a beautiful wife, and an elegant house in a desirable neighborhood with similarly situated neighbors, or "people like oneself" (*gente como uno*). Although Carlos Morado demonstrates the work ethic valued by the official discourse that mythologizes Costa Rica as a democratic, middle-class nation, this value is seen as a threat when displayed by a "social climber" who has come into wealth by winning the lottery and investing in an exclusive piece of property in order to ensure the financial future of his son.

When Morado refuses to sell his house to Don Emilio for more than what he paid for the property, Don Emilio destroys the Morado family's livelihood as newspaper vendors in the city by staging robberies, rapes, and assaults and placing the blame on Morado, his wife, and young son. Morado is also accused of being a kidnapper, an arms dealer, a communist, a narcotrafficker, and a terrorist. This forces the resilient Morado to rent out rooms in the large house and to use part of the property to raise chickens to generate income. Don Emilio and his upper-middle-class neighbors go to the national assembly to push for legislation to keep the popular rabble from the "gente decente" (good and decent people) of his neighborhood. He ironically declares to Sanch, "I have nothing to lose and if I had something to lose, I wouldn't care. What matters is order, hierarchy, the role assigned to every part of society." ("Yo no tengo nada que perder Ingeniero y si tuviera algo que perder no me importaría. Lo que importa es el orden, la jerarquía, el funcionamiento acuerdo de cada una de las partes de la sociedad." *TR* 74). He in fact does have much to lose—his class position, his name and reputation, and his economic security that depends on situating Morado and those like him in a position of inferiority.

At the conclusion of the drama, Don Emilio and Sanch rest comfortably believing that they have been successful in their effort to drive Carlos Morado from the neighborhood when explosions are heard. Morado bursts in calling Don Emilio and his company "rats." He demands the two million pesos he paid for his house from Don Emilio and makes a tearful statement saying that the house was a sure investment, and "It was a way to make a rise to pull my own bootstraps. On my own, without the help of no one else but Papa God. It was a question of keep on working, keep giving work to the three of us." ("Era una manera de trepar, de trepar solo. Uno solito, sin la ayuda de nadie más que de Tatica Dios. Era una cuestión de seguir breteando, seguirle dando trabajo a los tres." *TR* 84–85). The house symbolizes a chance to move up the social and economic ladder by owning a nice house in an area where they would not be harassed by their less fortunate neighbors for handouts. He made the move to protect his family, not ruin them. Police officials then come and take Morado away and we learn through Don Emilio's maid that Morado's son died in the explosion. Her last words to her patron, Don Emilio are, "You are an assassin rat. A dirty assassin rat!" ("Usted es una rata asesina. ¡Una maldita rata asesina!" *TR* 85).

In *El trepasolo* a marginalized group is transformed into a grotesque Other that must be destroyed, particularly when the group challenges the prevailing ideology. As Taylor states, "Aside from the imposition of centralized, vigilant order . . . societies in crisis also set in motion a mechanism of exclusion; they invent differences and convert members of society into grotesque and apparently threatening others" (Taylor 1991, 58). The death of the innocent—Carlos Morado's son—that closes the work is startling. In the theater of crisis marked by oppression and violence, symbolically "the many die to secure the stability and harmony of the few. Moreover, the deaths are not portrayed as morally uplifting, aesthetically beautiful, or cosmically inevitable; they could have and should have been avoided" (Taylor 1991, 8). The tragic outcome at the end of the play depicts an act of violence that moves the reader or public emotionally and call attention to the disconnect between the dominant ideologies of race, class, and caste and the fallacy of their "naturalness" for the socially or economically marginalized.

In comparison to *Hotel de vagabundos* (1955), a dramatic work by Afro-Colombian writer Manuel Zapata Olivella, Quince Duncan's is not as revolutionary, largely because of the era during which the text was written and the political history of Costa Rica. While Duncan does not add the dimension of race in *El trepasolo*, he does however, examine the unrealizable desire of the "social climber" to transcend the rigid social order and limits of class in Costa Rican society that constitute an enduring legacy of colonialism.

Although challenges to the dominant order are met with violence and death, *El trepasolo* questions the permanence of what Louis Althusser defines as "a representation of the imaginary relationship of individuals to their real conditions of existence" (2001, 109). Quince Duncan expresses sharp criticism of the socioeconomic structures in democratic society, principally criticism of the ideologies and systems that sustain inequality. *El trepasolo* challenges the myth of upward social mobility in a free and democratic society by exposing a firmly rooted social order that places the cultural and economic power in the upper class and denigrates the working class, particularly when the latter attempts to enter the middle class. The dramatic text presents the vision and voice of a character who has been marginalized because of social class and signals the desire for inclusion over exclusion for all members of society.

Duncan, who Costa Rican writer and critic Albino Chacón calls "a writer who makes black culture visible in Costa Rican history," also has produced texts that do not exclusively focus on Afro–Costa Rican culture or racism. Nevertheless, *Final de calle* and *El trepasolo* continue Duncan's fictional project of addressing the official discourse that has produced a "strong ethnocentric character of the Costa Rican myth of nationality and democracy" that are very much a part of the contemporary national imaginary (Chacón 2006, n.p.). Both texts at their core are about Costa Rican national identity and question official discourse. *Final de calle* and *El trepasolo* demythologize the image of Costa Rica as a middle-class, peaceful, democratic, ethnically and ideologically homogenous state. In *Final de calle*, the post-1948 events reveal some open wounds still festering in society—namely, class differences that were clear before and during the revolution but that have since been smoothed over by middle-class illusions and the elevation of the peasant as the mythological founder of the democratic state, an image that we see challenged in *El trepasolo*.

Conclusions

At the book presentation for Quince Duncan's *Cuentos escogidos* (2004), an anthology of the author's short fiction, held on August 31, 2004, at Costa Rica's National Museum, literary critic and president of the Editorial Costa Rica, Albino Chacón Gutiérrez, made a series of accurate observations that are not often heard at public events. Chacón opened his presentation by openly declaring, "Costa Rican society is quite strange, paradoxical and one could even consider it unsettling due to the series of myths that have so effectively constructed and even now continue constructing the knots of its discourse of identity" (Chacón 2006, n.p.). Many of these knots of Costa Rica's national discourse of identity relate to the *leyenda blanca* (white legend), the nation's foundational myth that has its origins during independence in the nineteenth century. This myth posits the often-repeated assertion that "Costa Rica was a country of peasants, owners of small parcels of land. In Costa Rica, there were no slaves or servants; all were persons whose worth was in their quality of human beings" (Monge Alfaro 1966, 129). This often-perpetuated myth also asserts that this pacific peasant class was not only of Spanish origin, but also, because of the absence of plantation slavery that in many Spanish colonies depended on a massive labor force of black and indigenous slaves, the Costa Rican people, developed an egalitarian society that would serve as the base for its contemporary democracy.

The African slaves and indigenous peoples who historically contributed much to the colonial history of Costa Rica had to be discursively erased. To address their presence in early Costa Rica historiography would signal the existence of strict economic, social, and racial hierarchies, and thus impugn the saliency of Costa Rica's national identity as a white nation of poor peasants with agricultural roots firmly planted in the fertile Central Valley. This myth leaves no room for the historical presence of black, mulatto, indigenous, or mestizo populations who were nevertheless present from the conquest to independence. This myth also leaves no room for the inclusion of the thousands of immigrants of Afro–West Indian and Chinese origin who contributed to the construction of the nation's infrastructure and place in the global economy during the postindependence years. This myth makes its nonwhite and nonmestizo citizens invisible, "foreign," "folkloric," or somehow separate from the rest of the *Tico*-nation.

When Quince Duncan emerges as a third-generation, Costa Rican–born writer of Afro–West Indian descent in the late 1960s, his very presence marks the beginning of the difficult process of dismantling the *leyenda blanca* and making more visible the history, culture, and the citizenship of Afro–Costa Ricans with West Indian roots. As the first Afro–Costa Rican novelist to represent the fictional lives of people of West Indian descent in Limón Province, in the Central Valley, and beyond, Quince Duncan and his work continue to stand as anomalies in Costa Rican national literature. At the beginning of the twenty-first century, he remains the only novelist of Afro–West Indian roots to publish in Costa Rica.[1] His work remains significant, not only because of his unique position in Costa Rican letters, but also because of the introduction and incorporation of Afro–Costa Rican identities and cultures from an "insider's" point of view. According to Chacón, "While expanding the horizons of the Costa Rican literary canon, he [Duncan] expanded the same horizons of who we are, of how we identify and conceive of ourselves. Beginning with *Una canción en la madrugada*, to *La Rebelión Pocomía*, *Los cuatro espejos*, *La paz del pueblo*, and so many other texts by Quince Duncan, Costa Rican society and culture will never be the same" (Chacón 2006, n.p.). From his first collection of short stories published by Editorial Costa Rica in 1970, *Una canción en la madrugada*, through his publication of *A Message from Rosa / Un mensaje de Rosa* and *El pueblo afrodescendiente: Diálogos con el abuelo Juan Bautista Yayah*, he has placed the black experience in Costa Rica, Central America, and the Diaspora at the center of his work.

Throughout the author's work, there are three key elements that unite the diverse themes of Quince Duncan's prose fiction: (1) exploration of issues of ethnic, cultural, and national identity; (2) intrahistory or "a vision from below"; and (3) techniques and narrative strategies of the new novel. The fragmented, nonlinear narratives with their multiple and shifting perspectives and points of view reflect the themes of ethnic, cultural, and national identity that appear in his texts. Donald Gordon comments that Duncan presents "the great themes of our century: the absurdity of the world, interior solitude, and burden of time find themselves present in the technique that incorporates the disintegration of time, using flashbacks, interior monologues, with a rich and elegant vocabulary, and stylistic resources like the simile and the metaphor" (Gordon 1989, 14–15). The voices that surface in his prose not only face dilemmas and crises that lead them to question their identity, but they also engage with questioning the construction and stability of their multiple identities as Costa Rican, as Afro–Costa Rican, as an Afro-descendant, as a man or woman. The voices of these different characters and perspectives also present, as Dellita Martin-Ogunsola notes in her study of Doña Carmen in *Final de calle*, the "voices from under," the voices of those left out of the national imaginary because they are made invisible by the *leyenda blanca*, marginalized because of their Afro-descendant origins, or because they are voices of dissent that openly challenge these myths.

One of Duncan's most significant contributions to the literary examination of identity is the articulation of the concept of *afrorealismo* (Afro-realism). By center-staging the presence, history, memory, ancestral spirituality, and experience of the African Diaspora in the Americas, Duncan gives voice to an authentic black presence, not some exotic or imagined depictions of blackness. He provides a counternarrative to the *negrista* representations of blackness, which is an extension of the *civilización-barbarie* dichotomy "inherited from the colonial caste system, strengthened and re-launched by social Darwinism that cultivated the creole elites, and still exists in our times" (Duncan 2005, "El afrorealismo" n.p.). Duncan also takes to task the Euro-centrism present not only in his own country but also throughout the Americas. By focusing on themes primarily related to Afro-descendants and his six elements of Afro-realism, the author calls attention to Costa Rica's national myths (equality, democracy, ethnic homogeneity) and the historical and cultural exclusion of blacks from Costa Rica's national culture. Like his contemporary, Eulalia Bernard, attention is drawn to the disparity between the desire to belong and the reality of exclusion.

Additionally, Duncan's writing calls attention to the process of "cultural hybridization" that occurs as successive generations of Afro–Costa Ricans of West Indian descent embrace more elements and values of the Costa Rican dominant culture and retain fewer of those inherited from their West Indian immigrant forebears. The novels *Hombres curtidos* and *Los cuatro espejos* in particular display a shifting sense of identity, fitting Stuart Hall's assertion that identity is not a fixed or stable entity, but rather transforms and adapts over time according to historical and cultural circumstances. In the two aforementioned novels, ethnic, cultural, and national identity are examined in great depth. With *Final de calle*, the most "Costa Rican" of Duncan's texts, he questions the meaning of Costa Ricanness by looking at the discordant and dissenting views of the 1948 civil war. *A Message from Rosa / Un mensaje de Rosa*, one of the author's latest works, forms a transnational, diasporic vision of blackness that is unified by a collective struggle of resistance to oppression and invisibility across borders of time and space.

Albino Chacón's observation of the Costa Rican cultural environment acknowledges that although several changes have occurred, the old myths remain. Costa Rica now looks to embrace new concepts of multiculturalism and diversity that "seek to contradict the hegemonic idea of racial, cultural and social homogeneity of Costa Rican society and show its multiple, even conflictive character." Chacón asserts the need for the nation to be more realistic in its approach "and mystify less the concepts that we like to embrace so much of a pluralistic society that is open and tolerant. In reality, the Costa Rican cultural history has never been pluralist, open, nor tolerant" (Chacón 2006, n.p.). Chacón eschews the possibility of recreating a more modern form of the *leyenda blanca* by inventing new myths of an open, tolerant, and pluralistic society.

Duncan has played a major role in contesting the myths of Costa Rica as a white nation founded by democratic and peace-loving Spanish peasants, and that it is an open, tolerant, and pluralistic society. Duncan's prose fiction, which attracted increased attention in the 1970s, and Eulalia Bernard's poetry of the 1980s, brought Afro–Costa Rican themes into the limelight and rekindled interest in earlier black writers like Dolores Joseph and Alderman Johnson Roden and interest in newer voices in poetry like Prudence Bellamy, Marcia Reid, Shirley Campbell, and Delia McDonald.

The critical attention gained by Duncan's entrée into Costa Rican literature—with the publication of *Una canción en la madrugada* by a leading publishing house, the Editorial Costa Rica in 1970—launched the literary challenge to the myths, old and new. Duncan's novels, short stories, and essays collectively tell the history of people of Afro–West Indian descent in Costa Rica and Central America from the perspective of contract laborers who struggled to ensure that their descendants be recognized as citizens in the country of their birth. The author's body of work attempts to write the story of Afro-descendants into the literary canon of Costa Rica by presenting legends and stories of Limón Province that were once told by the enslaved Ashanti in the Caribbean and passed on by West Indian immigrants on United Fruit plantations, tales that introduce the complicated themes of language, Afro-realism, identity, citizenship, belonging, and cultural exile. As the country's first and only novelist to date of Afro–West Indian descent, Duncan provides an important point of view on the historical and social construction of Afro–Costa Rican identity that is still clamoring for visibility and also to be considered an integral part of the nation.

Notes

Introduction

1. Although there may have been writers of African descent in Limón before the publication of Duncan's first work, *El pozo y una carta* (1969), Duncan is often identified as the first Afro–Costa Rican writer because he has reached a large audience by publishing in Spanish. For additional information on English language authors from Limón, consult my *Place, Language, and Identity in Afro–Costa Rican Literature* and "Alderman Johnson Roden: Reconstruyendo su aporte en la literature afrocostarricense" by Karla Araya Araya.

2. "Afro–West Indian" is used in the text to refer primarily to immigrants of African descent who arrived from the islands of the British Caribbean and their descendants in Costa Rica before the 1950s, when greater numbers of Afro–West Indians became naturalized Costa Rican citizens. The usage of "Afro–West Indian" marks not only how Costa Rica viewed the population but also the gradual loss of individual island identities (Jamaican, Barbadian, St. Lucian) over time. The terms "Afro–West Indian," "black West Indian," and "West Indian black" will be used interchangeably in this study.

3. Several historical studies by Carlos Meléndez and Quince Duncan, Lowell Gudmundson, Rina Cáceres, Mauricio Meléndez Obando and Tatiana Lobo, Oscar Aguilar Bulgarelli, and Irene Alfaro Aguilar have challenged this view; these writers catalog the extent of African slavery during the colonial period. Slaves of African descent and their descendants during the colonial period and into independence were subsumed by the mixed-race (mestizo), Indo-Hispanic population either through miscegenation or legal categorization, giving the impression that blacks "disappeared" until the large-scale arrival of Afro–West Indian laborers during the late nineteenth and early twentieth centuries.

4. The law resulted from negotiations of the banana contract between the Costa Rican government and the United Fruit Company. These negotiations occurred during a major strike against United Fruit by Hispanic workers. Most West Indian workers did not participate "because they did not want trouble" (Harpelle 2001, 84).

5. A few Afro–West Indian families did settle in San José and other parts of the Central Valley. According to Carlos Meléndez, "there have always been blacks—a few perhaps, but tolerated by our authorities—in San José for example" (Meléndez and Duncan 1993, 88).

6. Unless otherwise noted, the translations are mine.

7. See Diana Senior Angulo's *Ciudadanía afrocostarricense: El gran scenario comprendido entre 1927 y 1963* (2011) and Ronald Harpelle's *The West Indians of Costa Rica: Race, Class, and the Integration of an Ethnic Minority* (2001) for detailed historical examinations of the path toward citizenship for Costa Ricans of West Indian descent.

8. Duncan was active in the formation and leadership of the center-left party, Partido de Acción Ciudadana (PAC) (Citizen's Action Party), a party that has notably disrupted the authority of the country's two leading political parties. The center-left Partido Liberación Nacional (PLN) (National Liberation Party) and the center-right Partido de la Unidad Social Cristiana (PUSC) (Social Christian Unity Party) have dominated political life in the country since the end of the 1948 civil war. The electorate's growing frustration with corruption and deepening social problems have led to PAC's success. In 2002, PAC's presidential candidate, Ottón Solís (a former member of PLN) forced an unprecedented runoff election between the major parties. Solís was PAC's candidate in the 2006 elections and was narrowly defeated by PLN's Óscar Arias by 18,000 votes (1.1% of the votes). This was a surprising challenge to Arias, who served as president from 1986 to 1990, and again from 2006 to 2010, and won the Nobel Peace Prize in 1987 for his efforts to broker a peace agreement to end devastating conflict and civil wars in Guatemala, Nicaragua, and El Salvador. In 2013, Quince Duncan was in the running to be the president of PAC.

9. "Anansi" is the Ashanti word for "spider." During the slave trade, many of the Africans brought to Jamaica were of Ashanti origin (present-day Ghana).

10. Fuentes's Mexico is haunted by the legacy of revolution and the massacre of protesting students on the eve of the 1968 Olympic games in the capital; García Márquez's Colombia is forever scarred with "la violencia" and its aftermath; Vargas Llosa's Peru is engulfed in government corruption and persistent inequalities; Cortázar and Cabrera Infante are forced into exile in Europe by dictatorships. Without a military, Costa Rica never experienced such political turmoil. Its last dictatorship occurred in the nineteenth century, and democratic normalcy was quickly restored in the five-week-long 1948 civil war with unencumbered political succession, prevailing anticommunist ideology, bourgeois growth, and close ties with the United States.

11. As the keynote speaker, Duncan addressed the College Language Association (CLA) annual convention in April 2004 with "The *Afrorealista* Manifesto." He also presented a version of the lecture, "El afrorealismo: Una dimensión nueva de la literatura latinoamericana," at the VII Congreso Centroamericano de Historia later that year in July 2004 in Honduras on a scholarly panel on literature and history. The lecture has been published in the January–June 2005 volume of the electronic journal *Istmo*, "El Afrorealismo: Una dimensión nueva de la literatura latinoamericana." http://istmo.denison.edu/n10/articulos/afrorealismo.html, accessed April 10, 2013.

12. *Muntu*, a Bantu word Afro-Colombian writer Manuel Zapata Olivella frequently uses, and *samamfo*, an Ashanti term that appears in much of Duncan's work, are terms

that describe the coexistence of the living, the not-yet-born, and the ancestors. *Ebe yiye* is a Twi expression Afro-Panamanian writer Carlos Guillermo Wilson (a.k.a. Cubena) uses that affirms that the "future will be better." *Yemayá* is the Yoruba goddess of motherhood and oceans.

13. Dellita Martin-Ogunsola published translations of Duncan's *Canción en la madrugada* and *Rebelión Pocomía* in *The Best Short Stories of Quince Duncan / Las mejores historias de Quince Duncan* (San José: Editorial Costa Rica, 1995).

Chapter 1

1. The English titles for the short stories from *Una canción en la madrugada* and *La Rebelión Pocomía* are from Dellita Martin-Ogunsola's translations in *The Best Short Stories of Quince Duncan / Las mejores historias de Quince Duncan* (San José: Editorial Costa Rica, 1995). Unless otherwise noted, the English translations are from Martin-Ogunsola and quotations from her text will be cited parenthetically.

2. In *El negro en Costa Rica*, a historical anthology by Carlos Meléndez and Quince Duncan, Duncan observes various cultural differences between the West Indian and the "criollo" (mestizo Costa Rican) during the early years of the railroad construction and banana plantation. He writes of this period: "The blacks construct their homes on tall posts (African heritage) in order to avoid the problem of animals and of humidity. They polish their floors. To spit on the floors of the house was considered one of the worst offenses. The creoles build their homes flush with the ground, their 'floors' are of earth, they spit on the floors of his house without inhibitions" (Meléndez and Duncan 1993, 102).

3. See Martin-Ogunsola's "Translation as a Poetic Experience/Experiment: The Short Fiction of Quince Duncan" (1991) and her *Eve/Hagar Paradigm in the Fiction of Quince Duncan* (2004, 36–41) for her detailed analysis of the shifting linguistic levels in the text, as well as Ruby's manipulation of discourse.

4. Also known as Cuminá/Kumina, an Afro-Christian practice that relies heavily on spirit possession and the intercession of the ancestors. In Costa Rica, the religious practice is also derisively called Cocomía, and Pocomania. Ronald Harpelle notes in *West Indians of Costa Rica* that "both terms reflect an effort to label pocomia insane and potentially violent" (2001, 207n4). Although the religion is commonly known as Pocomania, as well as Pukumina in Jamaica, Paulette Ramsay notes that Duncan's use of "Pocomía" is an act of "literary marronage," seeing the linguistic alteration as "the author's method of overthrowing the racist attitude with which the Afro-derived form has been viewed, even before it was transplanted to Costa Rica" (Ramsay 1994, 33). The story is an effort to recover the presence of the religious and vindicate its significance for its practitioners, in spite of official efforts to erase its practice.

5. In *El negro en Costa Rica*, Duncan states that Minor Cooper Keith, the American businessman responsible for the contract to construct the railroad and the creation of the United Fruit Company, "passed for British" and gained the loyalty of the West Indian workers. Their loyalty was such that "many times he was unable to pay their salaries, with a simple and frank explanation of his situation, the workers continued without pay for

weeks, and at one time for eight months. They believed in him and his word" (Meléndez and Duncan 1993, 104). See also Harpelle (2001) and Chomsky (1994 and 1996).

6. "Intrahistory" addresses the history of the common people, which is of particular importance when the official history of Costa Rica excludes the contributions of West Indian immigrants.

7. Other sources, such as Ronald Harpelle (2001) and Aviva Chomsky (1996), do not specifically document the occurrence of the Pocomía Rebellion. However, they do record attacks on Afro-Christian Revivalist cults such as Pocomía, which coincide with the 1910 St. Kitts strike and hostility toward these religious groups by middle-class West Indians, United Fruit, and the national government.

8. For additional information on A. J. Roden, see Gordon (1983) and Araya Araya (2012).

9. Kumasi is the modern capital of the Ashanti region in Ghana, known for its large deposits of gold, and the name of the ancient Ashanti kingdom. There are references in the story to the celebrated king, Okomfo, the legendary Golden Stool, which represents the soul of the Ashanti and must never touch the ground, as well as the Royal Palace of the Ashanti. The Ashanti presented strong resistance to the British presence in their territory, and four wars were waged between 1826 and 1896. Kumasi, once the capital of the Ashanti Confederacy, finally fell into control of the British at the end of the nineteenth century. The Royal Palace of Kumasi was destroyed during the fourth Anglo-Ashanti war.

10. Martin-Ogunsola in *Eve/Hagar* notes that the name Lucy may be symbolic in the story because it means "light" (2004, 76).

11. For more information on Anancy stories, see Ramsay 1999 and Mosby 2003b.

Chapter 2

1. There are orthographic inconsistencies in the novel. The grandfather's name also appears as Jake. The name Jakel will be used in this study because it appears most frequently in the text.

2. A lodge during the time of the West Indian enclave was a fraternal organization that assisted contributing members with burial expenses.

3. Mestizo describes a person of mixed Spanish and indigenous descent.

4. *Paña, pana*: derogatory term for Hispanic Costa Ricans, derived from the Spanish word España (Spain).

5. *Cholo*, an often-considered-derogatory word, is used to describe rural mestizo peasants and their culture. The term often implies lack of education, poor habits, and lack of sensibility and culture. It may also mean an indigenous person who has assimilated Hispanic cultural values but maintains what are considered by the dominant culture as crude customs. Jakel is careful to note that West Indians were literate and possessed "civilized" habits like having polished floors, praying before meals, having a richer diet, and Protestant religious practices in contrast to the Costa Rican peasant's dirt floors, bland diet, and Catholic religious beliefs.

6. Clif's wife is an undeveloped character and appears tangential to the novel's narration. At first glance, her question appears to be a device to convey the possibility that the

wife is of a different ethnic group or part of the small population of blacks living in San José before 1948; however, Clif's wife appears in a more developed form as a trained nurse in *Los cuatro espejos*.

7. "Hansen's law," although still relevant, is not entirely unflawed, unproblematic, or as universal as the author advanced it to be because of intervening variables such as race, color, and the host culture's racial ideology. During the 1930s, Hansen concentrated his research on the Americanization of Scandinavian immigrants in the United States, placing particular value on the individual, and did not engage with the "Negro problem," Native Americans, or non-European immigrants or collective experiences of these groups. By providing an example of Margaret Mitchell's *Gone with the Wind* as a third-generation novel of the post–Civil War South, "Hansen's selection of *Gone with the Wind* as an exemplar of his 'law,' however unintentionally, gave historical credence to the Southern stereotype of blacks" (Lyman 1990, 129). The editors of *Memory and Cultural Politics*, in their criticism of Hansen's theory, state, "Hansen's confidence in assimilation of the second generation is unqualified; he did not consider race and color as issues affecting the immigrant experience" (Singh et al., 5). Additionally, "Hansen's understanding of the largely European predicament did not take into account the historical conditions affecting the lives of Native Americans, Mexican Americans, and African Americans; nor did Hansen anticipate the racial, ethnic, and gender complexities that affect the lives of new Americans of color" (Singh, Skerrett, and Hogan 1996, 17). Nevertheless, in spite of these critiques, we can extract some applicable meaning from his postulate to contribute to our discussions of contemporary migrations and diasporas.

8. Costa Rican scholars Franklin Perry and Kathleen Sawyers Royal coined the term "nowhereans" to describe the difficult position of the second and to some degree the third generation of people of West Indian descent in Costa Rica who were not Jamaican, Trinidadian, or Barbadian because they were not born there and they were not considered citizens of Costa Rica.

9. Intrahistory describes the perspective that privileges the experience of the "ordinary" individual rather than the historical discourse constructed by the dominant group that usually presents officially sanctioned events and individuals. This perspective gives voice to the experience of the marginalized. For a more in-depth explanation of the concept, please see Mosby (2003a, 13–16).

10. One of the points that can be made is the underdevelopment of the female characters. While we know Gretl and Grace play pivotal roles in the Duke family, we do not get the same scope of their characters as the family's patriarch, Jakel. Another issue is the chronology of Jakel's death. While it appears evident that he is in a hospital in San José, it is not clear if Clif already has his own family at that point in the narration or the amount of time that passes between Jakel's death and Clif's return.

11. This sentiment is also expressed by Richard L. Jackson in *Black Writers and the Hispanic Canon*. He states, "Duncan believes that *Kimbo* (1990) . . . is his best, but I think that *Los cuatro espejos* is most important because it goes to the heart of the identity issue, on both personal and national levels, touching on interracial relationships and the place of Blacks, especially non-Hispanic Blacks of West Indian or *antillano* origin, in Costa Rican society" (1997, 72).

12. Martin-Ogunsola also notes that "neither the primary nor the secondary threads develops in a linear fashion" (2004, 83).

13. The "marvelous real" (lo real maravilloso) was examined by Cuban writer Alejo Carpentier in his 1949 essay "De lo real maravilloso americano," which appears as the prologue to *El reino de este mundo* (The Kingdom of This World). As a counterpoint to European surrealism, Carpentier posits that writers of the Americas do not need to invent images of the fantastic, but rather the fantastic, or the marvelous real, is an inherent part of American reality largely manifest through Afro-descendant and indigenous cultures. "Magic realism" is not necessarily attached to a correspondent reality outside the text, but treats the supernatural and the fantastic as quotidian events.

14. An obeah man practices obeah, "an African-derived belief system that uses the power of the supernatural and the occult to effect change in the life circumstances of an individual" (Mosby 2003b, 103).

15. This malevolent spirit is known as *duppy* in Jamaican Creole.

16. For more on *afrorealismo*, please see the introduction to this volume.

17. See Tinney (1989).

18. A good example of this phenomenon is *Vejigantes* (1958) by Puerto Rican playwright Francisco Arriví. The play features Marta, the light mulatto woman who hides her black mother in the back room of their upscale apartment. Marta conceals and covers her dark curly hair under a turban and covers her face and hands with powder to appear lighter. She encourages her light-skinned daughter, appropriately named Clarita, to marry a white southerner from the United States in order to continue to whiten the family and escape any association with blackness. Marta attempts to explain away her olive complexion by passing as Mediterranean.

19. Pelé, the famous dark-skinned Brazilian soccer player, has been frequently cited as an example of achieving whiteness through wealth. Eric Telles contests this notion, citing public racist criticism of Pelé for his appointment to a government ministry and his courtship of the blonde bombshell Xuxua. He accurately observes, "Although money may whiten in some cases, its effects are limited to persons with phenotypes in an ambiguous zone that separates persons who are clearly white from those clearly non-white" (Telles 2004, 98).

Chapter 3

1. Cumina/Kumina is called Cuminá in the works of Quince Duncan, especially *La paz del pueblo*. In Jamaica the practice of Cumina becomes part of the syncretic revivalist movement in Afro-Christian sects like Pocomania that Duncan refers to in *Rebelión Pocomía*. According to a report, "Africa Live in Kumina," by Kesi Asher in the Jamaican daily *The Gleaner*, "Kumina, otherwise known as kalunga or kaduunga, features flat-footed inching of the feet (or the kongo step), a steady, but often subtle forward-thrusting of the hip with the rib cage and arms moving against the hip, followed by wild spins and sudden breaks, signaled by the lead drum. The dominant elements of kumina are dance, music, spirit possession, healing and the use of herbs" (n.p.).

2. Martin-Ogunsola observes in *The Eve/Hagar Paradigm in the Fiction of Quince Duncan* that Sitaira's name holds special significance in association with her ubiquitous laughter. She writes, "Her name (from the Latin *cithara* or Greek *kithara*) is derived from the term for 'a 30-to-40 stringed lute or musical instrument similar to the modern guitar.' This appellation identifies the young character as a person filled with laughter, music, and vitality" (2004, 112). Pedro's name is derived from the Greek word *petros*, meaning "rock."

3. Although older Jamaican burial rites sometimes engage the practice of passing a child three times over the coffin or grave of a recently deceased parent or relative to prevent the spirit of the deceased from inhabiting the child, the situation in *La paz del pueblo* seems to be reversed here. The couple, Mariot and Cornelio, seems to want grandchildren to carry on their spirit and to remember them as ancestors.

4. Martin-Ogunsola translates the title of "La paz del pueblo" as "For the Sake of Peace" (2004, 109).

5. All quotes are from the English version of the text.

6. Maroons (*cimarrones*) were escaped slaves who established settlements called *palenques*, often in remote areas out of the reach of European settlers. The historical Yangá or Nyanga was an African who became the leader of rebellious slaves near Veracruz, Mexico, during the late sixteenth century. After efforts to negotiate a peace with the Spaniards failed, Yangá's people engaged in a vicious battle with Spanish troops in 1609. After additional negotiations, Yangá secured a peace agreement with the Spanish, and Yangá's descendants were guaranteed land in return. In 1630 his descendants established San Lorenzo de los Negros, which was renamed the town of Yanga in 1932.

7. Rey Miguel (King Miguel) is also known as "El Negro Miguel." In 1552 he led a group of maroons who escaped slavery in the mines west of Caracas.

8. Benkos Biojó (also spelled Biohó) was an African-born maroon leader of *palenques* in La Matuna and Montes de María in the southern part of Cartagena province in Colombia. The settlement in La Matuna became known as San Basilio Palenque and was the first region of free blacks. Spaniards breached a treaty between King Benkos and the royal Spanish authorities. Benkos Biojó was imprisoned, tortured, and executed in 1622 by Spanish authorities.

Chapter 4

1. *El trepasolo* was adapted and produced by an Equatorial Guinean theater troupe, Bocamandja, in Malabo at the Centro Cultural Español in February 2011.

Conclusion

1. Poet and literary critic Dlia. (Delia) McDonald Woolery has written a manuscript for a novel; however, it is unpublished. In 2011, Lic. Karla Araya Araya, a graduate student at the Universidad de Costa Rica, found an unpublished novel written in English by first-generation Afro–Costa Rican writer Dolores Joseph.

Works Cited

Works by Quince Duncan

Short Stories and Anancy Stories

1969. *El pozo y una carta*. Goicoecha, Costa Rica: DLEH Editores.

1970. *Una canción en la madrugada*. San José: Editorial Costa Rica.

1976. *La Rebelión Pocomía y otros relatos*. San José: Editorial Costa Rica.

1985. *Voice of a Limonise*. Miami: Latin American and Caribbean Center, Florida International University.

1988. *Los cuentos de Jack Mantorra*. San José: Editorial Nueva Decada.

1991. *Los cuentos del Hermano Araña: Tal como los cuenta el famoso Jack Mantorra, alias La Cotorra*. 2nd ed. San José: Editorial Nueva Decada.

1995. *Las mejores historias de Quince Duncan / The Best Short Stories of Quince Duncan*. Translated by Dellita Martin-Ogunsola. San José: Editorial Costa Rica.

2004. *Cuentos escogidos: Cuentos*. San José: Editorial Costa Rica.

Novels

1971. *Hombres curtidos*. San José: Cuadernos de Arte Popular.

1973. *Los cuatro espejos: Novela*. San José: Editorial Costa Rica.

1978. *La paz del pueblo*. San José: Editorial Costa Rica.

1981. *Final de calle: Novela*. 2nd ed. San José: Editorial Costa Rica.

1989. *Kimbo*. San José: Editorial Costa Rica.

2007. *Un mensaje de Rosa / A Message from Rosa*. San José: UNED.

2012. *El pueblo afrodescendiente: Diálogos con el abuelo Juan Bautista Yayah*. Bloomington, IN: Palibrio.

Drama

1993. *El trepasolo*. Teatro para el teatro. San José: Teatro Nacional.

Essays

1972. *El negro en Costa Rica*, with Carlos Meléndez Chaverrí. 10th ed. San José: Editorial Costa Rica, 1993.
1975. *El negro en la literatura costarricense*. San José: Editorial Costa Rica.
1985. "El modelo ideal de la mujer: Un análisis ficciológico de estereotipos sexistas en la narrativa costarricense." *Káñina* 9 (July–December): 97–101.
1986. *Cultura negra y teología*. San José: Editorial DEI, Departamento Ecuménico de Investigaciones.
1987. "Visión panorámica de la narrativa costarricense." *Revista Iberoamericana* 53: 138–39 (January–June): 79–94.
1995. *Historia crítica de la narrativa costarricense*. San José: Editorial Costa Rica.
1995. "The Race Question in Costa Rica." In *African Presence in the Americas*, edited by Carlos Moore, Tanya Saunders, and Shawna Moore. Trenton, NJ: Africa World Press.
1996. *Un señor de chocolate: Treinta relatos de la vida de Quince*. Heredia: Programa de Publicaciones e Impresiones, Universidad Nacional.
2001. *Contra el silencio: Afrodescendientes y racismo en el Caribe continental hispánico*. San José: Editorial Universidad Estatal a Distancia.
2004. "The *Afrorealista* Manifesto." Keynote address at the College Language Association (CLA) Annual Convention, Nashville, Tennessee, April.
2005. "El afrorealismo: Una dimensión nueva de la literatura latinoamericana." *Istmo* (January–June). http://istmo.denison.edu/n10/articulos/afrorealismo.html.

Essays with Others

1987. Duncan, Quince, et al. *Dos Estudios sobre Diáspora negra y racismo*. Heredia: Instituto de Estudios Latinoamericanos (IDELA), Universidad Nacional.
1988. Duncan, Quince, and Lorein Powell. *Teoría y práctica del racismo*. San José: Editorial Departamento Ecuménico de Investigaciones.

Interviews

Duncan, Quince. 1997. Personal interview. November 11.
———. 2002. Personal interview. August 23.
Edison, Tomás. 1999. "An Interview with Afro–Costa Rican Writer Quince Duncan." *Afro-Hispanic Review* 18 (1): 29–33.
Rodríguez Cabral, Cristina. 1998. "A Conversation with Quince Duncan." *PALARA: Publication of the Afro-Latin/American Research Association* 2: 113–18.

Cited Sources and Sources of Interest

Althusser, Louis. 2001. *Lenin and Philosophy and Other Essays*. Translated by Ben Brewster. New York: Monthly Review Press.
Anglin Edwards, Joice. 1993. "Anancy in Limón." In *El negro en Costa Rica*, edited by Carlos Meléndez and Quince Duncan. San José: Editorial Costa Rica.

Araya Araya, Karla. 2012. "Alderman Johnson Roden: Reconstruyendo su aporte en la literatura Afrocostarricense." *Boletín de la AFEHC* 55 (October–December). http://www.afehc-historia-centroamericana.org/index.php?action=fi_aff&id=3238, accessed April 10, 2013.

Asher, Kesi. 2005. "Africa Live in Kumina." *Jamaica Gleaner*, October 9. http://www.jamaica-gleaner.com/gleaner/20051009/ent/ent1.html, accessed April 10, 2013.

Bennett, Louise. 1966. "Me and Annancy." In *Jamaica Song and Story*, edited by Walter Jekyll. New York: Dover.

Brenes Molina, José Jacinto. 2003. "Tres novelas en busca de un juicio histórico." *Comunicación* 24 (1–2): 50–63.

Cañas, Alberto. 1981. "Final de calle." *Káñina*: 131.

Chacón, Albino. 2006. "El sentido de la literatura de Quince Duncan en la historia cultural de Costa Rica, a propósito de la publicación de sus *Cuentos escogidos*." Editorial Costa Rica.com. http://www.editorialcostarica.com/quinceduncancomenalbino.htm, accessed August 11, 2007. Available April 2013 at http://www.alianzabolivariana.org/modules.php?name=Content&pa=showpage&pid=1433.

Chacón, Albino, and Danièle Trottier. "La Inscripción de las mediaciones institucionales en 'Lázaro de Betania' de Roberto Brenes Mesén y 'Caballo De Trote', de Quince Duncan." *Letras: Revista de la Escuela de Literatura y Ciencias del Lenguaje* 35 (2003): 197–209.

Chang Vargas, et al. 1996. *Cuentos tradicionales afrolimonenses*. San José: Editorial Costa Rica.

Chase, Alfonso. 1975. *Narrativa contemporánea de Costa Rica*. Vol. 1. San José: Ministerio de Cultura, Juventud y Deportes.

Chevannes, Barry. 1978. "Revivalism: A Disappearing Religion." *Caribbean Quarterly* 24 (September—December): 1–17.

Chevannes, Barry, and J. Besson. 1996. "The Continuity-Creativity Debate: The Case of Revival." *New West Indian Guide/Nieuwe West-Indisch Gids* 70 (3–4): 209–28.

Chomsky, Aviva. 1994. "West Indian Workers in Costa Rican Radical and Nationalist Ideology, 1900–1950," *The Americas* 51 (1): 11–40.

———. 1996. *West Indian Workers and the United Fruit Company in Costa Rica, 1870–1940*. Baton Rouge: Louisiana State University Press.

Clark, Anna. 2005. "Twilight Moments." *Journal of the History of Sexuality* 14 (1–2): 139–60.

Davis, Lisa E. 1984. "The World of the West Indian Black in Central America: The Recent Works of Quince Duncan." In *Voices from Under: Black Narrative in Latin America and the Caribbean*, edited by William Luis, 149–62. Westport, CT: Greenwood Press.

DeHay, Terry. 1994. "Narrating Memory." In *Memory, Narrative, and Identity*, edited by Amritjit Singh, Joseph T. Skerrett Jr., and Robert E. Hogan, 26–44. Boston: Northeastern University Press.

Eagleton, Terry. 1976. *Marxism and Literary Criticism*. London: Routledge.

Edison, Thomas Wayne. 2002. "The Afro-Caribbean Novels of Resistance of Alejo Carpentier, Quince Duncan, Carlos Guillermo Wilson, and Manuel Zapata Olivella." *Dissertation Abstracts International, Section A: The Humanities and Social Sciences* 63 (1).

Gordon, Donald K. 1983. "Alderman Johnson Roden: The Tailor Poet." *Afro-Hispanic Review* 2 (May): 9–12.

———. 1988. "The Sociopolitical Thought and Literary Style of Quince Duncan." *Afro-Hispanic Review* 7 (1–3): 27–31.

———. 1989. *Lo jamaicano y lo universal en la obra del costarricense Quince Duncan*. San José: Editorial Costa Rica.

———. 1999. "Lo africano en algunas obras de Quince Duncan." *PALARA: Publication of the Afro-Latin/American Research Association* 3: 94–99.

Hall, Stuart. 1997. "Cultural Identity and Diaspora." In *Identity and Difference*, edited by Kathryn Woodward, 51–59. London: Sage Publications.

Hansen, Marcus Lee. 1990. "The Problem of the Third Generation Immigrant." In *American Immigrants and Their Generations*, edited by Peter Kivisto and Dag Blanck, 191–203. Urbana: University of Illinois Press.

Harpelle, Ronald. 2001. *The West Indians of Costa Rica: Race, Class, and the Integration of an Ethnic Minority*. Montreal: McGill-Queen's University Press.

Jackson, Richard L. 1976. *The Black Image in Latin American Literature.* Albuquerque: University of New Mexico Press.

———. 1979. *Black Writers in Latin America.* Albuquerque: University of New Mexico Press.

———. 1988. *Black Literature and Humanism in Latin America*. Athens: University of Georgia Press.

———. 1997. *Black Writers and the Hispanic Canon*. New York: Twayne.

Joseph, Dolores. 1984. *Tres relatos del Caribe Costarricense.* San José: Programa Regional de Desarrollo Cultural (OEA), Ministerio de Cultura, Juventud y Deportes.

Kivisto, Peter, and Dag Blanck, eds. 1990. *American Immigrants and Their Generations.* Urbana: University of Illinois Press.

Lavou, Victorien, ed. 1997. Les noirs e la discours identitaire Latino-Américain / Los negros y el discurso identitario Latinoamericano. Perpignan: CRILAUP, Presses universitaires de Perpignan.

Lobo Wiehoff, Tatiana, and Mauricio Meléndez Obando. 1997. *Negros y blancos: Todos mezclados.* San José: Universidad de Costa Rica.

Luis, William, ed. 1984. *Voices from Under: Black Narrative in Latin America and the Caribbean*. Westport, CT: Greenwood Press.

Lyman, Stanford M. 1990. "Hansen's Theory and America's Black Birthright: The Historical Novel as History and Collective Memory." In *American Immigrants and Their Generations*, edited by Peter Kivisto and Dag Blanck, 126–41. Urbana: University of Illinois Press.

Manzari, H. J. 2004. "Rompiendo el silencio: Entrevista con el escritor costarricense Quince Duncan." *Afro-Hispanic Review* 23 (2): 87–90.

Martin-Ogunsola, Dellita L. 1987. "Invisibility, Double Consciousness, and the Crisis of Identity in *Los cuatro espejos.*" *Afro-Hispanic Review* 6 (2): 9–15.

———. 1991. "Translation as a Poetic Experience/Experiment: The Short Fiction of Quince Duncan." *Afro-Hispanic Review* 10 (3): 42–50.

———. 2004. *The Eve/Hagar Paradigm in the Fiction of Quince Duncan.* Columbia: University of Missouri Press.

Meléndez, Carlos, and Quince Duncan, eds. 1993. *El negro en Costa Rica.* 10th ed. San José: Editorial Costa Rica.

Molina, Iván, and Steven Palmer. 2004. *A Brief History of Costa Rica.* San José: Editorial Universidad de Costa Rica.

Monge Alfaro, Carlos. 1966. *Historia de Costa Rica.* San José: Imprenta Trejos Hermanos.

Morera Salas, Marta, and Mario Víquez Vargas. 1997. "El muñeco de alquitrán atrapa al ladrón: Atisbando en el discurso narrativo de Quince Duncan." In Lavou, *Les noirs et le discours identitaire Latino-Américain*, 225–35.

Mosby, Dorothy E. 2003a. "Dolores Joseph Montout's 'Limón on the Raw': A Study of Language, *Intrahistory*, and Afro–Costa Rican Cultural Identity." *PALARA* 7 (Fall): 13–16.

———. 2003b. *Place, Language, and Identity in Afro–Costa Rican Literature.* Columbia: University of Missouri Press.

Nerad, Julie Cary. 2003. "Slippery Language and False Dilemmas: The Passing Novels of Child, Howells, and Harper." *American Literature* 75 (4): 814–41.

Perry, Franklin, and Kathleen Sawyers Royal. 1995. "Costa Rica." In *No Longer Invisible: Afro–Latin Americans Today*, edited by the Minority Rights Group, 215–25. London: Minority Rights Group.

Persico, Alan. 1991. "Quince Duncan's *Los cuatro espejos*: Time, History, and a New Novel." *Afro-Hispanic Review* 10 (January): 15–20.

Ramsay, Paulette. 1994. "The African Religious Heritage in Selected Works of Quince Duncan: An Expression of Cultural and Literary Marronage." *Afro-Hispanic Review* 13 (2): 32–39.

———. 1998. "Quince Duncan's Literary Representation of the Ethno-Racial Dynamics between Latinos and Afro-Costa Ricans of West Indian Descent." *Afro-Hispanic Review* 17 (2): 52–60.

———. 1999. "Representations of Anancy in Selected Works of the Afro–Costa Rican Writer Quince Duncan." *Afro-Hispanic Review* 18 (2): 32–35.

Salas Zamora, Edwin. 1987. "La identidad cultural del negro en las novelas de Quince Duncan: Aspectos temáticos y técnicos." *Revista Iberoamericana* 53 (138–39): 377–90.

Senior Angulo, Diana. 2011. *Ciudadanía afrocostarricense: El gran scenario comprendido entre 1927 y 1963.* San José: Editorial Costa Rica.

Singh, Amritjit, Joseph T. Skerrett Jr., and Robert E. Hogan, eds. 1994. *Memory, Narrative, and Identity.* Boston: Northeastern University Press.

———. 1996. *Memory and Cultural Politics: New Approaches to American Ethnic Literatures.* Boston: Northeastern University Press.

Smart, Ian I. 1982a. "Religious Elements in the Narrative of Quince Duncan." *Afro-Hispanic Review* 1 (2): 27–31.

———. 1982b. "The West Indian Presence in the Works of Three New Central American Writers." In *Design and Intent in African Literature*, edited by David F. Dorsey, Phanuel A. Egejuru, and Stephen H. Arnold, 119–32. Washington, DC: Three Continents Press.

———. 1984. *Central American Writers of West Indian Origin: A New Hispanic Literature.* Washington, DC: Three Continents Press.

———. 1985. "The Literary World of Quince Duncan." *College Language Association Journal* 28 (3): 281–98.

Smith, Valerie. 1994. "Reading the Intersections of Race and Gender." *Diacritics* 24 (Summer–Fall): 43–57.

Taylor, Diana. 1991. *Theatre of Crisis: Drama and Politics in Latin America.* Lexington: University Press of Kentucky.

Telles, Edward Eric. 2004. *Race in Another America: The Significance of Skin Color in Brazil.* Princeton, NJ: Princeton University Press.

Tinney, Oscar Byrne, Jr. 1989. "Social Criticism in the Novels of Quince Duncan." Dissertation Abstracts International 49 (9): 2676A. University of North Carolina–Chapel Hill, 1988.

Villalobos, Ileana. 1982. "*Final de calle*: Perspectiva desencantada." Master's thesis. Costa Rica, Universidad Nacional.

Wright, Richard. 1944. *Black Boy (American Hunger): A Record of Childhood and Youth.* Reprint, New York: Harper Perennial Restored Edition, 1993, 355.

Index